P1

Brooks Running

Whether you are an avid runner, race organizer, or a born-again Christian, you will be enthralled by this work of Coach Brooks. He has reached the perfect balance between the physical aspects of running and the spiritual pursuit of finishing his personal race with grace.

— **"Cap'n Bagel" Bob Dyjak**, originator of the Bagel Bunch running group in Greece, NY, and race director for the Rochester Thanksgiving Day "Race with Grace" 10K for 25 years.

***

Why we run… it is often asked and often discussed. **Brooks Running** explains why one runs and why running is a parallel to life in more ways than one. Brooks knows about life's highs and lows and how to stay the course. Life is a marathon, not a sprint. Words of wisdom come from the pages, thanks to a well decorated marathoner. Brooks makes running look easy, which is why so many people have followed in his footsteps. Come along on this incredible journey with him as he retraces his runs through some of the most memorable courses and recounts the blessings that life has to offer. **Brooks Running** is a story of one man's perseverance and dedication to all things that matter. And, when you hit the proverbial wall, Greg shows you how to run through it with grit and gusto.

—**Chris Boshnack**, Founder of Gold Rush Runners, Rochester, NY.

***

For sure he's had a very interesting life! Maybe what I like best is Greg's caring nature compounded by a great sense of humor! Greg is a terrific contributor to the people of Rochester in so many positive ways, such as his coaching, running over many years, and his reaching out to learn about blind people and their cool form of baseball. With 20 Boston marathons and numerous ultra races around the USA, Greg surely has bragging rights, but he doesn't brag; he looks to be a support for others. I loved his story of his family's dog, Brigitte, which brought tears to my eyes,

i

just as it did to Greg's. His message is short; let's treat each other with respect and kindness!
— **"Boston Billie"/Bill Rodgers**, Olympian record holder in the Marathon, with four first-place finishes in both the Boston and New York City Marathons.

***

This book is written from a genuine place. It fills the reader with curiosity about Greg's life tale as well as a sense of connection to everything we ask ourselves about our faith, our capabilities, our past, and our expectations for the future… It communicates the feeling that we are not alone in the emotions that go along with all of that.
—**Nancy Perry**, music therapist for Greece Central Schools, NY.

***

As an acquaintance, contemporary, fellow vet and runner, and local church pastor in Brooks's hometown, I can identify closely with his carefully written story. Greg tells four essential truths about his life and experience— he knows what he believes and why; he is secure in the fact that he belongs to the One who created him; he recognizes that he is a part of a cause greater than himself, worthy of lifelong pursuit; and he is certain that he must fill his days with hope for the future. That hope is not a thing but a person—Jesus Christ! This is an open, honest, truth-filled, compelling account of the life of an exceptional man, Greg Brooks.
—**Pastor George Grace**, First Bible Baptist Church, Hilton, NY.

***

Brooks Running is the witness of how a man grew in his reliance on God, and how God helped him through the hills and valleys of his life. It is a wonderfully open, honest, true story of Greg Brooks's journey of life, running, addiction, and faith, and how they intertwine together. It was God's presence that helped bring Greg out from the depths of addiction to experience joy in running. Through his account, Greg shows us how God is always with us, even at the times we are unaware or don't acknowledge God…I loved that he shared his father's poems. They were perfectly chosen for each chapter in Greg's life, and through them he shared his father's life as well. What a great encouragement ***Brooks Running*** is for all of us.
—**Pastor Dorothea A. Tierson**, Lincoln Baptist Church, Macedon, NY.

***

In so many ways, we can all relate to Greg's story. We all face discouragement, sickness, depression, and death. In the midst of it all, we're not alone! In your race in life, look to the One who loves you and forgives you. Put your trust in the One who created and saved you. And keep your focus on the One who is with you every second of the journey. The most important part is to realize that God has a plan. And that even though we all fall short, he's the God of second chances. May you be blessed as you see how God has worked and is present in your life.

—**Pastor Matt Canaday**, Trinity Lutheran Church, Crown Point, IN.

Brooks Running

Memoir

Greg Brooks,
Heather Beck

Published by KHARIS PUBLISHING, imprint of KHARIS MEDIA LLC.

Copyright © 2021 Greg Brooks, Heather Beck

ISBN-13: 978-1-63746-070-2

ISBN-10: 1-63746-070-8

Library of Congress Control Number: 2021909781

All KHARIS PUBLISHING products are available at special quantity discounts for bulk purchase for sales promotions, premiums, fund-raising, and educational needs. For details, contact:

Kharis Media LLC
Tel: 1-479-599-8657
support@kharispublishing.com
www.kharispublishing.com

This book is dedicated to my late friend,
Bill Hearne.

Table of Contents

PREFACE

"Life's Journey"

Life is ever flowing,
A leaf caught in a stream.
Starting on a mountaintop,
And ending in the sea.

Lives are strings of eddies
That spin and whorl with style,
Telling of life's passages,
And lingering for a while.

Do your little pirouette,
And then you must move on.
Step aside for young leaflets
And follow those now gone.

Paths are tortuous journeys
That follow each small bend.
Some reflect a straighter track,
Though reach inevitable ends.

Will we lead our lives
And search out every hole? —Or—
Do we ride the stream of God,
Surrendering all control?

No, this book isn't some pastoral idyll about beautiful blue *brooks*, God's aquatic creations moving slowly along, full of tiny flora and fauna, with Bambi stopping to take a refreshing drink of that pure mountain runoff. There'll be no little rivulets melodiously bubbling along for frogs to play in and children to skip over moss-encrusted stones. That would be nice in a fairy tale sort of way. Sorry if that's what you were expecting, but no. Pure and simple, it's the memoir of a regular guy named Brooks doing his part to grow old—well, and a bit about a runner's exciting life getting there.

This is a book as much about me and who I've been as it is about the past itself. See, when we run, we put things, including the past, at a distance. We move away from what we've said and done perhaps faster than we normally would in daily life, at least in our runners' minds. Maybe it's an avoidance technique, really, or maybe it's a coping mechanism.

In that brook of life depicted in the poem above, the forces of gravity and momentum inexorably pull its waters downhill, picking up speed. Life starts out with us as individuals unsure of who we really are until we get the ball rolling. Then, people say, as we age, time starts to slip away faster and faster. What a cliché, right? But it's true! The inherent struggle in a race is that it is timed. The clock "runs" down. In my case, that is certainly true in one respect. There's only so much time for me to get this book done now that I am old. I've got to get this sweet thing down, in writing, before the bitter pill of regret comes calling.

They also say that "time flies when you're having fun." But that concept is a bothersome contradiction in my life these days. If you're like me and have had a decent or even great first part of your life as a young person for whom the world was your oyster, but you also look back on a less-than-stellar second part as you got along in years, well, you can see the irony here. Time for you and me doesn't fly anymore. The first half of my life went quickly—when I was having fun. The second part, and where I am today, not so much. I guess I defy gravity.

Time is going slowly now, perhaps a bit too slowly these days for a guy who was all about speed. My right "leg" is a cane that likes to saunter at best. I'm not fast anymore; I can't run—at all. I can't put the past behind me anymore; it's caught up to me now and wants me to have a conversation with it. I invite it to sit down with me and chat. I have time to sit in my chair, theoretically enough time to do everything and anything I want to do in the future. But the energy of youth required to accomplish these things has gone to a place of no return. I have time to burn, and my past knows this. So, I've modified my activities to fill up my hours. I think. I reflect. I ponder. I wake up, and already the next day is here. Then the next and the next. Yes, perhaps in their own, deceptive way, my final years are going more quickly than I think, considering I move so slowly now. That's bittersweet.

I felt psychologically and spiritually that it was important to get my story down. First, I thought it was essential to leave something behind so my dearest family, followers, and future generations could understand me and my life and what I had tried to accomplish. The inspiration for this book came from a journal I wrote while climbing Mount Kilimanjaro fifteen years ago detailing the preparation and execution of the trek plus a safari and African marathon. It was an adventure of a lifetime.

Brooks Running

I decided that this book should also be something for other runners that might interest them and they could profit by. So *Brooks Running* is also for those fast-of-foot athletes—young and old, coming up or slowing down, serious champions in the making or casual folks who just love to run as a hobby.

But there's yet another, wider audience. This book is also for anyone who's Christian and doing that tough Christian "climb," anyone who is a mentor of people in any capacity, or anyone who is existentially standing before the brink of old age. The poems woven throughout were written by my dad, Loder Brooks—my hero, my muse, my Christian exemplar—when he was elderly. He's passed away now, but it was my tender wish that I incorporate his timeless sensitivity and spiritual insights into my book. In the preface to his book of collected poems he published years ago, he says by way of introduction, "I bare my soul, I present my words candidly, for what they are worth, that you may know who I am." I hope by giving you a glimpse of his soul I can make my memoir his memoir too. So in all, it's my hope that this book reaches whomever it needs to reach, the readers God will bring it to for a reason. If you're reading this right now, then one of them just happens to be you.

I've always tried to be someone who follows his conscience and felt that sports provided clear situations in which to do so. As we go along on our little running trail that is my book (although it felt like an ultramarathon to write it!), I'll ask you to reflect with me. I invite you to put this memoir's experiences to work for you. *Run* with them. See if you can use what I've said to bring along on your own spiritual journey as you move from Point A to Point B. The process itself is key. Remember, it's the journey, not the destination, as they say. The journey is archetypal: I think you can see it most obviously in any old person's life well lived. Passing away and moving into eternity is the final destination, but that's not difficult if you believe in Jesus. *Living* is the hard part. *Enduring*, like a marathon runner, is the challenge—to be fully present in the life you were given until your appointed time to go.

I've taken the journey that nature/nurture, free will/fate, and Time have carved out like a brook into that mountain rock formed long ago. Has the brook sometimes meandered by itself? Sure. Have I made it run in my certain own directions? Yes. Has God approved at great junctures when it was gushing full force to make him proud? Absolutely. Has God shaken his head at other checkpoints, when the floodwaters were out of control and my sins were leading? Undoubtedly. As you read, we'll go up and down the mountain together; we'll run the race of life. As God's children, we're all in this moving, flowing, earth-bound experience, seeking a rest for our souls—a destination—together. I've run lots of races on foot, but the most

xi

important one, and the one I most want to share with you, is the race I'm running today—the one of my soul.

If we look at the conflict for a moment, the crux of my book, it's the classic Christian struggle—person versus a temporal world. But it's also person versus self. That's the way it had to be, after the fall of Adam and Eve, who sabotaged themselves and left us with a sin-filled legacy. You know the story.

And yes, this book is going to be one of those reads with all the parts of a good tale. There's a protagonist (yours truly) and several antagonists (drugs and alcohol, many different races, a mountain, etc.). There's a rising action (my corporate promotions and recognition in the running world) and a climax (literally, I'm on top of the highest **single free-standing mountain in the world!**). There's a falling action (I actually do fall a couple times during races but also trip myself up on a big life thing or two). And there's a denouement that remains to be seen (it's in God's hands). The setting for all of this is Rochester, New York, a mid-sized city in the northwestern/central part of the state, during my lifetime from 1947 to present.

The theme, of course, about the runner's journey, both sublime and agonizing, is to never, *ever* give up. This book is as much about the clear paths of life as it is about the snags, the twists and turns, the blind paths I've had to navigate. I've learned to do the hard thing and embrace the defeats as well as the victories. I'm "a work in progress," as they say. And so are you.

The memory of all those miles still lingers. Let's dust it off, fire it up, and see what's really there. God will be right here, cheering us on. Are you ready, running buddy? Let's get going! Come run with me on our epic adventure. Let's do the highs; let's do the lows—the joys, the sorrows, the "straighter tracks" along with the "tortuous journeys" that my dad spoke of in his poem.

I told you the race is timed, though. The clock is ticking, remember? We've got places to go, people to see. So…

On your mark, get set, GO!

Part I

PREPARATION TO RUN

Family History

"My Author"

Who is the one who writes my life?
Who can the author be?
Do you suppose that if approached,
He'd share the end with me?

I think that I will ask him that
And see just what he'll say.
I doubt he'll grant my bold request;
I'll ask him anyway.

Why has he been so good to me,
Supplied my every need?
Without my even asking him,
Responds with rapid speed.

But maybe, now I think of it,
Don't want myself to know—
I guess I'd rather be surprised,
Just live to watch the show.

Here we are now, in this adventure together, partner. They say that the journey of a thousand miles starts with just one step.

Looking at the above poem by my father, Irving Loder Brooks, Jr., you might have pondered the opening question: "Who is the one who writes my life?" Did you think it was God? Well, you're right. So I think I should start by acknowledging him, of course—almighty God the Father. God is my author, and he is *the* author we all have in common. He is the creator of us all. We have a common ancestry; we really are all related, when you think about it. You and I are siblings, all deriving from the same first genetic code. The link is there. That is why I think my memoirs may speak to you.

1

Along with my heavenly Father, my grandfather (Irving Loder Brooks, Sr.) gave life to my earthly father (the "junior" version), so these men are both "authors" as well. In his own memoirs, my father pondered, "Did our progenitors think about us, their issue, as they lived their lives, or did they just do what they were programmed to do by the nature of survival? In any case we must think about the hardships they endured in order that we now exist and have what we have, made possible by their efforts." So before I begin much more, I'd like to take a moment to recognize, through my dad, all the many forefathers (and foremothers) I've had who have brought me to this moment. While the purpose of this book doesn't include presenting an extensive family tree, let us note that all of us have them, and all of us should be aware of the lives that our ancestors led, including their sacrifices.

Father's Day and Mother's Day are great holidays to preserve memories, but Memorial Day is even better. It asks for a moment of your time to reflect, be grateful, and wonder. Perhaps a time to investigate, if needed, so that we can hold on to the waning echoes of someone's identity who would have loved us had they known us. It gets harder as time passes to be able to relate to our progenitors; they fade back into mysterious waves of inaccessible oblivion. Besides, it seems that too few people in today's world display active interest, care, and reverence, and forgivably so, as there usually isn't much information recorded about their ancestors. Also, today we have the technology to assist us in this difficult inquiry but rarely the time, with our busy and complex lives, to utilize it.

My dad did one day sit down and begin to write his story, in an effort to be considerate of his children and future generations. His autobiography weaves back into countless others. My father wrote down memories from oral tradition as far back as his great-great-great grandparents in America, but before this, all stories have been buried with unknown people. Wouldn't it be wonderful if grandchildren could know their ancestors' stories much further back? If not for that, those ancestors' hopes and dreams, their defeats and heartaches, which are a rich source of our own personal understanding, will forever be lost to us in an occluded mirror. . . I suppose I have a lot more to go on than many folks, even if it's only on the paternal side; I do know some things stretching back at least a little into the seemingly limitless expanses of time. These may give you a frame of reference to see how my personality and life's patterns grew out of many others', how God shaped my destiny even before being in the womb.

My family history includes some interesting figures way back, as all families do. I'm descended from a long line of English and German stock, mostly pastors and farmers. Dad was named Irving Loder Brooks, but he always went by *Loder* for his first name, as it was a family surname passed through interweaving generations and he was proud of it. Loders, Brookses, and Chapins were the mainline names in our sprouting American family tree. Dad said in his writings: "I, for one, would have loved to have been privy to the thoughts of, say, Gad Chapin, serving the king of England during the Revolutionary War, and any words from Thomas Brooks while in the service of General Washington in the same conflict [opposite side]. I should think that with an understanding of where our ancestors came from, it might make the study of our American history more meaningful."

In fact, like many Americans would be able to say today if they scrutinized their family tree hard enough, we had ancestors who came over on the Mayflower in 1620 and settled in Plymouth, Massachusetts. My family are not direct descendants of the Mayflower settlers through the Brooks line; however, we have a direct connection through the Chapin line, back to Capron and Tilley Chapin of Plymouth Colony. If you look back, it's likely you'll discover similar iconic and even colorful characters in your own heritage.

The Trunk: Great-Granddad Edward

If those generations were my American roots, then my great-grandfather, Edward Irving Brooks, was the tree trunk. Going way, way back, I don't remember him, but my father, Loder Brooks, took careful notes and documented that man's life rather thoroughly. During the Depression of the Thirties, Edward lived in a home chock-full of people: his wife (my great-grandmother); his son (my grandfather, Loder, Sr.) and his daughter-in-law (my grandmother); and his grandsons (my father, Loder, Jr., and my uncle). We always rolled our eyes and told my dad that he had quite the "grandfather stories." For instance, my dad related that my great-grandfather, his paternal grandfather, had a signature phrase, much along the lines of "children should be seen, not heard." He said it often. "You're supposed to be good for nothing, not good for something."

Can you see the delicious double-entendre there, reader? On the one hand, it is a bit of a whimsical joke. A never-do-well, mischievous child would be called "good-for-nothing," but my great-grandfather would never have promoted naughtiness. It is comical language, a reversal of what kids would normally hear from an adult's mouth. What parent would tell a child that he or she is supposed to be a "good-for-nothing," dirty, rotten little rascal? Every kid would know how to read that funny idea backwards to see the true intent, an admonishment to children that they should be "good for *something*." That something would entail, of course, being of use to someone else such as a parent for chores, etc. Or, it might refer to being worth something of value to the larger society. Here, the word *for* in Great-granddad's phrase is acting as a preposition and carries meaning in relation to the person the child answers to. Plainly said, without the funny twist, the statement means that children should be worthy, period. That's one side of the meaning.

3

Now, from the other side of its meaning, where the double-entendre comes in powerfully, it still simply means that children should be good, but it reaches into something more subtle as well. We can interpret it in the way my wise forebear intended: *Good*, instead of meaning of *use or value* to *the parent/society*, would mean *appropriate* in terms of the *child's own* behavior. This means that the children were supposed to behave well for *no outer reason* at all ("nothing"), that outer reason being a possible reward or bribe given to the child by parents, teachers, or elders. In this case, the *for* is used to mean *in order to get*. This outside imposition of rewards and punishments by parents and the seeking or avoiding of them by children is what educators and family therapists of today call "extrinsic motivation," and it's not ideal for short-term behavior modification or long-term character development of a child. Rather, this saying reminds children that they are supposed to behave for an *inner* reason, just because they want to be good—what experts call "intrinsic motivation." That translates to internalized value, a matter of principle within the child's own conscience. It is a feeling of God being aware of one's actions and a decision to behave well to please him.

So it turns out that that funny little saying was more than something silly to make us laugh. It was truth, a very serious maxim. If children have to be given an artificial "carrot" on a stick to do the right thing, then when that outward prize is not there (and it often won't be in life), it seems there's not much reason to display honorable conduct. Apparently, as my grandfather told it, my great-grandfather would say this phrase, laugh, and not explain it. Could that be like Jesus who would present a parable and then let people figure it out? The challenge there is a powerful teaching technique. Great-grandpa's meaning: Don't always expect to be paid for doing good. Just do it. Do it because you want to. That moral instruction, given to me sideways through an old saying, has been of the highest worth to me. My great-grandfather practiced what he preached. He really, intrinsically *wanted* to be a good man; he wanted to love and nurture his grandchildren (my father and his sibling). I know this because my father wrote that although he (my father) had eleven grandchildren of his own (counting my twin boys and my daughter), he "was not able to give to them [as a whole] the attention that he [alone] got from his grandfather." That's saying something quite remarkable, if you ask me.

The name Loder comes into our family history in that my great-granddad Edward's wife was Gertrude Loder. "Gertie" was a cultured, refined, classy person from a family of some elevated social standing. "She was a genteel lady, who came from a positioned family," my dad wrote. "She was always very proper and taught me how to do the table settings, among other social graces." Her father, Edwin Loder, seemed to have been a very successful businessman who owned a sandpaper company. From that position of power, he was also a political and community leader in Rochester. He served in the state legislature of New York (the New York Electoral College) and also as a United States ambassador on diplomatic missions to a European country. He was a Grand Master of the Rochester lodge of the Masonic Order and an officer of an artillery battery in the Civil War. He was in the battles of Harper's Ferry and of Culpeper's Courthouse in Virginia.

I expect that as his daughter, Gertie may have found it difficult to marry into a family of "farm folks" like the Brookses, who didn't have a chance to go to church because all their time was spent on agricultural labor. My great-grandmother Gigi, as Gertie was later called by my dad as a child, was a devout Christian and a regular churchgoer. She was brought up in the Episcopal church of downtown Rochester, and she saw to it that my father (her grandson) went there too. My dad, however, would, according to him, "feign all sorts of illness on Sunday so as not to have to go to Sunday school." It wasn't the reason that kids normally gave, though. "Not that I disliked the ritual, or the studies," he said, "but because we were made to read out loud and recite, which embarrassed me beyond words. You see, I could not read very well, and that reading disability coupled with shyness made me freeze up. In those days, dyslexia was not understood."

Gertie must have been frustrated that her farmer-husband, Edward, as I said, never went to church (and that, by the way, was out of line with his great-great-great-grandfather, the Reverend Thomas Brooks, the First, who was the pastor of a church in Brooksfield, Connecticut). However, Edward apparently had a strong sense of rightness and fairness. After his farming days, he was a game warden and on occasion was called upon to transport or extradite prisoners for the local sheriff. So Gertie, along with her husband, lived the Christian ethic, but she more so as a matriarch really helped to mold my dad in his holy walk, even if he kept it under wraps later as an adult. I guess she had planted just enough of a seed that her wishes for her family did eventually come true, specifically in my case, as I know and honor the Lord in unabashed, overt ways.

Other Branches in the Tree

Still on my dad's side, but on the other side of the family tree in reference to my great-grandparents, Ambrose and Ordelia Dano (born in the 1860's) were my grandmother's parents. Ambrose's father was James Dano, and his father was Joseph Danaut, before the spelling was changed to anglicize it. They were born in New York State but seem to have lived most of their lives in Canada, farming along the St. Lawrence River. This piece of information becomes very relevant in one of my final chapters, the one about the parcel of land that has remained in my family for generations. It is up on Grindstone Island in the Thousand Islands. Grandpa Loder (Sr.)

built his summer home and named it "Da-Brook" after the two ancestral families named Dano and Brooks who had always owned the land. It was with his own hands that all the mortar was mixed, the blocks laid, the boards sawed, and the nails hammered. The old place is still there, a memorial to him and his wife and their forebears.

That Dano daughter who was his wife, my paternal grandmother, was named Jessie. She was quite a woman. She was a strict disciplinarian, though always fair. She never punished my father without cause and without a precept to be learned. "Switching was a well-remembered method, not to inflict any lasting damage, only to [curb] the ego of an unruly boy," wrote my dad. The worst part of it, he said, was when he had to go and cut his own switch! But other methods were subtler, many times, in teaching my dad right from wrong. He learned early on that telling the truth was the best policy, as often this would lead to more genial punishment. The lessons were never forgotten when they were taught with love and understanding.

When he was around ten years old or so, my father would often want to know when he would be able to make some of his own decisions. My grandmother would say that when my dad could best her in a foot race, then he could do what he wanted. "Anytime you're ready," she said, "just let me know, and we'll race out to the garage," which was about seventy-five feet or so from the house. He failed many of these challenges throughout several years, he said. "As I remember, when I finally did prevail and win the race, I felt sorry for being able to beat her and never would claim my prize." But by then, he was mature enough to do what he wanted and not get in trouble anyway. "Funny thing—I never wanted to do anything that I felt would not make her proud of me," he said. So I guess the running gene and the running ethic were instilled in me from at least a couple generations back.

Now back to her husband—my paternal granddad, Irving Loder Brooks, Sr. He was quite a character as well. In his youth, Granddad was a powerful, barrel-chested boy, whom I'm sure could bench-press considerable weight. I never saw him do it, of course, as an old man. He and my dad "would stand over six feet tall if our legs were not so short," they would humorously say. However, the whole family was still extremely fast of foot over short distances, thus accounting for my dad's athletic bent that I will discuss more of later.

Granddad was a salesman and a real estate developer. His honesty and fairness, as noted by my father, were "above reproach; his word was his bond." He is said to have derived no greater happiness than when he was helping someone with a chore or a problem. His credo was: "Everyone wants something, and you can get more of what you want if you can give him what he wants." That has always seemed very wise to me. Maybe it carried over into what I did and still do today in some humanitarian efforts (as you will see in some of my later chapters). That truth had also earlier come to my father when he found his professional life as a dentist. Loder, Jr., enjoyed his relationships with his clients and friends more than the money his job provided. My dad said, "The secret that I kept from my patients was that I would have gladly performed my work for free. I felt like a thief taking money just to do what I loved. However, somehow the bills had to be paid."

Both my father and I learned a lot of positive things from my grandfather. Neither my dad nor I have any painful memories of him, except for one. Eventually, we saw the giant in our lives crumble. Time chipped away at him in its inexorable effort to reduce him to dust, to be put back into the rich Brooks soil from whence he came.

Me

My heavenly author, God, and my earthly authors, Dad and Mom, had initially set me down September 8th, 1947, onto the giant running track of life. I had joined the human *race*, with all of the other "contestants" whooshing by me. I was born here in Rochester, New York, into the early years of a good, healthy, and well-adjusted home life. Thanks be to God. My dad was a great guy, my mom a gem. Dad was an all-around athlete, excelling and earning varsity letters in basketball, soccer, track, and swimming. He later was not only that skilled and caring dentist I mentioned, but a sensitive poet and a loving husband and father. He raised us three boys and a girl; I was the firstborn son. He had been the firstborn of his tribe too, and my grandfather the firstborn before him as well. We were all first of our siblings, and you know what they say about firstborns: they're driven.

I can relate my early years in an autobiographical nutshell. I grew up in the fifties and sixties. I had what you'd call a typical childhood. We lived here in a suburb of Rochester called Irondequoit. I attended West Irondequoit High School. My early years were like those of the normal "boy next door"—fun and wholesome, with Boy Scouts and athletics. My parents were strong, stable, supportive influences in my life, but not openly pious.

Now that I've established my family background and briefly presented my younger years, I'd like to move right on to my running years, which were most of my life. Yes, this is where it all began. "How did you start running?" you ask. Well, as a kid I was always hiking on some type of adventure in our suburban jungle, where there were plenty of wild areas needing exploration. As I grew older, our territory expanded. Trees had to be climbed for lookout perches; forts needed to be constructed for defense from imaginary enemies. I was a scout conquering the land, hiking. I also would spend the summer months at the family property on Grindstone Island, about three miles wide and ten miles long, on the St. Lawrence River. It was our playground where we (my friends and I) discovered hunting and fishing. I'll always remember the sound of the mighty, roaring water. It was a lot of territory for a kid, but we were given free rein to hike and swim. With no paved roads, just farmland there, we basically had to run wherever we wanted to go. I remember a church (which still has services today), a cheese factory, and a school (the last one-room schoolhouse in New York).

Besides these formative outdoor experiences, my dad's athleticism influenced me. Although he ran, his forte was swimming. He had been a high school and college champion swimmer. He went to Kent State and enjoyed a great tour of athletic achievement. Of course, he would have liked it if I had followed in his footsteps. I did, for a bit, but it wasn't quite the right fit. It just wasn't me. But my wonderful swim coach, an easygoing, kind guy called Coach Rocco, just happened to be also the track coach too ("God moment" here). He got me into running, and the rest is history, I suppose. My dad wasn't fazed; he let me spread my wings, my brook take its course. So I participated in two different sports in high school—swimming and running—and received three different varsity letters: in track, cross-country, and aquatics.

The high school years brought me an opportunity to be an exchange student to Mexico, and I know that experience shaped my running years also. This was my first *real* adventure, I felt. It was the summer before my junior year. Off I went! I left my family and flew to Mexico to live with a family I knew nothing about. I was such a greenhorn, roiling in teenage adolescence. I grew up fast in Mexico. But that is another story.

While I was there, I met a Mexican cousin or friend of theirs—I can't remember, but it was a peer who piqued my interest to climb a volcano, either Mount Popcatepetl or Mount Iztaccihuatl, both dormant, of course. I guess when I was touring around Mexico with my Mexican family and I could see these snowcapped giants in the summertime, it begged the question: could I get there? I was strongly advised by my exchange family "Forget it! You must get *permiso* from *su familia*." These volcanoes still loom as someplace I may want to return to someday. I would like to revisit them because of the sheer impression they made on me as a kid. I still have enough *lengua (language)* in my cranium to be comfortable speaking and getting around Mexico.

Most important in my upbringing should have been my spiritual development. Alas, I was not raised in a God-centered home or church environment. I rarely attended church as a youth. My parents weren't officially religious. Sure, they believed, but there was basically no church involvement. Things were vague and left mostly unspoken. No "graces" at meals, no praying at difficult times, no reading of the Bible. I had no structural foundation of spirituality, only a potentiality that could go either way. Unlike my coach's loud and strong voice to move forward with the sport of running, God's was only a little whisper in my head. My belief just sat there, waiting for a push of some kind. Unfortunately, that push wouldn't come till much later.

WARM-UP

Young Adult Years

"Ode to Captain Morgan"

My Captain Morgan is a friend
Who comes a'calling now and then.
I welcome him here to arrive
When I so sorely must revive.
This is my favorite time of day,
So hopefully he'll opt to stay.

He comforts me and clouds my brain.
He numbs my body of the pain.
And then he winks, subverts my mind.
He dulls my senses 'til I'm blind.
He drags me down into a hole.
He buries me and steals my soul.

It is the ending of my day.
And now it's time to hit the hay.
He soothes me into blissful sleep,
Yet robs my dreams of counting sheep.
And when my senses I retake,
It's then that I do jar awake.

Tomorrow I will do my work
Before this time that is his quirk.
I know I will anticipate
When we together will libate.
Because I'm hooked, I'll always yearn
For Captain Morgan's stealth return.

Well, this chapter isn't going to be easy, gentle reader. I bet you might already know what's coming…
　　　　Let's start with the sixties and seventies. I graduated from

10

high school in 1965. Contrary to my earlier years, as a young man I was confused, in disarray, although I'm sure I didn't recognize the full extent of it back then. Before this, I had been a kid, and kids are generally optimistic, even if that optimism is just naivety. The fact of it is, as I grew to be an adult, America was in chaos, and that, of course, had an effect on me. It contributed to my personal sense of unsteadiness. Vietnam was looming; the Civil Rights Movement, though needed, was ushering in full-blown strife. Life—it all just "happened" to me in these two blurry, turbulent decades. The whole disorienting thing was mitigated, or at least I thought it was, by my relationship with Captain Morgan, my fatherly "friend" who came "calling." He comforted yet subverted me. He soothed yet metaphorically robbed me. With his help, I felt ambivalent about all that was going on around me.

Like lots of hip dudes, my favorite musician was Bob Dylan. He was our poet-singer, an icon of the cultural revolution of worldwide love and peace we young people were promoting. The songs of the Doors, Janice Joplin, the Grateful Dead, Jimmy Hendrix, Pink Floyd, The Who, and others played through our heads constantly. **The psychedelic tunes urged on the cloudy mayhem. Music was a big thing that encouraged drinkin' and druggin.'** It was the flower children era as well, when everything was shared. Illicit substances were given and taken freely by just so many people. Timothy Leary, guru of LSD, was known to most. Woodstock, in my own neighborhood of Upstate New York, drew hundreds of thousands of people—four hundred thousand, to be more exact, and drugs were a big component of that experience. The pervasive drug scene infiltrated other parts of the culture too. To say this epoch was a mess because of drugs, Vietnam, and the birth pangs of civil rights struggles is an understatement. Often with drugs, people were trying to find their souls—and the soul of a nation.

College

With no idea where I was going in life, I wandered spiritually, but I somehow retained my thirst for exploration and the knowledge that comes with it. The beginning of my undergrad studies took place at Missouri Valley College, a tiny Midwestern liberal arts institution of higher learning. It was Presbyterian, based on fundamental religious values that called for good behavior. (Remember what Great-grandpa Edward said?) But the year was 1965.

The college had only fifteen hundred enrolled. My advisor, the cross-country coach, got ahold of my record and strongly encouraged me to join the team. The first college meet I ran, I won the whole thing. That same year, still as a freshman, I went to the Small College Nationals, part of the

NAIA (National Association of Intercollegiate Athletics). I was doing great in this physical respect.

However, in being a college student and joining a fraternity, Alpha Sigma Phi, the camaraderie involved a lot of drinking, and it just swept me away. I was drunk more than I was sober. I got kicked out of the school halfway through my junior year. I was expelled for drinking, or so I thought. The dean sat me down and promptly said, "Well, I guess you better not come back here." I only guessed what it was due to, as I thought I had kept my habit pretty well hidden. My grades were okay, but because of my involvement with drinking and drugs, getting sucked into the whole mess, come to find out they thought I was dealing drugs on campus. But I wasn't. Honestly, I wasn't. It was more that I was *doing* drugs on campus and had gotten a reputation. And I just must have stuck out for who I was, anyway. Those of us from the East were the wild rebels—not shady guys necessarily, but different from the people of the Midwest. But I didn't know better than to be me. I didn't know better than not fitting in if I wanted to stay there.

At that juncture as a young man I wasn't furious; I was actually glad to go. I didn't like to get asked to leave because of my behavior. Once they told me to go, I was happy to be rid of a place and group of people that would be like that. We were just on different wavelengths, I suppose. It was those Midwestern attitudes I just couldn't get by—those parochial, narrow-minded beliefs. They were what we called "a drag." However, I was mad at myself in a way for this incident. I wasn't able to finish something that I started, a common thread that would show up at several points in my life.

True, those Midwestern farm values were much different than those of the "cool kids" from the East Coast like New York and New Jersey, such as I believed myself to be. Come on, now; we were the cats who brought the party to Missouri! Today, weighing in on the experience with maturity under my belt, I give more credence and respect to those wholesome values and wish I had had the foresight to embrace them, or at least to have been open to them. It was kind of like what F. Scott Fitzgerald implied about conservative Midwestern ideals in his classic American novel *The Great Gatsby.* That book's narrator, Nick, has an epiphany, through a journey from innocence to experience, that he must return from a morally bankrupt existence in New York City to his Midwestern roots and the pure mores on which they were forged.

The Military
College expulsion took me to the army in '68, and of course the recruiters did their best to make it seem appealing. When I left school, they had my number, all right! I got drafted into the military right away. So back in a tent I went (I'm linking this to my Boy Scout days only to be sarcastic). Long

hair shorn, drugs all stashed, and on to basic training to prepare for Vietnam. I was excited—NOT!

I was in a big-time mental struggle with this one. I did not support the war but didn't want to run off to Canada and get hauled back to jail. I wanted to be a conscientious objector, not a deserter, as I was a pacifist, but my competitive spirit would not allow me to back down from the challenge of the army. But then again, I really didn't want to support a war I didn't believe in.

I hung in through basic training with my newfound friends from all over the country. I believed we were then going to a base in Canada, but we ended up being assigned to Korea. I had "lucked out" with an easy, non-combat assignment! Aha, another adventure on the horizon! Yes! I totally engaged this one. As long as I had to serve, no violence was fine with me. I knew I could do a year overseas in this country, which was stabilized at that point in history.

So, after basic training, on our way to Korea during the Vietnam era, 1968–1969, we had really been quite fortunate. There were many dissenters among us in the ranks, and there were enough of us in our unit who were against the idea of going to Vietnam that we could have really raised hell. I surmise that there would have been a rebellion had they (the government) kept on sending troops there. We believed in love, not war.

We went into advanced infantry training (AIT) from there. Although not in a place of direct fighting, I was a "combat engineer"—those are the guys who build bridges and dig ditches for possible war efforts. I was sent to Korea because of the DMZ (demilitarized zone on the border between South and North Korea). Those two countries were and still are at odds with each other about communism.

Korea turned out as expected, a cakewalk. Back in the saddle again, so to speak, I had few goals or passions except for the usual drugs and alcohol. Like I said, while in the USA, it was a very difficult time in everybody's life, if you were an American. And that feeling stretched all the way over to us in Korea. All the conflict back home was immense, and we knew it; it psychologically trickled down to us too. But over here in Korea, a world away, we were ironically sort of immune in a way to the realities of the conflict. It was easy duty. It was as good as it could be. Maybe we soldiers felt guilty and wanted to push that from our minds. There was plenty of opportunity for drinking, drugs, and girls to do just that. There were lots of beautiful Korean girls. Most of them were prostitutes. You have to realize, it was a big industry there. I might have brought one home to the States, but I didn't. Everybody—every serviceman—was lonely over there.

But that was nothing. Our brothers sent to Vietnam were being maimed by Viet Cong, chewed up and spit out by Uncle Sam, and scorned by their own people when they returned to home turf. Today, I humbly reflect on the 2,700,000 American men and women who were involved in the Vietnam War. It was a war that many didn't believe in, and because we ultimately surrendered anyway, it was the first war in which we failed our objective. These soldiers were patriotic and did their duty, though. I can't say for sure, but what I imagine was even more heroic, however, is how they combated the societal negativity when they came back home. Rather than being publicly lavished by the parties and banners and yellow ribbons around trees we see today when our loved ones return from deployment, they were shown hostility and contempt and mostly ostracized. What they suffered at the hands of many of their own countrymen was horrible, despicable, unconscionable, and just not right.

If you are a younger person reading this, you can view the movie *Born on the Fourth of July*. It does an excellent job exploring the heinous and deplorable treatment soldiers received when they got back from military service in Vietnam. This 1989 film starring Tom Cruise is based on the true story of Ron Kovic and gives a glimpse into the reprehensible manner in which our country took its troops back onto American soil, with no plan as to reintegrating them into civilian life. The gripping irony, in Kovic's case, was that he had originally been a true, idealistic patriot just raring to go serve his country. Seemingly incarnated to fulfill a heroic American destiny, he had even been born on the nation's supreme holiday—the Fourth of July—signifying the freedom he wanted to fight for to protect us all. Men like him were fighting the perceived threat to America of globally expanding communism.

Instead, men like Kovic had been used up and discarded, deemed pariahs of society, sneered at, and denied necessary medical benefits like prosthetics, physical therapy, and counseling. And even though many of them had sustained major, extreme physical and emotional trauma including lost limbs and post-traumatic stress disorder (PTSD), they were basically just ignored or, worse yet, persecuted for fighting—as if being drafted had somehow been their choice! These men deserved and still deserve our utmost respect. I think of them as awesome, as in the old context of the word: they fill me with *awe*. My brother-in-law was in Vietnam, a tough-guy Marine who saw a lot of action. I have a good friend too, Ward, who still carries shrapnel in his body due to Vietnam. In addition, he lost his hearing because his tank got barraged with deafening shots and bombs. He's older than I am but still running, believe it or not. What resilience he's displayed! But not all have. Vietnam vets struggle with high rates of unemployment, addiction, homelessness, and suicide.

Landing (Mostly) On My Feet Post-Military

As I said, I was spared from the horrors of Vietnam. When I got out of the military, I was whole. I had to move on with my life and become a regular citizen. I took a civil service exam and did very well. I became a letter carrier for the Post Office, walking all over the place the year of 1970. I didn't like it there, though. Quite political. I was still a hippie in my mind. The "good-old-boy" milieu that operated there wasn't compatible with my mojo.

At this time, I was looking around for something else. Like my dad, I had been a biology major in college—for my first three years before being expelled. I really wanted to be a medical technician. So, I went to the nearest hospital and got a job in their pharmacy department. Little did I know, my future wife was also working at that hospital, Strong Memorial. But Strong is so huge that there's no way we would have ever seen each other in passing. I worked there about three years. I was still drinking and doing drugs.

During my time at the post office and pharmacy, I always had a camera in my hands, and that has been one of the major themes of my life (you'll see deeper connections in subsequent chapters). I had had a camera in the army as well. My paternal grandfather always had a movie camera in his hands to make old family films, so I think it was in our blood. Today, I still possess reels and reels of his sixteen-millimeter films from early motion picture days of the 1930's that I've collected. Anyway, around this time of my narrative, I had taken a night course at the U of R (University of Rochester) in basic photography, since Strong Memorial where I worked is affiliated with them. The class pricked my interest in the arts enough that I wanted to get out of the pharmacy. All I had been doing was wandering around the vast hospital's halls, pushing a cart, delivering medication. That wasn't my cup of tea.

Dick Rowe, owner of Rowe Photography, came looking for me one day. He was a close friend of my younger brother. He was a nice young guy, and he knew I had an interest in photography. Maybe I had gone into his place to buy film once; I don't know. The Rowes were a fairly well-known family, liked around Rochester. They had started their small business when film first came out—around the turn of the century. I worked for them a short time. Since then, I've taken thousands upon thousands of photos, many of them to chronicle my life and adventures. I didn't know it then, but that little job was going to open the doorway to my life's main profession.

THE SIN-SICK SOUL

Substance Abuse

"My Prison"

My prison bars are self-imposed,
Existing in my mind.
They press upon my attitudes,
Restrictions so defined.

I sense incarceration here,
A box that won't unseal.
When without warning, I should see
The bars, something, reveal.

My keeper has a set of keys
With which to set me free.
I plead with him intently now,
Allow their use by me.

He never heeds the yearning cries
Of my sincere request,
But when I least expect it yet,
He grants me my behest.

I don't know how this happens so
Or what entraps my mind,
But when I find my soul in angst,
The bars dissolve in time.

The old hymn "A Balm in Gilead" has a line in regard to "sav[ing] the sin-sick soul." But hold on, wait a minute—we were just talking about my days as being one long string of mindless, drugged-out moments that were basically okay with me, given the low degree of responsibility in my life at that time. I was as content as the times would allow, I thought. So what gives?

Well, underneath that easygoing veneer, I was sick and didn't know it. My outward life could have appeared to be all right; however, my soul was anything but. Deep down inside, things were very wrong. I was a drug user, an alcohol abuser, and I would have to come to own those facts. I would have to "get real." Because of guilt or simply a lazy attitude, many abusers can't ever simply admit that they have a problem, and that is unfortunate for them and everyone else around them. That's because once substance abuse gets its grip on you, it doesn't like to let go. And then even after you conquer it, it can on occasion come back for a visit, sometimes longer than you expected. Remember Captain Morgan? Well, he's fictional. *I* was the one who was making me sick. My "prison bars" were indeed "self-imposed," like Dad's poem says.

The Alcoholic Gene

I am going to begin by talking in detail about my particular experience with substance abuse, along with my observations and conclusions about drug and alcohol habits in general. This is not easy for me, but if it can help someone, then it needs to be done. At the end of the chapter I will also briefly explore what I think to be true about addiction in terms of what the Bible has to say. The best authority in all life matters, of course, is the Bible. God's Word is timeless and remains the ultimate source of wisdom for all problematic situations. Plus, you might be surprised to know that the ancient people of biblical times grappled with substance abuse just like we do.

Although there aren't very many references in the few bygone records we have, drugs and some drug addiction did exist back then. Substances like glycerol, opium, mushrooms, and hemp definitely were around. There was even an extensive drug trade set up, according to History Extra's article "Happy Plants and Laughing Weeds: How People of the Ancient World Used—And Abused—Drugs." In fact, as this source tells us, "Careful investigation over the past two decades has begun to reveal patterns in the use of these drugs, previously unsuspected even by twentieth-century classical historians." So, just like the book of Ecclesiastes says, there's really nothing new under the sun, is there?

Fast-forward to my lifetime. My paternal grandmother, Jessie, was an alcoholic who hid the truth for many years. There is a lot of covert behavior in the entire family unit that goes along with most addictions because of shame and desire to avoid conflict. The addicted person's relatives "go along to get along." Today, we call this "codependence"—when family members buy the abuser's evasive denial and turn a blind eye to the concerning behavior. I suspect that there were several previous generations in our family tree who also bore that burden, that dark family secret. I don't know for sure. It wasn't talked about much. My uncle tells the story that my grandmother hid her booze in the toilet tank... hmm, I've never thought about that trick! I think Dad had some stories too. But I am not trying to be cavalier here. What I'm trying to illustrate is that alcoholism was and is a common thread in the tapestry of many families, a pervasive dysfunction that is pushed aside and not really dealt with, more often than not.

Yes, that tendency to abuse, or "gene" as we will call it, can spread over many iterations. I'm sure it caught me, but none of my siblings ever seemed to evince it. Geneticists today think that there actually is an alcoholism gene—in fact multiple ones—an organic reason behind what causes a person to become an alcoholic. This is still mostly theoretical, but there are some very convincing studies that have been conducted as we unravel the immensely complex workings of the human genome. The belief is that the genes do not directly *cause* someone to become an alcoholic; rather, they indicate only a *propensity* toward the problem. If they do not open the door, they unlock it, so to speak. Genetics are only 50 percent of the equation, says a 2008 meta-study conducted by the National Institute on Alcohol Abuse and Alcoholism (NIAAA).

What I'm writing here is not a scholarly study of genetics or physiology or brain chemistry or behavior, so I'm going to leave it at this: The American Addiction Centers (AAC) says, "If a person is predisposed to metabolize alcohol in such a way that the pleasurable effects are more prominent than feeling nauseous, overheating, or experiencing mood swings, the person may be more likely to develop alcohol use disorder." In other words, and these are my own, if you just naturally, for example, really like the taste of ice cream to begin with, you're likely to eat more ice cream. And if you like ice cream more than you are worried about other things, like sugar putting on excessive pounds or contributing to diabetes, then you are going to eat more ice cream still—maybe lots of ice cream. It's a vicious circle of rewards and consequences, but in the mind of the person with the addiction, the rewards seem to hold more sway. Some people call this having an "addictive personality." My substances of choice were primarily alcoholic beverages such as beer and liquor, followed by recreational drugs.

The AAC website tells us the extent of alcoholism in the United States. Here are some statistics: "As many as 18 million adults in the country struggle with alcohol use disorder; that is one in 12 individuals. Around 100,000 people die every year because of alcoholism, including deaths due to cirrhosis [of the liver] and other organ damage. Chronic heavy drinking also increases the risk of kidney disease, diabetes, and several cancers." It is also possible to acutely overwhelm oneself with a single overdose of alcohol, called "alcohol poisoning," or to asphyxiate on one's own vomit in the body's attempt to rid itself of the poison. Why would someone do this to themselves? These consequences are very large. We even call them "sobering." The payoff would have to seem *very large* indeed to make them seem palatable enough, or at least endurable.

The Alcoholic Environment

So, what about the other 50 percent of the equation? Our answer is the environment.

My mom and dad were quite into the suburban social culture of the fifties. This environment encouraged people to drink and smoke, not to excess but just occasionally, for mild social lubricant. That's what they did on their time off to socialize, to unwind a bit. As kids we were exposed to secondhand smoke and firsthand drinks. Nobody was going to bat an eye if you had one. If you wanted to act like a grownup, you smoked like the Marlboro Man (cowboy) and drank like the Crooners (certain Hollywood entertainers who always had a cocktail glass in their hand).

Today we have a huge opioid dependence problem in our country. The kids in today's generation start the train much earlier and enter the world of substance abuse with much more serious gateway drugs. Obviously, they are introduced to the drugs through other users. In terms of peer pressure, I remember smoking as a teen with my friends, but luckily I had other interests to deflect me from the magnet of partying. I was more targeted on sports and fitness than carousing. But as a high schooler, the temptation was always there to dip your toes into that dark water. Once that engine started, there was no stopping it. Enter the sixties with "sex, drugs, and rock 'n' roll" all around you and blanket social permission, and we had a recipe for trouble. I do clearly remember the first time I got drunk—not just inebriated but smashed drunk. Throw in marijuana and girls—see ya! Inhibitions gone…As I said, I was able to temper that influence with school and running, but as for what most kids did at that age, drug and alcohol use beyond their parents' casual patterns was somewhat considered okay. Rebellion to the rules of parents and society was a common form of behavior back then.

So I used substances in high school, my first round of college, the army, then when I resumed civilian life. "Everybody was doing it." That's my excuse. I really started smoking heavily in the army, though. I smoked like a chimney for about five years, total. Would you believe that I, someone who liked running, was smoking like a fiend? It's hard to believe that a guy who was even only a dilettante runner, needing lungs in fairly good shape, would do such a thing, ever. I didn't do any running in the army; my body was a disaster—weak, flaccid, and a chemical wreck. But I should have known better. We didn't really know the size of the problem, what cigarettes could do to a human body long-term, either.

Substance abuse was never an angry part of my adult life, because I was a "nice drunk," a placid pothead. I had just always been "having fun"—or so I thought. I didn't do it to quell embittering feelings of boredom or inadequacy, either. Smoking dope and drinking had been my thing for quite a few years, just because they could be, I guess. Although there may have been a touch of Grandma's strain, the activity was mainly social for me. In the army, I was basically safe from harm, and it was like a picnic. Wine, women, and song… and woah, we were flying high with our buddies. Personally, there was a little guilt mixed in there for me, as mentioned before. But when I got out of the army, alcohol had turned me into quite a different person in terms of who I really was. I felt somewhat isolated, and my lifestyle didn't feel as fun anymore. After I realized that, I came to not respect myself so much.

Because I wasn't violent and causing problems for others, and I had plenty of people around me doing the same thing, no one was telling me to address my problem. But it was growing and growing. I was descending. I would go so far as to say that addiction was the dark demon of my early adult life. When I was moving in the direction of what people refer to as "rock bottom," I had to accept that an issue existed.

Bottoming Out

I eventually dropped like a dead weight into an enormous pit of self-loathing. Up until then, I had tried unsuccessfully to push away any sense of responsibility I may have felt for the hold alcohol had on me. No matter how far and wide you try to run away from a drug addiction, however, you're likely to circle right back to yourself as the root problem. As they say, "You can run, but you can't hide."

Everyone trips up sometimes in life. But Hebrews 12:1 states, "Let us strip off every weight that slows us down, especially the sin that so easily trips us up. And let us run with endurance the race God has set before us." Basically, we don't have time for drugs, the Bible says—not if we've got better things to do. My addiction was my weight that passage speaks of, my stumbling block. As it advanced, other people were starting to catch on too. I had gotten a name for myself as "Greg the Tripper." That pun wasn't too funny to me; it was downright embarrassing considering I was a runner! I suppose the element of irony is what made it so hilarious to my associates. But in my own view, it marked my shame. Isn't addiction just like that? Self-defeating? I have to say that as I was increasingly smoking and doping, the doctors, trainers, and coaches did notice my huffing and puffing, my reduced lung capacity. My friends and family saw it too. But they didn't say much, other than to make that little joke, because it made them feel uncomfortable.

There are many rationalizations that people with addictions try to get by on. For example, we say that the next guy is worse off, further into it. Looking at it that way, in comparison to some others I knew of, I wouldn't have agreed that I was an abuser if you had asked me at that time. I wasn't a "drug addict"—no way! Well, just wait a minute. I'm not personally proud to say it, but I *was*. I surely was. The recreational marijuana I often did throughout this period of my life had me in a constant subjective haze and craving more. I was experimenting with other things too. But aside from all that, the substance that hurt me the most was alcohol—because of the extra addictive quality of it that chemically seemed to fit my individual makeup. It fit my hand like a glove.

Alcohol. I drank after work at bars and at home. I drank here; I drank over there. I was never a counter, but that was just another way I duped myself. I drank: Every. Single. Day. Scotch was my go-to selection, although I drank a lot of other types of stiff drinks as well. I drank Captain Morgan, believe it or not, just like my dad's poem. And I drank Irish whiskey. Oh man, once I discovered that, that was the end of the end! Boy, I really loved that. I drank only about three generously apportioned drinks a night, but again, it was *every single night*, not a couple times a week. It became rather habitual, to say the least. If I didn't get a drink that day, I was going nuts. No doubt about it—I was a functioning alcoholic, and as long as I could perform at my job and hold down my other responsibilities, it seemed like no big deal. That was a second rationalization.

It's hard to admit that I was an alcoholic for another reason as well: because my wife, Donna, was my drinking buddy, and sitting down with a few shots was a "special" time for us—time for talking and relaxing, not time for keeping track. Time for unwinding, for chatting about the day's events, for bonding more, for growing more emotionally intimate with each other. A space in which to share our joys and grievances. It was an activity we associated with each other, even with our love for one another, as odd as that might sound. I had love then. Alcohol didn't take my love away; in a skewed way, it appeared to add to it. I actually thought it aided me, that I was being a good husband, a good father with it. I don't know exactly what my kids would say, but I don't think I neglected them much. We could have been lackluster parents before our twins were age three (when we got saved and stopped), but they didn't seem to be suffering, or even noticing what we were up to. But who would expect them to, in their baby minds? Do you see the errors in my thinking, which seemed so logical to me at the time? I'm sure things would have gotten much worse as time went on, the way things were going.

So, Donna and I weren't exactly bar flies, especially after we got married. We had backed somewhat away from that scene before we had the kids. But I was still hurting myself, and she was still hurting herself by drinking at home. It went beyond the emotional too—Donna fell a few times and ended up in the ER getting stitches. She would try to hide this from people. We were closet drinkers. We didn't even talk about it between ourselves.

But talking about it is key in today's world. Get it out in the open to understand its draw and power, the part of it that decimates our self-control. Interventions are more successful when people don't feel as much of the stigma to discuss their experiences, when they have more ability to communicate and get support. When there's more loving acceptance that opens the door to self-empowerment and correction. Not approval. Compassion.

Addiction as Thief

As a kid I didn't really know about evil. My parents never talked about it—about sin. It just wasn't part of our family's language or thoughts. Remember, our orientation was just slightly in the believer zone.

And because I didn't know what evil was or looked like, I wasn't on my guard; I easily fell victim to it. But as I wised up, I began to dread the worst possible scenario, the one that can never be undone. Addiction derails many a life and even brings some to their graves. The end result is bad, potentially lethal. In one case, an addiction to OxyContin pain pills was the cause of the suicide of a relative of mine. Some people overdose with the substance itself, accidentally or on purpose, in one last, huge, "glorious" high; some people execute themselves in other ways just to be rid of the nightmare. This is something I wish had never been let loose in the world, unleashed from the mythological Pandora's Box of evil. It devastates countless numbers of today's families. I fear that you, dear reader, have a similar story, a connection of some distressing and tragic sort.

Being addicted simply means that whatever the attraction is for you, you have no say over the habit of engaging it; it orders *you* around and tells you if you will live or die. At the least, it impairs your life. It gets in the way of other things you need to attend to or want to accomplish. It robs your soul, like Dad wrote.

The Spiritual Antidote

All is not hopeless, really, if you have a problem. There is a biblical principle, a central tenet of the Jewish and Christian religions, that can help us with addiction. In fact, it is the very first item in the list of the Ten Commandments that Moses was given. Exodus 20:2–3 and Deuteronomy 5:6–7 say, "I am the LORD your God...You must not have any other god but me."

What does that mean, though? That's ancient language. This law was originally commanded by God to prohibit the worshipping of gods other than him (Yahweh)—that is, false gods. Today, Jews, Christians, Muslims, and followers of some other religions ascribe to monotheism, not polytheism. (*Poly* means *many* in Latin, *mono* means *one*, *theo* means *God*, and *ism* means a *school of thought*.) We Christians believe in one almighty God, so this commandment obviously doesn't apply in the original sense. The point is moot. In fact, for today it seems totally unrelatable—at first glance. According to Harvest.org, "This is one commandment most of us do not think we ever break. We tend to imagine an idol worshipper lying prostrate before a carved image."

Yet, the commandment is much broader than that. An idol as we think of it nowadays is any person who is so highly esteemed as to be almost "worshipped"; think *teen idol* or the show *American Idol*. That's the kind of idol that's probably innocuous enough, as it is only a hyperbole. What the commandment more aptly refers to is any one thing that takes the place of God in our lives. According to Harvest.org, "It is anything—an object, idea, philosophy, habit, occupation, sport, or person—that is your primary concern, or that to any degree decreases your trust and loyalty to God."

Drugs are obviously pleasurable to areas of the brain, inducing a sense of euphoria. Alas, that is violating the boundaries and sanctity of our holy temple that God created to be the clean and whole vessel for our spirit. But it can't end there. People look to repeat the euphoria any way they can. They must possess the drug only to be possessed *by* it, ironically. So it necessarily becomes a sought-after possession. One of the evils of drugs is that they cause so much crime and violence in the endeavor to obtain them.

We don't need to read the commandment "Thou shalt have no other gods before me" as punitive, though. Psychology tells us that positive reinforcement usually works better than negative reinforcement. Mary Poppins said, "A spoonful of sugar makes the medicine [here, meaning advice] go down." So taken less legalistically, the first commandment is a helpful aphorism for life. In the spirit of its meaning, the first law of being a God-fearing human suggests that to keep things running smoothly, you've got to maintain your central objective properly. That's your focus on God. Imagine it as a guardrail for a driver. Go off the path and hit the guardrail, and the guardrail reminds you that beyond it there's certain danger. Go off the path, hit the guardrail, and break through that guardrail, and you know you are in serious trouble. The commandment is a reminder to make the Lord first, and all else will then fall into place—safely. It makes sense, because God has all the answers. To let him reign supreme in your life is to be wise and to avoid a life of pain. Allow the Lord to control you.

This is not said to be judgmental of anyone. I don't mean to suggest for one second that I could walk in the shoes of everyone with addiction. They could have faced even greater lures or pressures to succumb. There are things I may not understand or have the full story on. I'm not a doctor or psychologist, so my discussion is inherently incomplete. I don't profess to know it all about correcting drug addiction. I'm just saying that God wants to be the center of our lives no matter what.

Final Thoughts

Many addicts are initiated into their current condition because of socioeconomic reasons or traumas that they never asked for. They are victims of something larger than themselves. But they must fight. The Bible tells us that Satan is prowling around like a lion in search of souls. He wants to steal yours; he wants you miserable. Resist him! You can shove him away. You can put your foot down and simply decide to get the reins over your life. Don't even go *near* that guardrail God is providing you with, if you can help it. God's will is for us to stay connected to him. So stay in the game. Stay in the race. And if you are addicted, never, ever give up trying. It's your life, so claim it.

Okay, one last thing, a question I've been asked: can one be addicted to *running*? Remember the definition of *addiction* from Harvest.org? It mentioned sports. I've heard of some people taking running too far, which really is too bad. That usually happens when someone becomes addicted to the endorphins being generated through running. (These create the "runner's high," which we'll examine in an upcoming chapter.) There have been lamentable stories of people becoming desperate to run marathons back to back, runners so inseparable from their activity that they've ravaged their bodies and died through exhaustion. Or runners can become very thin. I'm sure every sport has its ability to create problems like these in its own unique way. Regardless, there is such thing as excessive wear and tear that our systems were never designed to take. A runner who just passed away recently, David Clark, has an incredible autobiography called *Out There: A Story of Ultra Recovery*, about his transformation from drug addict to recovered person *to running addict*. He didn't die from running; he died during an operation to repair a herniated disc, but he believed that he eventually would die from running itself. So sad.

I never had an addiction to running. Thankfully, I was able to have a healthy relationship with my sport. God placed it in my life as a joy, not a curse. I was always able to keep it in balance. It wasn't my focus; it was just something special God gave me through his love. It was my release, my friend, my entertainment…but never my *god* with a lower case. Here's a thought for you. Never take something that was beautiful in your life—a blessing—and let it get out of hand. Remember, "All things in moderation." This phrase was first stated by the ancient Greek poet Hesiod, although there are short passages from the Bible written earlier that approximate the same notion. It's been around a long, long time. So even if your "guilty pleasure" is something as harmless as frequent oversleeping or binge watching too much Netflix, be careful. Anything that started out good but now gets in your way could potentially ruin you. That distortion is a perversion of what God first gave you to enjoy, among other things.

CAN WE START RUNNING ALREADY?

Getting Saved

"Clean Sweep"

I don't like to wake up
To yesterday's dishes.
I'd rather have prospects,
A new day's great wishes.

And what is left over
From yesterday's hassle,
I'd rather forget—leave
There back in the prattle.

I'll now ask my thinking,
The day not to rehash.
I don't want to live with
My yesterday's grim trash.

Forget it tonight, cast
The memory long gone,
To start out tomorrow
With bright, brand-new heart song.

Substance abuse went on dismally in my life—until I got saved. All the years up until then, I had had a relationship with Captain Morgan, but all along, it should have been instead with Jesus Christ. Finally, through little doing of my own and really only the Lord's grace, there was the day, *the* day, of the classic "a-ha!" moment. The day that Donna and I recognized that what we were doing was bad and walked down the aisle from our sin-sick seats in the church pew to give our hearts to the Lord. We both would turn the corner at that point, praise God!

That's when I cleaned up everything! Cut my hippie hair short and stopped all cigarettes, alcohol, and drugs. My wife and I—we had been inveterate alcoholics; then the next thing, as born-again Christians, we were pure as the white driven snow. And we never looked back.

Now let me insert a brief parenthetical note here, though, because the "never looked back" part needs a little qualification. Sure, to be fair, I had minor relapses a time or two. For example, when we left the big church we had gone to for years, and passed through a transitional phase in which we didn't have a church family, that wasn't a happy time for several other reasons as well, and I started drinking again a bit, for a few years. Not heavy drinking, just the soft stuff, wine and beer. But that was bad enough. That's why it's important not to lapse in church attendance. What pulled me out of that time was a gradual process of recognizing that I had to really make it an ongoing commitment not to drink *anything, anymore*. My wife and I had made the decision together after another spiritual dawning, but more about that later.

Now don't jump to conclusions and think that's the end of that story. Today, if alcohol were to be in my house, I'd still want it. For sure. If there were even a small amount for cooking use, like brandy in the cupboard, I would hit it. It's that strong of a snare. So we don't keep it around. We don't invite temptation.

Coming to Jesus

So, back to my wonderful conversion, my awakening. How did I come to God, you ask? Become born again? Well, it was 1976 BC. Yes, not AD; I said BC. *Before Christ*. Before my coming to Christ. It was my brother, two years younger—my best friend, Jeff—who got me hooked on Jesus, and that got me clean. But, as you'll see, Jeff originally seemed like the least likely person on the face of this earth to have performed that role. Jeff had been a musician, a consummate roadie who lived in Hollywood trying to make it big as a rock star and expert guitar craftsman. He was my *idol* (yep, there's that word!). He was a fellow druggie just as thick into it or more so than me. He had been my drinking and doping pal.

But then he did something weird. He got saved. I said, "Whatever happened to Jeff, the guy I used to smoke dope with and get high with?" He didn't know. He had become rather conservative.

One day, he did something even more strange, totally mind-blowing, and invited me into his faith. He was a new Christian on fire for the Lord. Always preaching to me after he got saved. He had made such a dynamic turn in his life that he had wanted me to follow him. Proselytizing and assertive were his ways. He started to witness to me by pushing all sorts of high-minded books my way, knowing I liked to read. He told me to read the Bible especially. I didn't want any part of it at first. It was obvious that this all was just a come-on. He was trying to brainwash us, me and Donna, to lure us in.

He kept trying to reach me. I know he wanted me to make a "clean sweep" of my behaviors and morals, like in Dad's poem I opened with. Applying a little more effort, he introduced me to Christian books not as intimidating, and those started to speak to me. I read about the amazing concept of being "born again." That sounded good, like it could be a washout of all my history with illegal substances. The well-known, canonical Christian apology *Mere Christianity* by C. S. Lewis caught my interest and attention, then I gave the Bible another try. It all was making sense now. I had started with the book of John. That was the catalyst, the ignition. It was the first Scripture I had ever read in a meaningful way. It's all about love, you'll remember, and that's what spoke to me. You know what passage I'm talking about. In the end zones of football games, they hold up the banners that read "John 3:16: 'For this is how God loved the world...'" That is a verse so many people know and treasure. It is popular for a reason.

And that's when the lights went on. Oh. My. God. (I'm not taking the name of the Lord in vain here; instead, I'm saying that I finally saw that God was phenomenal and could be something of *mine!*). I had discovered the Lord; I wasted no time then in coming to Jesus and getting born again. I used to call myself "The Born-Again Hippie." I'm being funny here, self-deprecating, but the principle is as serious as they get. I doubt that anyone of sound mind wakes up one morning and declares, "This is the day I make my decision to become an addict." That is not natural. God wants us to be in our good and natural state, the one in which we were born, not the one that's been corrupted by life. If you've allowed drugs to get the upper hand, or anything else for that matter, it doesn't have to be permanent. God and Christianity had finally come onto center stage for me, and they can for you too. I had somehow "found religion" through the back door, so don't be surprised if God saves you that way too.

With this newfound revelation of God's love for me, I saw that he was about to give me better purpose and direction in life and abolish my connection to drugs. The books of Psalms and Proverbs next really resonated with me; Psalms talked about wandering in darkness, and Proverbs told me how to get out of it. (I take no glory for myself because without God I would still be wandering in darkness.) So in 1976 at twenty-eight years old, when I started my Christian walk, a new existence began for me.

And then my brother did a third weird thing. He invited me to his church, Faith Temple in Rochester, New York. We (my wife and I) started attending Jeff's spirit-filled church and one day responded to an altar call to accept the Lord. That was the official fork in the road that led us "cold turkey" away from drugs and alcohol. I started to spend a lot of time in church after that.

My First Spiritual Home

Faith Temple was very big on preaching the Word, and I say I got my basic training boot camp there. The book of Acts is the story of the church and the beginning of the history of Christianity as a formal religion. It is about Christ's apostles receiving the gifts of the Holy Spirit to assist them in going out and spreading the gospel and being soldiers for Christ; it's about them healing people like Jesus did and establishing the first church communities. Because Faith Temple was a Pentecostal-type church, they embraced the full experiences of the early church—like being born again, receiving the gifts of the Spirit, doing hands-on healing, and speaking in tongues. I was on fire for God there and told everyone evangelically about my new relationship with All Things New. I was excited to witness to anyone who would listen to how God rescued me. Donna and I had a ministry there, and I still do it. I go to the hospital to visit people who are sick. As a disciple of Christ, I will lightly touch them, my hand on their forearm, in my mind exuding a healing spirit through that contact, praying for them silently.

Besides developing my personal relationship with Jesus, reading the Bible, attending church services, and engaging in service, I took some adult Sunday school classes at Faith Temple. I took a class called "Understanding God," vital for all new Christians of various ages and backgrounds. Later in my journey, I became the teacher and department head for that class. I did this for ten years, and the enrollment was always around sixty or seventy people. This was an important part of my function in ministry and eventual church leadership as an elder at Faith Temple. I was also involved in a men's group, and we had a meeting every week. I eventually became its vice president. It was called FGBMI (Full Gospel Businessmen International), and we would have breakfasts and an altar call at the end of them.

There was another runner there, a friend. Lew Proper, a "proper" Catholic man, had lapsed in his journey, but I brought him back to the Lord through that group. He was integral to my life, to my own spiritual development, as we were in that walk together. Because I was responsible for him, not only myself, he kept me on the right track, and I'm forever indebted to him for reciprocally helping me toward salvation.

As I said, I was known by my fruit of separating from many years of darkness. I received a renewed body and soul and was launched into a spiritual life I never knew existed. We were all flowing together at that church in God's grace, building the church and seeing converts added daily with signs and wonders. I was participating in a wonderfully diverse fellowship of believers, and I felt truly cared about.

In our process to get clean and recover from addiction, any one of us can get support like that from others, as in Alcoholics Anonymous or

Narcotics Anonymous. I was never in these; I've dropped casually into AA meetings to see what they were about. I think it's a great organization. They connect people up with sponsors, who are former alcohol abusers who can be there for them when the going gets rough. I know people who are really staunch believers of that system, and I admire them. It works for many, many people. Their program explains that when it comes right down it, we must *want* the change. We must acknowledge our powerlessness and rely on a higher power. We must be authentic in our decision to stop doing our own thing and trust in the Lord.

It's our free will that determines how we'll wake up the next day—a prisoner of our most egregious fears, insecurities, and baits, or a liberated child of God standing firm with self-restraint. It's good at this moment to reflect on the well-known and treasured "Serenity Prayer" by American theologian Reinhold Niebuhr that was adopted and popularized by AA and other such twelve-step programs: "God, give me the serenity to accept the things I cannot change, the courage to change the things I can, and the wisdom to know the difference." It's like in my father's poem where the persona is requesting serenity with a "clean sweep" of his soul. With setting aside substance abuse, I had the courage to change the things I could.

So, at this point I was living clean and had a clear purpose in my life. A roadmap of sorts had appeared. I understood God and his role in my new existence, and he understood me. He had *always* understood and cared for me, though I wasn't aware before then. Now I felt confident that he believed in me, that he was taking a vested interest in me. And this transformation was about to propel me forward in other ways. I was on my way to becoming a serious runner.

Health was not the reason for me quitting smoking. As I mentioned earlier, once we got saved, and the boys were three or four, I cleaned up my act, thoroughly. I changed from a two-pack-a-day smoker to someone with not a single cigarette in his possession. Then I saw a neighborhood guy running around and around the block and got inspired. Health *was* the main reason for me beginning to run again. My first post-drug road race was the Irondequoit Five Mile, right on my own turf, on roads I was familiar with growing up. I was just beginning my renewed love for competitive running while detoxing from my happy hippy lifestyle. It was a hot summer run on a particularly challenging course, the last half-mile up a steep hill to the finish. I landed in the top ten.

Then I read a book about running and decided I'd like to attempt a marathon. So, I started reading more voraciously about training. I trained for a year, faithfully. From there, my friend Steve signed us up for a Syracuse event called the Burger King Marathon. (With good humor, I realize that today this name looks antithetical to solid nutritional support for a runner.) I wasn't the holder of a peak physique or burning the roads up or anything, but both of us ended up in the top ten. It was a great accomplishment to even finish, because we'd never attempted one of those long races before.

I had wanted to get in shape, but I didn't take it as earnestly as an Olympic athlete. It was a physical by-product of everything good that came along with the Christian lifestyle. I always put my training in perspective, in balance with other areas of my life. After the marathon finish in Syracuse at 3:13 or so, then it was on to the Rochester Marathon. I ran that race in the city and suburbs, did pretty well, and then started gearing up more. I had been bit by the bug of competitive racing! This was during my marathon prep phase when I started running three marathons a year, getting my sights set for Boston. I was getting close to Boston qualification and ran the Skylon in Buffalo the same year, where I finally achieved my goal.

Reader, I ask you to reflect on that past we keep moving away from, the one I spoke about in the preface. If you've not yet turned to the Lord, never fear; away-facing flowers eventually grow towards the light. What would it take to have you come to God, if that could be done right here, right now—today?

MIGHTY MENTORS

Crazy-Good Heroes

"Something Left Behind"

I think that I will fade away,
Not strive to be so pined.
To be acclaimed—less who I was,
More what I left behind.

It might be just some simple thought
I've managed to complete.
One day, someone will find these things
That I hoped to bequeath.

Of seeds I've planted there are few,
Yet flowers, they do thrive.
As long as they are given care,
The memories will survive.

It's like a note left on the stand,
"Gone shopping, back at noon."
The student will remember me;
I'm coming back real soon.

* * *

When Teacher's gone, and you are 'lone,
Go find something they've left.
Just know that they are still around,
Don't feel yourself bereft.

"To be acclaimed, less who I was, more what I left behind." That phrase from my dad's poem strikes to the very heart of mentorship. My mighty mentors on my track of life were many and humble. They wanted to be known not for *who* they were but for *what* they brought to the world, what they left behind. In most cases, that was inspirational deeds and knowledge imparted to future generations. These teacher-types didn't want to *give* "the fish" away; they wanted to teach their students *how* "to fish."

My Local Running Inspirations

Like King David, there are many people I've respected in life. Those include, as I've shared with you already, my great-grandfather, great-grandmother, grandfather, grandmother, my father, and my brother Jeff. As far as my running career, I'm going to now discuss the people who were most impactful, from near and from afar.

First, I'll speak about my homegrown mentors. Back in high school, Roger Goodman was my first cross-country coach. Reed Kepner was my first college cross-country coach. Those were my only formal coaches over my whole career. These two guys molded and generally impressed me to a large extent.

Locally, my inspirations for marathon running in particular were two special nearby men. Don McNelly was the first. I recall Don fondly. A neighbor, he was my friend and a friend of my dad's, an apiarist (beekeeper) like me and my father, and a winemaker. Dad met Don through me. Don was *always* running. He had run a thousand marathons and other races before he died! Well, not that many, but as an icon of running, Don actually did approximately eight hundred events. He has the distinction of competing in the most marathons locally for anyone over the age of eighty. There is a book called *The Runner, The Madman* about him and his prolific accomplishments as an older person. Norm Frank was another nearby inspiration for whom I could say much the same. But for mega-marathons, more commonly called "ultramarathons" (races with distances beyond fifty kilometers/thirty-one miles). Norm introduced me to this brave new world. Don McNelly and Norm Frank were two Rochesterian role models I was fortunate to have—my closest mentors.

They both taught me that running could be a fun, social experience, reconnecting me to the part of myself I had lost during my drug abuse. But—and this is more important for the competitive athlete—they taught me about persistence. That means getting up every morning and running, even when you don't feel like it. Being regular about following a defined regimen is essential. Running can be fun, but you have to work hard. You have to put the drudgery away mentally and just think of the work. You are training for a goal, so that helps. You think about the future achievement and how to get there.

For example, if I'm looking at a training schedule, I have to plan for it to be "hard, easy." That means that one week will be hard, one easy. One month will be hard, one month will be easy. One year will be hard, one year will be easy. It gives your body and your mind time to recover. You've got to have "zero days," days you just rest. When I was training like a banshee,

Sundays were always my days off (you know, Sunday, the "day of rest"). I was pretty adamant about that. Later on, when I was a trainer, I would set up schedules that would be hard-easy, like interval training, for people. Again, this was for the recovery factor, so you could patch yourself up from the assault.

My National and International Running Exemplars

Next, I'm going to talk about people I didn't personally know, but who were my idols, in the correct sense of the word (I admired but did not worship them). The runner who has my greatest respect is Dr. George Sheehan, a medical doctor. He bravely served as a physician in the navy during World War II, on a destroyer, the USS Daly. He is also a *New York Times* best-selling author who wrote eloquently and convincingly about the sport of running in his book *Going the Distance* (1996). In addition, I admire Jim Fixx and his blockbuster *The Complete Book of Running* (1977). Fixx is thought of as the father of the 1980's American aerobic fitness craze; he showed us the health benefits of jogging and was the guy who really made running popular as a sport. He was a very wonderful resource for me through his smash-hit writing about running as a discipline, and I was fascinated by that idea, especially in my earlier years. These books I've mentioned are excellent manuals about running, and I recommend them highly.

After I'd been running for a while and was into the Boston Marathon, Bill Rodgers became a hero of mine. To me, he was more of a "local" (accessible enough to at least see from afar as we ran the same race), but still formidable. He won several straight victories in both the Boston and the New York City marathons in the late seventies, even setting record-breaking times. He became an Olympian and elsewhere won twenty-seven out of thirty races he ran in 1978. That's incredible, considering all that competition! He finished his career having run fifty-nine marathons in total, winning twenty-two of them, half of which were clocked at under 2:15. "Boston Billie"—he's a legend. He's come to Rochester to speak before. He's written a book; he got so very many endorsements. Everything was named after him. If he were a football player, he'd be a multimillionaire.

There were more runners I greatly looked up to for their superpowers. The famous four-time Olympic gold medalist Jessie Owens and "The Four-Minute Mile Guy" were widely acclaimed, high-profile gents of the thirties and fifties, respectively. The latter was **Roger Bannister**, who broke the "sound barrier" of the four-minute mile with a time of 3:59.4 (that's written, in the runner's world, as minutes, seconds, and tenths of a second). Yes, that was down to the nitty-gritty, and that's how we do it. Six-tenths of a second are what gave him the edge. Wow.

Well, I'm not going to sit here and say that I attained the likes of any of their greatness—the people I just spoke about—but I tasted speed. I made it work for me. It's a whole new dimension when a child first runs, a feeling of discovery, disbelief even. A feeling of confidence as the passing air rushes through our hair and freedom dips down from the sky to touch our very being. What I experienced as an adult was something like that.

Now, I want to introduce you, if you don't already know about him, to Yiannis Kouros, who also was a huge icon of mine. You are going to be blown away by this guy! I'm not sure that he's even human. He has been my biggest inspiration and that of many other runners around the world. He's performed some pretty incredible feats. He's the man alive today who is considered the paragon of all runners. In fact, he's known as "The Running God." He's also called the "Golden Greek," just like Hermes, the Greek god of running. Yiannis Kouros. His is the name that inspires awe in the mind of all ultramarathon runners. He did his first Spartathlon (annual long-distance race in Greece) in 1983, and everyone thought he cheated by taking a shortcut or two because he ran so fast that people literally didn't believe it. Of course, he hadn't scammed them, though. But his time was so outrageous that from then on, race officials had to watch him to make sure he in fact didn't cut out any of the course. If his running doesn't impress you enough, know that in his spare time he's a poet, musician, artist, and philosopher as well.

Let's get some figures on this guy. In 1984 Kouros set a record that caught the breath of every person who heard about it. He ran the 153-mile Spartathlon in twenty hours, twenty-five minutes, and zero seconds (20:25:00—with no one near you, no need to get down to tenths of a second here!). That's an amazing mile every eight minutes, meaning about eight miles per hour at a constant speed for about a day! Here's another way to put it. Kouros has run about two minutes faster than the average of all marathon runners in the world, but he, as an ultramarathon runner, has also done it for about six times longer at a time than they have. And he did that four times! Sure, he's beaten himself, but no one else ever has. He's the king of time and distance combined *and* has broken many, many records for faster speeds over shorter distances. Of course, Kouros was the natural choice to play the Greek Pheidippides in the movie *The Story of the Marathon: A Hero's Journey* in 1991. Pheidippides, legend has it, was the ancient Greek who dropped dead after running incredibly fast to bring Athenian commanders the message of Greek victory over the invading Persians at the city of Marathon.

In case you're wondering, the top female record for the Spartathlon has been an incredible 24:48:18, set by Polish Patrycja Bereznowska in 2017, and there is a Greek goddess of female runners, named Atalanta. Greek mythology contains women who would be equal to or often outshine their male counterparts. The deity's name derives from the Greek word *atalantos*, meaning *equal in weight*.

Villains

Not everybody's a hero, though. Let's talk about cheating for a moment, the kind that officials thought Kouros might have done. Obviously, it's very bad to cheat, because those who do it are slighting other hardworking runners. There's not just recognition and a trophy but large cash prizes involved in many cases. For example, thousands of dollars for the Boston, Chicago, and New York City runs are at stake. You also get endorsements like I said, just like in football or any sport.

In addition to awards for sheer time, there's those for specific age class and gender too. Master's Level is forty years old and up. In a race I ran in Dublin, Ireland, when I was in that category, I was pretty furious about the lack of ethics some runners displayed. Besides getting the money, standards and propriety become important if you are trying to get admitted to big races like the Boston Marathon. This was the case for the Irish race, which as a forty-five-year-old I needed to run in less than 3:30 (three hours, thirty minutes) for a Boston age-group qualification. At this particular event in Dublin, I came in at 3:31, which was one minute too late. That was frustrating, but even more so than you'd think because there were guys who made the cut who were blatantly cheating, like literally not running fully around corners! So unfair. I guess that's where we get the phrase *cutting corners*.

I had to repeat my quest for qualification at another event somewhere else. But I never complained. I wanted to take "the high road" and press on. I wanted to be like the heroes before me.

A "KODAK MOMENT"

My Occupation

"The Photograph"

A picture's worth a thousand words,
Or so the poets say.
Well I saw one just yesterday
That blew my mind away.
It was a picture of a girl,
Whom I knew long ago.
So when I gazed across the frame,
The memories then did flow.

The photo holds a red-haired girl—
That made the memories start.
I was so starved for someone's love,
With ease she stole my heart.
She was a lovely, tender flower
Who briefly touched my life.
But who, so many years ago,
Became another's wife.

She'd offered me her love one day,
A prize I did refuse.
Because I didn't visit her,
Her true love I did lose.
She asked if I would come see her
And stay a day or two.
I was too shy to figure out,
To know, just what to do.

I failed to grasp the magnitude,
The offer I'd received—
Allowed the rose to wither there,
The blossom go to seed.
How could I tell her different, that
The trip I couldn't make?

It wasn't for the lack of love
The plum I would forsake.

It was my youthful innocence
That caused me to refuse.
It was the lack of worldliness,
My first real love to lose.
She never spoke again of that,
Or paid me any heed.
What could have been a raging fire
Just cooled and did recede.

I think of her from time to time,
Though time has dulled the mark.
I guess I'll always harbor her
In corners of my heart.
It makes me think of loves I've had
(And I have had a few).
I've learned from each experience
What to or not to do.

So live each moment to its most,
For time may bring you sorrow.
For chances that you let slip by
Can't be reprised tomorrow.

A simple, single photograph… it can hold so much meaning. As an enhancement of memory, it captures the magic of the moment and makes it permanent, relivable in a way. It defies the limits of time. A favorite photo is like a wormhole of the universe to another dimension because it tells a story that was once so real.

Photography is one human invention, quite recent, that has dramatically shaped our lives. It's a recorder and preserver of history. It's proof that some person, place, or thing existed, or some event truly did take place. Among its capabilities, it has not only given us lasting representations of deceased loved ones and historical figures, but it's evolved into a tool for gathering evidence in legal matters and conducting scientific research for which our human eyes aren't sophisticated enough. I'm talking about everything from shots of microscopic organisms to telescopic astrophotography of galaxies. Photography has also enabled self-expression and entertainment. With its unique capabilities of portraying light and shadow, it's every bit art form as it is utilitarian. Taken as a whole, the contributions that photography has made to our technology and cultural experience cannot be overstated. Photography is a window into and out of the human condition, with a very special type of lens.

Rochester, Land of Plenty

I think it was destiny that got me involved with photography. It's interesting that I fell into working at Rowe Photos. As I said, it wasn't intentional; it was just a job offered to me by an acquaintance because I needed some work. After working at Rowe Photos for a while as a young, married man, I decided I needed more money for family expenses. Money was pouring and pouring in at Eastman Kodak, the world's premiere photographic film company and our city's biggest employer, so I said, why not? I was in the right place at the right time.

Kodak made **photographic and motion picture film products. Begun in 1888,** Kodak rapidly became the seat of immense, and I mean *immense,* wealth. George Eastman, its creator, was a genius inventor, market innovator, and businessman. He could be compared to the likes of a Vanderbilt, Morgan, or Rockefeller. Like Ford made having a car a reality for the average family, Eastman brought cameras and film to all American households, which we of course gobbled right up. Kodak's slogan was "You push the button, we do the rest!" Strategically democratizing their low-cost product and promising ease of use for anyone, Eastman was handing out visions of the things everybody wanted—happiness, smiles, and love. Like today's selfies, photos then were representations of us in our "Sunday best," living the good life.

In case you're too young to remember what a "Kodak moment" was, it was a marketing phrase. It meant a perfectly ripe time for documenting an important scene from someone's life, a fleeting second of photographic opportunity that should not be missed. Whether it was a baby's first step or a Christmas gathering, Kodak reminded us that we should grab and hold onto it. The company produced many sentimental TV commercials in the sixties, seventies, eighties, and nineties illustrating this. The ads were so innocent and memorable, each with a little narrative like a snow globe of brief fantasy. It always incorporated that embrace of all-encompassing love one would want to keep and cherish. This would be a true Kodak moment.

Besides helping families grow closer, George Eastman was providing consumers with the new-fangled fun of taking snapshots, creating a simple yet gratifying hobby. Moreover, Eastman was making movie film, the medium through which our fascination with Hollywood came to life. Cinematography, the silver screen, was a huge part of the entertainment business.

Eastman's wildly successful empire rose quickly and maintained itself over a century. He didn't stop with cameras and film for both personal and commercial use. He created, as offshoot businesses to support those endeavors, the Eastman Chemical Company and the Eastman School of Music. He got into the music scene to provide the soundtracks for movies and so founded that world-class conservatory to feed his orchestras. In Rochester we have this internationally famous, prestigious institution that trained the musicians who would play the finest background music to go along with the film we sold, like one-stop shopping for movie producers. Most musicians consider the rigor of the Eastman School of Music to be second only to that of the Julliard School. Having a degree from Eastman says something. Besides still churning out superior performers—virtuoso symphonic players—today it also prepares eminent music historians, composers, theorists, therapists, and teachers.

And of course, these terrific players would then need somewhere elegant to perform. Besides, potential purchasers and investors would be flocking in from all over the world, so we needed to look good. Consequently, Kodak made the Eastman Theater, attached to the music school. If you've ever been in there, where the Rochester Philharmonic most often performs, you will be impressed by its grandeur. With its plush, red velvet auditorium chairs, its gleaming white marble balconies, and its golden fountains and other ornamentation, its colors are a feast for the eyes. With its immense crystal chandelier and its massive, scrolled columns accentuating its expansive interior height, it was and still is an enviably large theater for any city to have. Its classical murals of Grecian nymphs and hunters and ceiling of astrological designs showcase a sumptuousness that is the paragon of taste and luxury. The place vibrates with rich culture and emanates an aura of success. The world's greatest talents have performed there, like at Carnegie Hall.

We were booming as a city because of this company, raking the dough in hand over fist, like I said. It was putting us on the map. As Kodak's wealth visibly spread out through the city, like a fragrance filling a room, Rochester's streets became the portrait of many opulent Victorian mansions. Prosperity was gracing us with her wings. When I was employed there, seventy years after Kodak's inception, Rochester had grown to be the third largest city in New York, the Empire State, and it was just lovely.

The film industry was basically monopolized by Kodak. Making money exponentially, we were a Fortune 500 company from 1955 when the designation started, all the way to 2005. These were the halcyon days of Kodak. We were the crown jewel of Rochester, of New York State, of the United States, and one of the top three companies of the globe. We were world dominators. Nothing could stop us! We were firing on all pistons, so to speak. We were worthy to be a photographic portrait hung in history's Hall of Fame.

To get a piece of the pie, the American Dream Kodak was promising to every eager employee, all you really needed was a high school education. Positions were plentiful and easily obtained. **Kodak Park was a gigantic employer, itself the size of a small city, at its max with something like 50,000 workers of every shape and origin.** Everyone got a great career with great job security and would receive a great pension. People had lucrative, stable employment because of this exploding industry.

Damage Control

Thirty years was the total time of my gig at Kodak. Before I got saved, I worked there for three years as a quality control technician to begin with. I did shift work and was still drinking quite heavily. That's when I found the Lord and then cleaned up my act. I was then able to get a technical job doing safety research. I did this for about ten years. I was learning a great deal about chemical reactivity and fire and explosion hazards. It was really fun, as I was still living life on the wild side in a way, like a kid playing with matches. We tested *everything*. It was all about the raw materials in the film manufacturing process and seeing what they'd do. We tested the flammability of a lot of the products, especially those from China. If there were any objects that might be associated with Kodak film, like if a little teddy bear had a Kodak logo or was put with a film to sell, we wouldn't want them to catch on fire, of course, so we tried a lot of different things to see if they'd ignite.

Before I was in the safety group, one of the manufacturing processes had gone out of control, and the workers had blown up a building. People weren't killed, but many were very badly hurt. We ended up taking on one of the manufacturing guys who had been horribly burned. After he came out of rehab, he worked in our department. We were able to determine how the accident happened.

I wrote a paper on the film chemicals' dust explosivity factors, that is, certain characteristics of dust explosions, because those were not an uncommon safety hazard in the manufacturing of powders. Some of the chemicals that Kodak was making were impact sensitive (meaning the cause for ignition is a physical blow, as it happens with little kids' caps for cap guns). For instance, the employees might have a steel drum, drag it across the dust-covered floor, and just by the friction of doing that, it would sometimes burst into flames. We also designed all types of experiments that would determine what types of chemicals would be considered safe and inert. The chemicals being used, however, were actually more dangerous than thought and could usually be ignited under certain conditions—like those resulting from Murphy's Law. I'm being facetious here, but indeed things could happen unexpectedly. So we had to be ready for them, and better yet, be proactive in preventing them. All in all, I was carrying out my role well and was happy that I was doing something good to keep other people safe.

College the Right Way and Promotion

My Kodak years had bloomed, and I bought our first house, in East Irondequoit. I loved that place, starting a family there. It was a big old house that needed work, but we were handy. With gorgeous gumwood trim and moldings, it had so much potential. We had twins and filled up the house nicely. Rewinding in my story a bit, that was the time that I was doing trick work production, quality control in the paper film industry as a research technician. I worked three shifts, C-B-A. My wife and I alternated so one of us was always with the kids, not a babysitter. On occasion we received help from our parents.

After six years, my wife, Donna, got pregnant again, with our daughter Ashley. I was in my thirties. Superficially, I felt mostly like a success in my job. But deep down inside I still felt like I was a failure in this area of my life. At that point, it had been over ten years since I had been asked to leave my first college, where I had been a biology major. For years I knew I had the ability for more responsible activities at Kodak but was denied advancement because I lacked a college degree. So I got motivated and went back to college at Roberts Wesleyan for a bachelor's degree in Organizational Management. At this time, I was in my prime, doing EVERYTHING! I was running, I was racing, I was trying to be a good dad, I was engaging in my faith as a very active church member (three days a week), and to top it all off, I was going to school at night as a non-traditional student.

I remember that when I got that degree, it was a significant accomplishment because at that time in my life I had been starting a lot of things but not finishing them. To walk across the stage in cap and gown was a really big, big deal. When I was back at Kodak with my diploma in hand, I could demonstrate to my superiors that I was capable of advancing up the corporate ladder. And I would.

I started looking for a concrete path by which to rise in the company. There wasn't much opportunity for upward mobility in the department that I was working in (a few dozen people, very specialized work, as I said, fire and explosion testing for all Kodak chemicals). But there was room for more people in another department.

"You know what, Brooksie, you'd be very good in the industrial hygiene department. Why don't you come join us?" someone said. So I applied and got it. I had jumped a couple levels in "the ladder" right away. With an undergraduate degree, I was able to obtain a professional rating, meaning I was getting a salary. That was something to *talk about* at Kodak if you could work your way up from hourly to salary. With the acquisition of that bachelor's degree, well, wow, it was like being a floor scrubber and then becoming a supervisor! Quality Controller to Chemical Technician/Analyst to Industrial Hygienist. That's when I got my brand-new, shiny title. I literally now had the nifty nameplate "Industrial Hygienist" on my desk. But I knew that to hang onto it, I'd have to complete yet another hurdle: a master's degree. Although they gave me the job, I was expected to eventually cement my position educationally, officially, like most of the other guys had. But more on that later.

So, what exactly did that fancy IH crown entail? A natural outgrowth of my former position, it required looking out for all kinds of workplace hazards—health and safety issues—so as to protect the employees. But it was more than that. It was about being responsible for everything and everyone. I would observe individual people and follow along with them as they worked, studying them at their machines and the interactions between metal and flesh. I would scope out different environments they inhabited. It was me against the "bad guys" of the space, such as toxic chemicals, unsafe practices, etc.

There were hundreds of people I personally had to keep close tabs on, as Kodak in its heyday covered an enormous amount of workspace. Although there were lots of big ancillary buildings located elsewhere in the city, the main **Kodak Business Park** at that time was the largest manufacturing complex in the state. Beginning in 1890 and continuing over decades, Kodak Park was built and added onto numerous times to meet the massive demand for what America and the world wanted. The park would eventually become the biggest industrial filmmaking facility in the world. The physical size of Kodak Park, which ran along the Genesee River, was about four miles long and half a mile wide, totaling two square miles (not including the square feet of all the multiple floors in those buildings)! Spanning 1,300 acres, it had over **154 different buildings**. Technically, I worked for the Utilities Division, which covered most of the entire footprint of Kodak Park. My fellow hygienists and I had our work cut out for us.

I think, looking back, that I became an industrial hygienist, as a psychologist might say, because I had a latent desire after I had finished cleaning up my own act of drugs and alcohol and darkness to start scouring clean everything around me. Where better to do this than in the workplace and to get paid for my neuroses? I laugh now, but maybe that *was* really it. I wanted to preserve the orderliness, safety, and security of my life and by extension the physical environment of every coworker surrounding me. I cared about that, the health and wellbeing of my colleagues.

Eastman Kodak Running

Once I started being a real athlete after my spiritual conversion, I would run on my lunch hour outside of our industrial complex. We had sixty minutes to get in a workout, which was plenty of time for a quick five- or six-mile run. I didn't have to punch a clock, so I had a little leeway. Kodak Park was a giant place full of alleys, plus I had sprawling options all about town. I used a variety of routes. I sometimes went across the Genesee River. Then there was maybe a quarter-mile to Seneca Park with a mile loop around a pond perfect for repeats.

Being such a diverse and prodigious workforce at Kodak, there was a large number of people like me doing what was popular those days: running and socializing. There were so many, in fact, that we assembled a team to compete in local running events of six to ten miles. Our company had some very fast runners. We would compete in a race with other companies around town put together by a big national organization called the Corporate Challenge. From there, the CC also signed up the country's largest companies for regional challenges across the USA. This in turn culminated in an international championship race that was hosted by different participating cities around the world. Each year Kodak would easily win our city of Rochester race and go on to the regional and world races. I wasn't ever the top dog on our roster since short races weren't my specialty. Our group consisted of both a men's team and a women's team that were outstanding, though.

We would usually send one or both winning teams consisting of five to ten runners each to regionals and internationals. In 1992 we won the Rochester race as usual, and several runners in our B team went to a different city—Buffalo, New York—for the regional championship. I was chosen to be on the mixed team, two male and two female. There we swept up the competition again, sending two teams to New York City for the World Corporation Challenge. We filled two Kodak vans, and off to battle we went. It was a huge honor to take our team to a red-carpet event hosted by ESPN. We made TV and got all expenses paid. Our A team did okay as I remember, but the mixed team I was on came in second of many teams. It was time to celebrate!

Speaking of celebrate... our Rochester Kodak runners were quite well known, and we took many of them from our area to other large events around the state to compete individually. One such race was The Utica Boilermaker half-marathon, the largest and most well-known race that length in the nation, hosting thousands of runners from all over the USA. Rochester usually fielded a large contingent each year. I ran one year. The trip wasn't too far away—only several hours' drive. It was a very selective

44

event hosted by the Utica Beer Club. Free food and beverages afterwards. (I didn't want to drink the beer, but the food was delicious).

At the awards ceremony, the winner in each five-year age category, both male and female, was presented with an engraved pewter bowl. We Rochester individuals were overtaking everyone, it seemed like, winning most of the age categories. After each victorious runner was given a bowl, our tradition was to go to the beer tanker truck, fill the bowl with beer, stand in a circle with our cohorts, and pass it to the entire team to communally drink a sip or so. That was a ball for people, especially if you were a beer drinker. For me, it aroused temptation. I'm sure many stayed the night partying after that, too. I spent the return trip on a mattress in the back of a friend's pickup passed out—not from alcohol, but from physical exhaustion, a good day's run.

Nobody has a perfect life, but this was one of the best periods of my own, due to running and Kodak. I felt that God was blessing me with a plethora of uncommon experiences.

THE THRILL OF COMPETITION

My Early Races

"Accomplishments"

The day dawns blue with promises,
What great things will be done?
I hope to make a little dent,
But hours, they will run!

The sun's rays reach down from the sky
As if to shout their bidding.
There are so many things to do,
Yet here am I, just sitting.

What will the chores be for today?
What wonders to accomplish?
Will they be chances to construct?
Or things I must demolish?

If I should go on to delay,
By dusk I shall remark,
"It's just another wasted day,
And now I'm in the dark."

As a young man, I was primarily laid back. I was passive in some ways and had a just-go-with-the-flow mentality. Alcohol and drugs made me more so that way. Once I met God and removed that baggage, however, I was more clear-headed and started developing goals. Goals give you something to work toward and a chance to physically use some good old-fashioned elbow grease. Attained, they give you a culminating sense of satisfaction and self-esteem. They make you feel alive. When a person starts achieving, and feels vigorous and rewarded, it's a game changer. Goal setting begets more goal setting and is important for everyone. If not in regular life, in competitions I could be intense, but not so much in relation to other athletes. As a runner, I became an internally competitive kind of guy. I had goals to beat the me from earlier races. I guess you have to be that way; it's the nature of racing and self-improvement.

So somewhere along the line, I should explain to you, if you're not a runner, what the different lengths of the standard races are. There's a 5K (3.1 miles), a 10K (6.2 miles), a half-marathon (21 K or 13.1 miles), a marathon (42 K or 26.2 miles), and an ultramarathon (anything longer than 26.2 miles). Within the ultramarathon category, there is the 50K (31 miles) and the 100K (62 miles); then it goes from miles into hours, typically as far as you can run in twenty-four hours. Exceptional runners will run 100-plus miles in that timeframe, taking short breaks for naps and meals. Lastly, there are multiday races that occur over maybe a week (cross-country), in which athletes can sleep normal amounts of time.

In the beginning, I ran 5Ks and 10Ks just for fun and conditioning. I have a trophy room downstairs in my basement documenting these, but most of those races weren't wins. I'd have to say that my most triumphant moment ever in a race was when I was just starting out, ironically enough to say. I was in a short road race in Clayton, New York. It was called "Save the River." I came in first, and it was the first time I ever won a race outside of college. It was a watershed because I felt like I was an adult, competing in adult society.

As I've said, as I progressed, my thing became distance running. My early thirties were my big marathon years. I've run all kinds of marathons, all over the world. I've been to Africa, Ireland, and various faraway states, such as Alaska and Florida. I've set national age records in many ultramarathons and been inducted into the Rochester Runners Hall of Fame in 2002. I've been asked how many races I've run, how many times out of everything I've run that I've won, and for all kinds of statistics. I have to say, I never really was into that (more into the sheer experience of it), and I have a poor memory, especially now (I laugh at this). Remember, I told you I was not a "counter." But I know you might want to know, so, for the running enthusiasts reading my book, here are some of my records and run times, with the details as best I can remember. In this chapter, I'll also relate some anecdotes you may find entertaining.

You Can't Catch Me

In competition, I would regularly like to do the twenty-four-hour race at the U of R, on my home turf of Rochester, and I was the champion of that for many years. One year, there was a guy from Canada (we usually don't get people from out of town), a little arrogant and expected to win, to knock me down from my kingly status. He regarded me with animosity. To make a long story short, he made the mistake of taking a break during the race, like the hare in "The Tortoise and the Hare" fable. He came off the track, smoked a cigarette, then resumed. That infuriated me, especially since smoking was a personal bane of mine. Maybe he even somehow knew that, and used it to get under my skin, I don't know. Anyway, at the very least, it was like he was trying to brag or something about his speed and put me down. He thought he had so much extra time. So I channeled my fury and won. I never got beat by anyone in any long-distance marathon race in New York. When I blew by him, "Mr. Canada" was shocked. He might have even quit before he finished. I was called the "Hundred-Mile Champion" still.

Double Whammy

There was one race that almost turned out to be deadly for me, and I'm not talking about anything like a heart attack. In fact, I actually had *two* scrapes with death around the immediate time of that race. In November of 1986, I ran in the prestigious John F. Kennedy Fifty-Mile Trail Race through mountains in West Virginia along the Potomac River. It's notable because it was my first fifty-mile trail race. Trail races are different than track races, because trail races cover wilderness hiking trails, not smooth, flat tracks like at your local stadium.

The JFK race and hike began in 1963 and actually started as a fitness walk. Decades earlier in our American history, Teddy Roosevelt had required all military officers to hike fifty miles in twenty-four hours, so this was a later extension of that tradition. The hike trail grew in popularity in the 1960's and in 1968 became the oldest fifty-mile ultramarathon. Starting in Boonsboro, Maryland, it goes out of town up to where it picks up the Appalachian Trail headed to the Chesapeake/Ohio Canal Trail. Then in West Virginia, the race goes past Harper's Ferry and Civil War battlefields. It is quite historic and scenic. It finishes back in Maryland at Hagerstown.

My plan in executing this run was to meet with several of my Rochesterian ultra run celebs and participate in fifty miles of fun. Ultramarathon man/friend/neighbor and running mentor, Don McNelly, did most of the planning for the group since he was a past finisher of this race and knew the routine. Also attending were several of the local, age-fifty-plus men who previously had run a relay across the USA, setting a record for that. Rochester runner Joe George was one of those crazy guys and a past finisher of Western States One Hundred. He was, like Don, one of my Irondequoit neighbors. Joe was known to be quite a character, though.

Joe and I drove together in my car from Irondequoit to Hagerstown where the group had booked a hotel. We traded driving duties until we got to a small town along Route 17 in Pennsylvania. I was riding shotgun as Joe drove like a madman into a small, sleepyhead town. I don't know why he did that, other than that he was always one crazy dude.

48

Then something happened that would send us into a moment of the most acute panic, a tidal wave of fright. I glanced out the car window to my right and saw a vehicle barreling towards us, perpendicularly. I just knew we were going to get hit, and that I'd be the one who was going to be struck. My life flashed before my very eyes! (It's true—that really does happen!) And if I weren't going to die, my car at least would certainly be wrecked. It happened so fast…well, Joe was driving way too fast, so he was partly to blame. That other vehicle was coming directly at us, though, and there was nothing either of us could do to turn back time.

In fact, yes, the other driver hit us from the side even as Joe sped up to avoid the crash. We got blasted behind the back wheel on the fender, like a police pit maneuver. This spun us out into a dirt lot in a whirl of dust that left us stunned.

Rattled and upset, we got out to survey the damage. Local police came to file a report. In the final analysis, it was just a fender bender, nothing severe, and allowed us (meaning me this time) to still drive to our destination. The other driver was a very elderly man, probably just going to the local market to buy milk or eggs. It was nothing to be angry about.

Hoping to shake off this strange and distressing sideswipe, we continued on. When we arrived in Hagerstown, the whole Rochester group met up at the hotel, and we all exchanged happy and enthusiastic greetings (minus my news about the little accident). Then we prepared for a long next day.

The following morning we assembled insanely early in the local gym to pick up our run bibs and registration materials. Because of my fast run times, I was assigned a coveted low (single-digit) bib number, and I was psyched. We got our prerace instructions from race officials, changed into the gear we were to wear, chitchatted with other runners…and grew nervous and anxious, all in the dawn hours of the day.

The run started in town and snaked up a long climb to where the Appalachian Trail crossed going towards the Potomac. I was in new territory, doing a new event much different than the track ultras I had previously done. And—I didn't have the trail experience running that long of an event. **I knew it was a totally different beast.** I questioned my ability and stamina to complete it.

I tucked myself in mid-pack, knowing patience would be imperative, not charging off and then having to take too early a withdrawal from my energy bank. Once on the trails I was also paying careful attention to my footing, as I have been known to trip, you know, and the trail courses present lots of potential pitfalls—like uneven planes, mud, and roots.

The run/hike is in mid-November. It's cold—but not like Upstate-New-York cold. Wearing the right clothing for these long, cold races is paramount. I had a drop bag placed by one of my handlers at the ten-mile mark, where after running the first portion a shoe change would be required and gloves would help freezing fingers. The weather affected us in other negative ways too. The water offered at the stops had frozen right in the paper cups. *Ya, right…Pay attention, volunteers!* I said to myself, perturbed. Luckily I had packed my own Gatorade.

The long and flat part of the canal trail was good news for my speedy track—not trail—legs. I settled into a relatively quick seven-minute-per-mile pace, which seemed comfortable and not too dangerous. I was monitoring my pace and heart rate to measure my effort and progress. I was pleased by my performance so far, and the pain was doable, typical of ultra running.

Once the route left the canal trail, runners headed out onto a country road to the finish line. I did okay, finishing in seven hours, forty-seven minutes. I came in sixteenth out of the two hundred twenty-one runners. It wasn't a win, but it was a good start for having to adapt to a new kind of environment and be so nimble.

But the story's not done…Our plan was to clean up, change clothes, and hit the road for our return trip to Rochester. So who would drive—me or Joe? I was not about to let Joe drive my car after the accident. No way. But would I be up to driving after having run fifty miles in eight hours? Well, I had to be back for church with the family the next day. In driving such a long way, I'd be into marathon event number two.

Exhausted from the race but not knowing what else to do, I decided I'd go ahead and do it—push on through—to uphold my responsibilities. Joe lay passed out and snoring in the passenger seat, not being a very good travelling buddy. As I was driving my dinged-up car that had almost become our hearse on the way down there, I put two and two together to understand that we were now going to do the same terrible thing on the way back! Crash! See, it wasn't long until I realized I was losing it; I was asleep at the wheel! For two awful seconds, I guess I nodded off. I had drifted over into the oncoming lane but luckily jerked back awake, before something more than a scraped-up fender gave us and our loved ones something *really* unpleasant to remember.

Extremely irritated, I pulled over and got some coffee. Ah, coffee! It was like a welcome shot of amphetamine. And again off we went, to get back into Rochester at two in the morning. Hey, that's what ultra runners do—make the long haul. Although the race wasn't as bad as anticipated, the transportation to and from was unexpected and a bit harrowing, to say the least. It began and ended with near-death, for two different reasons but both vehicle-related. Oh, the irony. That certainly wasn't a great day, but in the end it was pretty good, I suppose, because we lived!

The Sweet Smell of Lilacs

Since I just shared a bad memory, let me share a few good ones now. Rochester is called "The Flower City" because of its fabulously fragrant lilacs in May. Because of their proliferation, we have the annual Lilac Festival that thousands flock to. It's in our beautiful Highland Park, winding around the high hill of the city's reservoir, which has a large, stately Roman-style fountain at its top. Music from bands of all sorts lilts through the air, vendors ply their wares and rich carnival foods, and most of all, the vivid purple, lavender, and white lilacs in the old bushes display their ode to spring. Everything is perfect. Everyone comes. If you haven't, you haven't lived life as a Rochesterian.

In November of 1985 I ran the Lilac City Race in Rochester. It is 50K (thirty-one miles), and I completed it in 3:31. It was held at Irondequoit High School track, where I used to run my high school races. This very legit race is certified by the USATF (United States of America Track and Field organization). Rochester is in its Niagara regional district. The USATF has all the records of anyone who's run a serious race in America. Here, I captured the single-age record for thirty-eight-year-olds. A single-age record is determined when the officials look at every single runner in *any and all* races of a specific length that year who is that particular age and then compare the fastest time of anyone to all previous years' records (again, in any and all races). So this means that up to that year, no other thirty-eight-year-old had ever run that fast for that distance for any race in America (not just the Lilac City one). But of course age records are time sensitive. That record indicated that I was the fastest long-distance runner of that age in the nation *at that point*. I don't know how long I held that record, but this was my fastest 50K ever, and I like I said, it was more about competing with myself.

"My Kingdom for a Flashlight!"

Here's another accomplishment I'm proud of in my running career. It's not so much about my time, but about an unforeseen obstacle that I and my running buddy had to overcome. And, ironically, that obstacle was really created, although unintentionally, by me, if I must admit it.

On June 12, 1988, I ran the Old Dominion trail race, which is one hundred miles through both the Shenandoah National Park and George Washington National Forest. It's very "outdoorsy"—all park trails and not much in my comfort zone. This is about as hard as it gets, folks. We started and finished in Front Royal, Virginia. Old Dominion was the event I chose to debut for my hundred-mile trail race category. My time was 21:42, and I placed sixteenth out of ninety-eight runners, but that's not the important part, really.

Historically speaking, that long-established race had started as a horse race and later morphed into an activity in which both horses and people were running simultaneously, a horse race along with a foot race. I met some neat people on horses there, and that's a cool thing for me, talking. I'd often have a conversation with a person on a horse while we were running. "What's your horse's name? How do you train a horse?" I'd ask, etc.

Trails are sometimes narrow at Old Dominion, going up a mountain. Here's a tip for you: when you are running on a path with a horse, don't ever get on the outside of the track, because if the horse gets spooked, it may give you a little nudge off the trail, and you could fall off the steep cliff, and boom! "Lights out!" It never happened to me or anyone that I know of, but I want to warn you about it in case you ever try that race. You have to realize, there are also on occasion rattlesnakes to beware of. Not only could they scare a horse enough to push you to your death (game over!), but they could cause a horse to trample you (game over!) or themselves bite you (game over!). Usually, the hundreds of runners' pounding vibrations scare them away, but you never know. I ran this race just for the experience, and it was a great one, but hair-raising at parts.

We started and finished in the dark, over not-your-typical terrain. It began at four a.m. Runners first, then a few hours later the horses started. Looking back at it now, I had no idea about what the course was actually like. I had no clue about any specific obstacles that needed to be overcome. Sure, I had lots of *track* race experience, but apparently not enough *trail* race experience to know of all the myriad hidden booby traps that might lay before me. However, I embraced the challenge, being young and stupid and not knowing any better. Yes, I had studied the maps to prepare for one of my most exciting runs ever. I knew it would involve trails with steep hills, rivers and streams to be crossed over, and creek mud to slog through, not to mention the summer heat. I was trained up for this physically, and mentally I thought I knew what I was doing.

It turned into a perfect day as we ran, a hundred participants or so in total. The first leg took us from the horse stables into the park trails. Then we arrived at the first expected obstacle: the Shenandoah River about seventy feet across. Forging that river was surreal because, just as we started to cross, sometimes knee-, sometimes waist-deep through slow-moving water, the horses and riders caught up with us and created a problem. Sweat was steaming from all of us being cooled by the water. It created a massive sauna effect in appearance—misty, only semi-transparent. Dangerous for that many congregated people trying to see where they were going so quickly.

On the other side were our drop bags which we had packed with fresh footwear and rehydration supplies. Official aid stations like those that held these bags were about every twenty-five miles, where the runners and horses had a brief medical check including weight, heart rate, things like that. It was like a pit stop. You got a change of dry clothes, you checked in with your support crew, you ate some snacks and drank some Gatorade, etc. Get the picture?

The next several hours went by as I concentrated on the path and felt more alone. As time had passed, the closeness of runners dissipated. Runners of an ultra get separated from the pack as the differences in their pace over long distances multiplies on itself. Everything is so stretched out. So you find yourself running more and more solo as time goes on, especially if you are one of the first ones, those in the lead. I knew that I would probably not be passed by anyone at this time, and it was unlikely that I would pass anyone else either. It was beginning to grow dark.

I knew that I would see signs of life eventually. No handlers (one's crew or other race assistants) could accompany runners yet. However, much later in the race, at seventy-five miles into the event, we could pick up a runner friend for moral support to help bring us to the finish line. At this checkpoint, the last official stop for refills of food and water, I picked up Lew, my New York brother in Christ.

It was fully dark again now at about midnight as we headed towards a near-complete cycle of twenty-four hours. The feelings of pain and hunger grew more intense for me. We crossed another river, which had a rope with gallon jugs tied to it as grab points for us. Then we would be off to climb up some hills and cross the Blue Ridge Parkway near the top. We would crest, and after that, we'd be going down a rocky, tree-lined trail six miles or so from the finish. Lew and I were using simple flashlights with regular batteries— "old school" compared to today's fancy, powerful headlamps.

Here we were, about to cross that parkway, still climbing slowly uphill...then—uh-oh, one light's battery died. That was a little unnerving. We were now functioning with only one light. (Was this poor planning?) I held the light as Lew followed way too closely behind me in an effort to stay with me. You couldn't run side by side because the path was far too narrow. Nevertheless, we kept on chugging and crossed the highway, really only a lonely country road, starting down the long trek that would bring us to the finish. Remember, this is now a little over twenty or so hours into the run. Did we have any legs or brains left? I was severely fatigued, but I knew it would be only a few minutes more.

We picked our way downhill though the trees and rock. Boy, was it ever *dark*. As dark as dark can get. Despite that, we kept going. It was looking like things were going to be okay. We were only a couple miles from the finish line, so, so close.

But then, more trouble. The second (last) light died. "Oh no!" we each screamed. There we were, on the pitch-black trail alone, trying to run. It was a horrible feeling. *Don't trip, Greg,* I said to myself, the worst possible thoughts flying to my mind. Would a root snag my foot and send me flying into a tree, smashing my face? The trees were like specters taunting me with frightening visions and mockery of my past shortcomings. Worse yet, would I step on a snake and it bite me? Suddenly, no inch of ground felt safe.

I knew now that the last few "minutes" would stretch out into centuries. What were we to do in these dire circumstances? They were basically of our own making, perhaps even more my fault because Lew was just a friend doing me a favor. I felt besieged and beleaguered by my own thoughtlessness.

It was like being stranded, but we knew it wasn't hopeless—yet. We could use our intellect to problem-solve. We weren't completely helpless. I said to my friend, "Lew, we better start praying." And so we did. "Oh Lord Jesus, we need help!" we both cried in unison. "We beseech you…" We were communicating directly with God—I'm sure of it. He helped us to remember his Word. As Psalm 119, verse 105 says, "Your word is a lamp to guide my feet and a light for my path."

Suddenly, we heard footsteps behind us—another runner coming along. Praise God! The sweet sound of someone else and, instead of ghosts, the vision of a friendly human with a light bobbing along! We conveniently tucked in behind him—you know, like when you drive in the wake of another car in a snowstorm to follow their lead because you can't see but somehow they can (we have lots of those squalls and dark blizzards in Rochester). But the guy quickly lost us, as he was very fast and obviously more experienced on this trail than us Yankees. Plus, since we didn't directly have the light on our own individual paths—he did—it still had proved too hard to see.

That happened again and again with several other runners. And we prayed time and time again throughout those covert pickups in which we did not notify the runner of what was happening and what we were attempting to do. "Please come to our aid, sweet Jesus! We need you now!" we pleaded. Proverbs 4:12 says when you walk, you'll not be hampered, and when you run, you'll not stumble. Well, we thought, where was that promise right now?

Much to our relief, Jesus would always send help. Each instance could have been our big rescue. But that help always slipped away. Most frustratingly, at one point we lost a guide with a light as huge as a car headlight. We were really beside ourselves right then.

So again we were praying out loud, this time even more vigorously. We were pulling out all the stops of our faith, and our remonstrance was vociferous, petitioning God or his Son to swoop down and save us, Deus-ex-machina style. I felt like crying out "My kingdom for a flashlight!" and bargaining away my whole soul—like the failing and desperately wild Richard the Third did in his final battle—after he was knocked off his horse, an essential thing for survival. "My kingdom for a horse!" he had famously screamed. But he never got another one from anybody, and he was killed...We were of course losing precious time in the race, but by this time we didn't care one iota. We just wanted to get out of there without a broken femur. We'd be lucky if we didn't have some injurious catastrophe that would prove to be the final outcome, with medical people eventually recovering our shattered bodies.

Eventually yet another runner came upon us and stopped. He had an extra light that he allowed us to borrow, thank God! A kind fellow competitor, an empathetic soul. With that we took off even though we had to share the one light. We went blazingly fast, tight together, passing all those who had previously passed us. I finished in less than twenty-two hours, well under the twenty-four-hour goal to get my commemorative silver belt buckle. That simple piece of metal is to this day one of my most cherished trophies. No, I didn't win, but I finished in the top twenty, the top fifth of a hundred. And my friend and I came out unscathed. I had trusted God to not only save me from the "storm" but to run right through it by my side.

I stood there watching the horses race over the line. I thought it was pretty neat that I had bested even some horses that were specially trained endurance animals. My pace during the flashlight episode had been only two miles per hour.

Watch Out for Bears!

On Labor Day of September 1988, at the Greater Rochester Track Club (GRTC) 50/50 race, I came in first place at a time of 3:30. The title 50/50 means 50 kilometers for a team or for an individual. I ran against a team. There were five members on a team; each member of the team ran 10K. In relay style, they would hand off the baton to the next person, then that person to the next person, and so on. I didn't have any team members; I ran it solo. In Mendon Ponds Park, I beat every person running individually as well as the Kodak team, and they were mad at me, very mad, because apparently I was a traitor. They weren't going to let me live this one down.

They harbored a grudge. So, I knew we would have a showdown at this same race a year later.

After twelve months of them stewing, here we arrived at the following year's same event. Labor Day of September 1989, the GRTC 50/50. As I said, in the first (1988) race, I came in first place for any individual, at 3:30. I thought I probably would again. But as for against a team, that was another story. See, Kodak had vowed to "get" me, and they strategized from the very moment they'd put their team together earlier that year. They were bound and determined that they were not going to let me beat them again, not going to lose to me as just one solitary runner.

The Kodakers had a secret weapon, I came to find out. The "Bear Woman," I called her—a very competitive, tough amazon, very intimidating—who at the end burst out of nowhere to catch up with me and "crush" me! It was torture to see her speed on by and overtake me. *Noooooooooo!* I was just about to win, and within a mile of the finish line, she had passed me with a mixture of fierceness, scorn, and glee in her eyes.

With her, they ended up winning their division for all teams and against me. But again, I still won the race as an individual and felt great about that. In the past, I hadn't beat all the teams, though I beat some. So I was used to losing to teams, no problem. I just didn't want to lose to the Kodakers because they had been viewing their former defeat with an axe to grind.

Curiously enough, I almost didn't win in the individuals' division, though, either. I had been running against a top-level ultramarathon runner, and after Bear Woman left me in the dust, he was beating me too. His name was Eddie. We were on the last loop, and then someone said that Eddie dropped out. So I won. I don't know if he ran out of steam or fell down. It was a mystery. So, lucky for me, nobody was able to beat me as an individual, and I again got the distinction; however, it was still more about doing my personal best.

Oh, Snap!

The following June, I believe, in the Lake Ontario Marathon out on Hamlin Parkway, Hamlin, New York, I ran 26.2 miles in 2:40. This was my own record, my best marathon time ever. It was my most rapid speed if we don't consider distance. The fastest on my feet. I remember the air was very, very hot! The whole key was to make sure you were hydrating enough, taking water at all the stops.

At this time, I was doing lots of regular marathons, trying to make each one my best yet. The incident I'm about to relate is about my participation in the Wine Glass Marathon, down in Corning, New York. It starts in Bath and ends in Corning. I had run the first couple of those races and done pretty well, being within the top ten finishers. I was in tip-top shape when this incident occurred. I was rushing by all the other competitors. I was on my way to running my fastest marathon yet! I thought I could beat that Lake Ontario Marathon time. The beginning of this Wine Glass Marathon is a long, slow climb out of Bath, then it goes up through the plains along the Chemung River, around the town of Painted Post.

In the beginning of the race, I was checking my watch and knew I was on track to run a really, really, *really* good race. Then, wouldn't you know it, calamity struck. By the time I got up to where the course leveled off to a flat plain, it felt like a rubber band had snapped inside my leg. I never sensed it coming. An injury like that will happen with no warning. It was my hamstring muscle. That's our biggest muscle in the human leg. I couldn't even walk. I fell onto the side of the road. I was in unspeakable pain. Someone drove by, picked me up, and took me to the finish line. They didn't load me into an ambulance because it was a smaller race, without that kind of medical support.

This was the only race I ever had to quit. It wasn't just a rough patch I thought I could power through. This one took me out. It could have been a career-ender. Instead, it was months that I couldn't run. I was fortunate to know of a physical therapist in my neighborhood who specialized in the treatment of runners and who turned out to be wonderful. His name is Tony Oliveri. We really clicked, and he brought me out of the weeds. With physical therapy and TLC from God and my family and running pals, I got back on my feet and was able to do the Boston Marathon of that same year. I knew God wasn't done with me yet.

So those are some of my best running tales, though an old athlete like me has many more. Fun and interesting times, you bet. They all seem a million miles away, now.

THE "RUNNER'S HIGH"

My Ultramarathons

"A Special Star"

It doesn't seem so long ago
The stars were in your eyes.
But now your stars are beckoning
From bright and studded skies.

The stars are ever calling you,
They're whispering your name.
And once you've heard their siren's call,
You'll never be the same.

Your dream a subtle mistress is;
She'll lure you to vague goals,
But once you've found your special star,
You will have found your soul.

My dad wrote that as a birthday present for my twin boys one year. It was his way of telling them as they grew to always reach for their best potential. Runners move away from the past, like I wrote in the preface, and toward the future, and they should do the same as Dad's poem instructs—reach for the stars. I guess you know you've really made it when you get some big awards. But if it's more of a spiritual thing with you, you'll find your soul, or experience nirvana, when you go into the trance that we call "the runner's high." It's a place in which you're in the flow and nothing else matters, except that you are running at that very instant.

We have endocrine glands that secrete some potent buzz-inducing chemicals. Much better than anything artificial, like drugs. Apparently, endocannabinoids (the body's own natural pain relievers) are much more prevalent in the morning than in the evening, so if you want the runner's high, try to go out in the morning to do your thing. That's some more good advice I can put out there. Luckily, I'm a morning person, not a night-owl, so I know this is for real.

58

The Emotional and Social "Highs" of Ultramarathons

That's the physiological part of the runner's high. There are other components of the runner's high, too, more long-term ones. I want to talk here about those involving self-approval, social approval, and fame. These came during the height of my running career. This is when I was truly at my emotional peak. It's when I was the best I think I could ever be physically, and I enjoyed the internal knowledge of it and the external recognition. Of course, that can be seductive and self-indulgent. Perhaps I was a legend in my own mind, a god in my own little corner of the universe. Stick around a bit and I'll show you the fawning that was laid upon me by sycophants. I'm just kidding, of course, but the praise and friendship I received from my many admirers was nice.

In my quest for upward mobility in the running world, my ambition had led me to the ultramarathon. That was my dream, my "star," my "mistress," my "siren's call" like in Dad's poem. Have you ever been so very excited about something that you can't wait to "run right out" and do it? Think Christmas morning and the feelings you got as a kid. That was me with an ultra. I couldn't wait to face the day. I couldn't wait to face the people! Physically and mentally, I was full of exuberance. I had more energy than I knew what to do with! I was shining, beaming, radiant—in essence, a powerhouse of joy.

By this point in my life, I was finally fully tasting the fruits of my labor, all that grueling training. I was coming in national champion of hundred-mile races. I was "Marathon Man." No, make it "Ultramarathon Man." In my early thirties, I was invincible, or so it seemed. I'm a long-distance runner primarily, but with ultras, I really found my true calling, my niche. Some people might think I was crazy. Would anyone want to count 425 laps on a typical quarter-mile track like at a high school while they practice-ran? Not really. Well, that's what it felt like to keep track when I'd venture to complete one hundred miles in one stint. (Again, I wasn't a counter anyway, like I keep telling you.) To describe people like me, one of my non-running friends said a short-distance runner friend of hers made this comical but accurate remark about ultra runners: "They're a different breed." I think some people are intrigued and/or bewildered by ultra runners, and maybe for good reason.

My Ultramarathon Times

In case you're wondering, here are my best times at some ultramarathons in which I gained notoriety and recall experiencing an emotional high: In May of 1985 I ran the 50K USATF race at the University of Rochester. I got two age records for the same event. I came in first place for the track age record of thirty-seven-year-olds. Also, I did the 100K tacked onto the end of the same race and got another age record, coming in at 8:32.

In May of 1986 for the next year's USATF hundred-mile race at U of R, I came in first over everyone at 16:43:11 and earned the track age record. This was my fastest personal record for a one-hundred-mile race. I was flying in that race. It turned out to be the best ever of all my longest races. It wasn't the fastest per second I'd ever run, but considering the distance, it was my best performance overall, ever.

In May of 1987 I did the McCurdy Department Store Run, a fundraiser for Strong Memorial Children's Hospital, on the U of R track. It was a 100K, and my time was 9:27. Those trophies are really special, uniquely embossed with a children's crayon drawing of a runner. They are lovely, very dear. In October of 1988 I did another McCurdy race, this time only 50K, and came in first place.

In another race for the hospital, the June 1989 Toyota Children's 24-Hour Run at the U of R, I took first place for 102 miles. The 1992 Strong Children's 24-Hour Run at the U of R brought me first place for 101 miles. These were the same race course, just with different sponsors.

I'm not going to lie—the adrenaline rush of crossing the finish line before anyone else is every bit as sweet as it sounds. It is pure exhilaration, knowing you did what you came to do. Realizing you have come in first place is a feeling like none other. Mostly, it's a feeling of accomplishment regarding all the effort you've made in disciplining yourself, and it's a time for being grateful overall for what skills God has bestowed upon you.

BOSTONIAN

The Boston Marathon

"Ice Cream Cone"

A little more left, now some more to the right,
A little more toward the shore.
I know that it seems to be moving around,
But I've always found it before.

That just might be it, to the left side, the port,
Its head there just under the waves.
Now circle around and then put the hook down;
Know here's the position to save.

Its old granite head is both dark orange and red;
Its base is set firmly in stone.
A hazardous sight, not seen there in most light.
We call the rock "Old Ice Cream Cone."

Now drop your bait just past the curious spike;
I'm sure that a lunker is there.
Retrieve it just right, then prepare for a fight,
And we'll have a dinner to share.

See off to the right is a grand flash of white,
And then the strong line starts to go.
The drag starts to sing a familiar refrain.
You've got him so tight—that I know.

The line cuts the waves, and it goes slowly down,
And whence round the old stone it goes,
It's easy to see; oh, your catch has gone free!
The fish is now headed for home.

One day we'll return to find Old Ice Cream Cone.
The fish will be gone, I'm aware.
We'll look to the right for that awesome, sure sight,

And know that the stone will be there.

In the poem above, the "Ice Cream Cone" is a big, tough rock under the waves that the speaker keeps returning to. It's a bit difficult to locate, but he always finds his way back. This natural structure was at an actual place near our family property on Grindstone Island. For me, the Boston Marathon was like that—always very challenging but always there and a charmer.

The "granddaddy" of all big American foot races is the Boston Marathon. According to the website BostonCentral.com, "The Boston Marathon is the world's oldest annual marathon and ranks as one of the world's most prestigious road racing events. The Marathon is run on the third Monday in April (Patriot's Day)." I ran twenty of them. The Boston was always there for me, no matter what other races I did. It was stable and comforting in that way, but it was really hard. To be honest, I didn't ever place real well there in Boston. That's the best of the best runners in the United States. For the Bostons it was so high level, so high class, that only the stars were there. Their times were really fast, and I didn't ever have a stellar record. Understand me: I wasn't a great marathon runner, but I was good. I'm more of a very long-distance runner, an ultramarathon man. There's less competition at ultras because, like I said, you have to be sort of crazy or "out there" to want to do one! So it was something even to qualify for the Boston Marathon with its stiff competition. I had heard so much about it, being the biggest American race. I was just so ecstatic to be part of that arena. I loved the marathon in itself.

Tips

True, I may not be as good as "Boston Billie" I mentioned in my section on running influencers, but I do have some good expertise with the Boston. I consider myself an honorary "Bostonian." People who know me still ask me for advice about the Boston. They ask for the how-to's of running the course. Every marathon is unique in its own way, but Boston is very different because it's not just a flat, quiet course or something predictable. It involves a massive participant body and big, loud crowds that you have to work around. It's twenty-six miles of wall-to-wall spectators, thousands of people standing close and interacting with the race. It's a rolling course, continually going uphill, going downhill. If you think of it more from a bird's eye view, though, overall it's mostly a descent.

You start outside of the city, in a town called Hoppington, and work your way in. You run through a lot of different suburban towns—Natick, Framingham, and Newton, etc.—then into the campus of the prestigious Wellesley women's college. Then you keep coming in towards the city and go right by Boston College. You end up in front of the Prudential building in the hub of the city. And that's it—*if* you make it.

What I mean by that is there is the infamous Heartbreak Hill I failed to mention. Heartbreak Hill is a signature concept, a physical place in the Boston Marathon that's a very difficult point on the course. It's a small, four-mile series of very steep hills that come between miles seventeen and twenty-one in the race, near the end. It's called "Heartbreak Hill" because it really breaks a lot of people, and I assume that would be very depressing. By the time they get done, *if* they get done, they are literally crawling through the finish line in the city of Boston. People I've coached most frequently ask me for tips on how to get through this particular leg of it.

And there's tough downhill parts too. What? you say. Downhill is tough? Naw, you insist. I know it sounds easy, but just listen to me for a minute. I was known as a downhill runner. I was good at that. But it's not easy, not easy at all. Believe it or not, the downhill parts are harder than the uphill. The downhill can be vicious, dastardly, in fact. The downhills will pound the body—badly. That alone will take gas out of your tank more than running uphill. It's easier, in fact, to run uphill. Most people will say, "Oh, I'm going to have fun running downhill now." You'd think that if you are running downhill, your lungs will have no problem, and you won't get out of breath.

True, it's going to feel easier, but only at first. The lungs are a smaller organ than your leg muscles, which are going to bear more of the brunt. What happens, though, when you are running downhill, besides sensing all of the painful, enormous pressure on your joints (toes, ankles, knees, hips), is that the blood must take in increased oxygen so that the muscles can work like shock absorbers. The oxygenation comes from the lungs, so they still have to work hard. If your legs are getting pounded, that pulls the strength out of your muscles, obviously, and hurts your endurance. The key to the Boston is preserving, or metering out, your metabolic fuel so that you have enough energy and muscle strength to get to the finish line. It's carefully calculated management of one's resources. I never dropped out of a Boston, but many people do, because they just can't get that right.

Running uphill is also more stabilizing for the feet, with less chance of falling than running downhill. The foot strikes the pavement in a more solid, secure way. Most all brooks in nature run downhill, not uphill, right? That's because gravity is doing its work. Gravity can do a number on you too, if you accidentally turn an ankle on a rock or pot hole, and come skidding down to your hands and knees. The road rash of skinned and bloody knees and lacerations or gashes on elbows and palms is not a pretty sight, nor is it particularly comfortable for the remainder of the race.

Gravity can also make you run away with yourself, so fast that you're getting out of control, and that kind of excessive speed is just plain scary.

For these reasons, the descent is harder than the ascent. I hope I've convinced you. You should long for the uphill climbs, because, paradoxically, they are less toilsome. I guess you've got to trust me on this one. I considered myself a true "Bostonian" because I was so well versed in this race and gained some specialized knowledge through the school of hard knocks.

I've given you some thoughts on what to expect from the Boston Marathon and how to handle this great big hairy beast. Oh, one last caveat…Be ready for whatever weather Boston can possibly throw at you. Some of my races were blistering hot and dry; some were windy, rainy, and cold. Be particularly careful with that heat, though. I got zapped on some of these Boston Marathons and found myself in the medical tent to get rehydrated through intravenous fluids and electrolytes. That means getting stuck with a needle and having a pint bag of replenishment pumped back into your veins. The process is about an hour, but it depends on the runner and the amount of attention he or she needs.

All in all, what you've got to deal with is really not that bad. The huge numbers of cheering onlookers and the bragging rights you bring home make up for the unpredictable weather and nutso hills. I'll never forget the first time I ran a Boston, one of the most famous marathons in the world. I was a basket case of nerves (good ones). And all the hoopla with bands, loudspeakers, and news helicopters flying around just added to the excitement. The Boston Marathon is like Old Ice Cream Cone Rock. It'll be there when you're ready for it. So what are you waiting for? Train, try out, and then run it! It will be a great experience for you, one no one can ever take away.

MAN'S BEST FRIEND

Brigitte

"Ode to Bentley"

Remember when you were a pup?
You'd make a mess; I'd mop it up.
You'd make a puddle on the floor;
I'd sop it up—it was no chore. . .
You couldn't help it.

You grew in stature, learned the rules;
I taught you what's not shown in schools.
You learned to trot and keep the stride
While you would follow at my side. . .
You couldn't help it.

You never learned to fetch a ball;
You hardly came when I would call.
You never learned to play a game,
But yes, we loved you just the same. . .
You couldn't help it.

You had an independent air;
You acted like, "Well, I don't care."
But not from lack of gratitude,
Just to maintain your solitude. . .
You couldn't help it.

Your loyalty was not in doubt;
You'd always follow me about.
You were content if you could be
Just by my side and there with me. . .
You couldn't help it.

Now somehow you have gotten old
And not so steady, not so bold.
Your eyes are dim, your hearing gone,

Your heart is young, though, full of song. . .
You couldn't help it.

The time has come, as seasons must,
To be returning to the dust.
But when it comes right to the end,
You were a faithful, loving friend. . .
You couldn't help it.

I have had dogs my whole life. It seems like growing up we always had a dog in our house. My mother had an affinity for animals which she passed down to me, so much so that later in life as a teen, I wanted to be a veterinarian. I was even a veterinary assistant during my college days.

In my married life, as we Brookses grew as a family, our first pet was a big lovable yellow lab named Missy. She lived a full life as the boys and Ashley grew up with her, and then she passed.

A friend at Kodak raised German shorthairs and asked if I'd be interested in a pup. Not knowing much about the breed, Donna and I went to investigate. Well you know how that was going to turn out. We brought home a wild-child puppy we named Dot, our first of two of that breed. She was a natural island dog, a great swimmer who loved to run the fields of Grindstone with me. We didn't do as much running together as I did with our next shorthair, Brigitte, though.

Brigitte was a German shorthaired/pointer mix and had the build and stamina of a runner, swimmer, *and* hunter. I think it was that little extra bit of the pointer genes that made her exceptional. You know, those that make the breed lean in a forward stance of alertness while spying prey. She would play Stick In The Water for hours on end, swimming till she couldn't fetch anymore. My Brigitte years were ones devoted to what we both loved best, though—running. I trained her to run on a leash with me when on our Rochester roads, but up on Grindstone she was free to run untethered for our longer exploration runs. Then it was always back to the cottage where we both went for a swim.

Besides being a free spirit up on the island, Brigitte was a socialite and also a professional with a competitive mindset when in the city. In preparing for races together, I would rise early for a training run with Brigitte. It was my praying, planning, and preparing time of day, my best hours, my quiet time to get ready to do business and battle. She shared that meditative space with me. We usually did three to five miles to wake up and roll, just Brigitte and I and an occasional wild animal. In the awakening of the dawn, the birds were starting to rouse as well, and traffic was gearing up.

My distances increased as goals became more and more in focus. I started ramping up the daily miles; I was running to and from Kodak as well as running during lunch hours with my speedy friends who worked there. We'd run at noon, logging as many as twenty miles a day, five days a week, and capping our workweek off with a long run on the weekends! That weekend run would call for twenty or more miles too. However, we always took Sundays off; that was church and family day. My big weeks were well over hundred-mile ones, my dog usually coming with me and my running fellows. Most of the runners knew her by name when I group-trained during the off-season.

I would also bring her to formal races to run alongside me if the event wasn't more than a half-marathon distance. Some races I even had her enter with a race bib. There were no divisional winners for dogs, but if there had been, we would have taken home all the awards.

Nowadays, most foot races don't allow dogs. Life is more complicated and regimented now, more "official" than it was when I was a young person. Back in my time, the looseness of regulations allowed man's best friend to participate no-questions-asked. Today, there is something exciting called canicross, though. It is the sport of cross-country running very popular in Europe in which the human and dog are connected by a bungee cord that reduces shock to the runner when the dog pulls, a natural instinct of a canine (think sled dogs). All breeds of dogs and all abilities and ages of people (including the elderly, disabled folks, and children) can participate. There is even an international championship for this activity. I know that if we had had the chance, my girl Brigitte and I would have taken up the challenge.

As time progressed, both Brigitte and I were getting older and slower. We both had health problems. She eventually presented an anal tumor which was diagnosed as cancer. She was having problems just walking. Brigitte could no longer be my running companion and was failing fast. The vet told us that the operation was going to be risky and costly and recommended we put her down. It was our decision that we were reluctant about making, but watching her suffer was painful for Donna and me.

We took Brigitte in to an animal hospital and arranged for her to be euthanized. With her in my lap, the doctor put the needle in, and, as her heartbeat slowed, she expired in my arms. I'm crying now just reliving that experience. In the book of Ecclesiastes, King Solomon gives some verses we are all familiar with: "For everything there is a season...A time to be born and a time to die...A time to cry and a time to laugh. A time to grieve and a time to dance" (3:1–4). Sometime, Brigitte and I will be singing, running, and dancing together, though not in this life.

God's animals reflect his eclectic creative abilities and love for us in providing them for companionship. My dogs have been important blessings in my life, supporting me emotionally and enriching my days, but Brigitte was my favorite. She really knew how to run. Never underestimate what a dog can do!

I once owned a dog named Brigitte. She was pretty, well-mannered, and loving. Brigitte Girl, my running star. She was beautiful inside and out and a gregarious creature if I ever saw one. Everybody knew her. Everybody loved and petted her, talked to her as if she were one of us. She had so much enthusiasm and must have thought that I was a super cool dog myself. I was her pack leader, and she was my friend.

"CHARIOTS OF FIRE"

The Olympic Torch in Rochester

"Dock Day"

The flickering picture of dragonflies,
The sun's sparks igniting the bay,
The dawn rising over the stately trees
Now signal the start of the day.

The sky is so clear, and the wind so soft,
A nice day they now do portend.
We surely do too have a treat in store,
At least by this pleasant day's end.

The Skylark*—she starts her light metal call
By clanging her halyard to mast.
The rhythmic soft dinging sure seems to say,
"How long will the day's fresh wind last?"

The sailing, at least for the moment's time,
Must wait till the work all gets done.
There are some slight chores that need tending to
Before we can join her for fun.

The sailors go out, and the swimmers sit,
With beach towels, some cushions, and chairs;
It's in for "first dip," and then when they're out,
There's blithe conversation to share.

Their bodies will hide from the chill of wind
In effort to get cozy-warm.
Then set with a grin, they'll all jump back in
And this is the beat of their norm.

Some snacks now appear for the friends so dear;
It's sandwiches, soft drinks, and beer.
When repast is done, we feel bad for some,

Those, sadly, who couldn't be here.

The sun now descends; it is losing warmth;
The shadows begin to get long.
The shortening waves flatten out the bay,
The Skylark is stilling her song.

The fireflies wink, just as do Sun's rays,
All over the tranquil, small bay.
The wind has let down, and the sailboat rests,
Thus ending a super "Dock Day."

*The Skylark is a type of small, fast sailboat. My family owned one.

Isn't that quite some image in my father's poem? I bet you have a memory of one such similarly magical "dock day," some perfect, long day at the beach. Unforgettable. Or perhaps you remember many days like that. More generally, think of any really happy day, in which you felt totally at peace and the world seemed so nice.

When they had the Summer Olympics of 1996, those were deemed extra special because they marked the modern Games' centennial. For the Olympic Games, just like for an opera or musical, there is an overture, an opener of sorts to the main proceedings. That overture is called the Relay. The powers that be of the Olympics brought their relay that landmark year through humble little Rochester, so we townsfolk were really pumped up. Each runner had their own torch and ran with it, lighting person to person. Then they lit our city's main torch, which would itself stay lit until the Games were over. Meantime, the torch generally travels onwards, but the proud people of each community hang onto their fragment of light, their little sidecars of the great train.

The torch goes through only places that symbolize human braininess and achievement, places of renowned history and culture. Now, because the organizers recognized George Eastman's brilliance and tremendous legacy, his enlightenment of the world, we have that claim to fame of the torch! Our stop was just one of hundreds of illustrious transfer stations. At each juncture, the race gets a fresh new torch that burns another reed on an aluminum base. Afterwards, bearers can buy the splinters for themselves as a keepsake.

The Associated Press covered the flame's arrival here by likening it, appropriately, to another "Kodak moment" in Rochester's history. "The Olympic torch took a picture-perfect...trail through Kodak country... borne a few blocks by George Fisher, chief executive of the world's biggest photographic firm... Thousands of spectators, many of them Kodak workers on lunch break, roared their approval as Fisher and his wife, Ann, jogged through the clogged downtown streets of Rochester, their slow progress overtaken by black clouds gleaming with distant lightning." So dramatic. And Fisher himself was a runner, so it must have been a considerably moving and priceless moment for him. Indeed, it was a once-in-a-lifetime spectacle for all of us, and it meant so much to so many.

"'When you see so many people smiling, yelling, and excited about something as positive as the Olympics, it's really beautiful,' Fisher said after transferring the torch flame outside Eastman Kodak headquarters." Sixty other people actually did the running to bear it all the rest of the way through town. They included a teacher with cancer and former Olympians—sailor Louise Van Voorhis and field hockey player Randolph Lipscher. That day was absolutely a "dock day." There's still the bowl for the flame up in the air on a pedestal at the corner of Exchange Boulevard and Plymouth Avenue, and when I drive by it, I always smile. It makes my heart happy, every time.

PLAN B

Kodak No More

"The Fire Dance"

The sun is setting behind the ridge.
The river is smooth and gray.
The night birds are piping flute-like trills
To signal the end of day.

The sun's rays, now they are bending low
Across the broad orange expanse.
God choreographs the red-pink flight,
A bright, wondrous fire dance.

Each cottage will now be set ablaze,
So lit by the setting sun.
The flint that strikes hot the melting clouds,
Igniting each, one by one.

Each window there on the distant shore
Aglow with the golden light.
While seen only by a privileged few,
It's truly an awesome sight.

Now slowly comes there the evening's snuff,
Extinguishes glittering sparks.
And each, in turn, will blink on and off.
It soon will look velvet dark.

The scene returns to a quiet state,
With waning of purple light.
Once more the shore is a tranquil place.
The river sighs, "Sun, good night."

The poem above that my dad wrote suggests something subsiding. An afternoon melding into dusk then turns to full night. A vibrant sunlit scene fades and is gone forever. All good things must come to an end, right? "The fire dance" is a term my family made up to refer to the setting sun that would paint a luminous picture on most evenings in the Thousand Islands. The sunset's rays illuminated the cottages' window panes two miles away on the mainland. The point here is not so much the end of something as it is the remembrance of the thing as it goes.

Au Revoir, Kodak

As Kodak employees, we rode the wave of good times. . .we were "ultra" profitable, pun intended. Until, that is, some of us saw the handwriting on the wall. For decades, there were concerning signs that Kodak as a whole was becoming complacent. As king of the hill, it believed it was untouchable. But it was starting to go downhill. Technology and consumer demand were changing, and Kodak was not adapting as quickly as it should have.

The first signs were visible when Fuji, a foreign film company, stepped into the market and was undercutting us significantly in price. Then more trouble came just at the beginning of the computer age, when inventors were initially developing the first digital cameras. Kodak jumped in too late and didn't catch up with other industries that were making those slick modern cameras. You know, the ones that stored picture data inside and that enabled users to electronically preview and delete pictures that they didn't like. No more stupid shots! No more red-eye. No more wasted film!

From then on, nobody was buying emulsion film for pictures, so Kodak simply stopped making film virtually altogether. George Eastman had long been dead, so he was not there to maintain his dream—to step up and turn the tide. Thousands of people, that is most all of the workforce, were given severance packages or pink slips and asked to leave. Their positions were eliminated because the golden age, the high noon of Kodak, was now over—basically vanished into the night. The colossal buildings became deserted and forlorn. Rochester was bleeding. Many, many people left our once abundantly thriving city to find work elsewhere. Finally, after struggling to hold on, in 2013 the "unsinkable" Kodak corporation, once a monopoly of the industry, declared bankruptcy.

The Worst Was Yet to Come

But besides the devastating personal job loss and the city's economic gash, the people around here were negatively affected in another, even more disturbing way. In my earlier chapter on Kodak, I told you about my own extent of working with copious amounts of chemicals at the job site. But in the final decades of Kodak, society in general was waking up to the worrisome issue of pollution, and Rochesterians would begin to have suspicions about the residual chemical footprint Kodak had imprinted on its community's surrounding land. People began to make allegations of

Kodak's unethical dealings in not caring for the environment. Cropping up overnight were very serious health issues, and the appearance and increase in numbers of sick people were just one more factor indicative of the beginning of the end for our once-great company.

Methylene chloride is not good stuff—it was a chemical solvent used a lot for a base in film products and also commonly found in paint removers. At the time I'm speaking of, methylene chloride was a suspected carcinogen. The EPA regarded it as one, although its cancer-causing connection has never been proven. Kodak officials said there was no scientific evidence of a link between this film manufacturing chemical and cancer. A company spokesman, James Blamphin, said to *The New York Times* reporters, "We've looked at it... We've watched these trends. Our workers have been exposed to higher levels than anybody, and we've never seen an increase in cancer rates." Wow, we used to handle that stuff everywhere and all the time—just about swim in it. But I can't say that any guys around me ever got cancer.

Nevertheless, I don't think Kodak was handling waste properly in general. We were easily the state's chief polluter. *The New York Times* wrote, "Concerns about the company's emissions peaked in 1988, when Kodak acknowledged that it had released 20 million pounds of toxic chemicals into the air the previous year." We dumped nitrogen oxides, sulfur dioxide, and microscopic soot out our stupendous smoke stacks. But in fact, the prime offender, coming in at just about half of those air-borne pounds, was that methylene chloride. Besides poisoning our air, all that crud was seeping into the ground around Kodak and going into ground water, which would become our drinking water. So many local residents in the area were claiming that it was resulting in a major public health hazard and that we had to do something about it.

Methylene chloride was supposedly causing too-coincidental cases of cancer within a small radius, "cancer clusters" specifically within the Maplewood neighborhood of Rochester immediately adjacent to the central plant building. Kodak got major lawsuits over this. As told in an article in *The New York Times* entitled "Rochester Parents Fret, And Sue, Over Cancer," there were about seventy children countywide who contracted a rare form of neurological cancer in just twenty years. Official investigations into these compelling and tragic cases began. The most extensive look into the cancer clusters took place in the mid-1990s, "when the Monroe County Health Department conducted an 18-month study amid allegations that toxic emissions from Eastman Kodak Co. caused brain or spinal cancer in children living near Kodak Park." But no verifiable link was ever found. "Though the county health department found no evidence of the claim, the families of five of the children sued Kodak twice [for $185 million], claiming that methylene chloride…caused the cancers. Kodak settled out of court with the families in 2004."

Apparently, it's difficult to scientifically prove that any alleged cancer cluster exists because there are many factors that can interfere with a direct cause-effect connection. Things can happen over years or even decades to set the cancer off and growing in someone's body. This latency period "complicat[es] the task of determining when and where a person might have been exposed to a particular carcinogen," states The *Rochester Business Journal* article "Investigation of Cluster Requires Strong Link to Cause" based on information from the Centers for Disease Control and Prevention. In other words, there are many carcinogens someone could be exposed to, and people who move in and out of a neighborhood over the years pose a problem to the analysis. People coming in could have contracted cancer through many other means, elsewhere. Or, people who contracted the cancer in our suspicious district could move to another locale, making it hard to trace them. I suppose what made this case so alarming was that the victims highlighted here were children, who make the point about long periods of time seem moot. Perhaps something was changing our DNA and passing from parent to child?

Once under the proverbial microscope, Kodak cleaned up its act, at least somewhat. Kodak repurchased some homes in the Maplewood area of people who wanted to get out and opened a community information center on its responsible handling of toxic chemicals. In just five years, from 1988 to 1993, the company "cut emissions by 63 percent to 3.3 million pounds, and it has continued to reduce them" ("Rochester Parents Fret"). That was thirty years ago, and I'm sure that the problem is nil in comparison to what it used to be, especially since Kodak's production is just about defunct. In a recent post on Reddit, a woman was wondering whether it is safe to buy a house in the Maplewood area now—whether the "cancer cluster" still exists. Another local user, KalessinDB of Henrietta, responded, "You're going to have trouble 'definitively' proving it's gone, since they could never 'definitively' prove that it existed. That being said, Kodak is a shell of its former self, which means that the cancer-causing chemicals are also a shell of their former selves." That logic makes sense.

Although Eastman Kodak may have been exonerated in these cases, many people believe that, taken in aggregate with all others, big polluting companies *are* responsible for creating an environment on the national scale in which everyone is generally more at risk. One such local citizen of this opinion interviewed by *The New York Times* was Mrs. Cusenz, whose husband worked at Eastman Kodak and whose son died of spinal cord cancer. She would keep a map of the city, with color-coded angels pinned to it representing each child who died by a different type of cancer. "Mrs.

Cusenz thinks the problem is bigger than any one company. She said that although she believes Kodak is not blameless, she thinks pollution by all companies, both large and small, should be examined."

When called into this mess in Rochester, the epidemiologists of the Federal Agency for Toxic Substances and Disease Registry recommended just that. While they found that past local studies had been scientifically sound, they called for further review beyond Kodak. "The problem may be part of a national trend, they said. Brain cancer in children up to four years old has increased by a per capita rate of 47 percent in the last twenty years." The agency was going to include Rochester in a three-state study of the occurrence of brain cancer, said *The New York Times* in 1998.

But even if all American companies over the past few decades have been dealing with our pollution problem, other nations may not be. Chinese and other companies put a relative of methylene chloride, methyl alcohol, in instant hand sanitizer that we are using nowadays for communicable disease prevention. They are distributing it to the world. Manufacturers are supposedly much more careful to examine these types of chemicals now, but I don't know much about this. I hope it is true.

Anyway, the collective though unspoken desire to make a respectful tribute to Kodak before it was too late seems to have manifested itself in that electrifying Olympic torch-bearing ceremony in 1996 which I explained. It was like someone's retirement party, an acknowledgement for a company in obvious decline. It was Kodak's fire dance and its swan song.

Brooks Coaching and Consulting

Overconfidence, inflexibility, foreign competition, pollution, and worry about a castle resting on carcinogens. Kodak had slipped away...we had had an amazing run, but it was over. The "Kodak moment" had disappeared. In fact, that term has been relegated by the newer generation to the status of a silly trope; it has even been redefined by the business world and now refers to the disintegration of a successful company due to obliviousness by leadership.

So, enter Plan B. I had to switch gears. It wasn't just a possibility that I might get laid off; it was a *certainty*. Every day that prospect was looming and giving me unrest. The announcers of local radio programs gave daily numbers of unfortunate workers dismissed, always accompanied by a gasp from whoever was listening.

When I reached the company's early retirement points for age (56) and years of service (30), I knew they were my exit tickets, time for pulling the plug on my Kodak life. I put a lot of prayer into my options. The corporation had offered me a package: one year of full pay and education benefits if I wanted to go back to school.

Okay, so I hatched this idea. I knew over my lifetime that I was good at two different, seemingly unrelated things: running and environmental hygiene. So, I would start my own business combining both. That's when Brooks's Coaching and Consulting for developing runners and marathon training programs, and for solving industrial safety problems, respectively, was born. The plan was to continue my coaching of runners one-on-one that I had been doing for years, work with community organizations to host clubs and races, and advise construction businesses who needed help with their health and safety programs. I had the opportunity to split my year's pay from Kodak into two years, which would give me some time to develop the business and not have to immediately worry about putting food on the table. Of course, gaining a clientele for my new setup was originally a bit concerning. But during that time, business came in at a moderate pace for both areas of my expertise. I was on a roll down a different brook, not sitting at a desk wondering when the axe would fall, yet still doing what I loved and was wired for.

In the running department of my self-employment, I was pulling training and racing plans together for individuals, doing racecourse certification, and organizing the Rochester Marathon. These were all activities I had already been doing through my time at Kodak anyway, so they provided for a smooth transition and a steady client base, thankfully.

In the industrial hygiene department of my own business, I also grafted on easily, finding clients I already knew through Kodak. Back in the day, I had been responsible for giving orientations to outside contractors coming into Kodak Park, for work such as underground digging and maintenance of our hazardous waste burners or coal-burning power generation facility. Contact with these people was refreshing in that it helped me meet a very different type of worker not at all like the manufacturing folks I had dealt with all my time at Kodak. They were a rough-around-the-edges construction crowd that I didn't have any trouble communicating with in my new business. They were cool, and it just all seemed to come so naturally. "Plan B" was working out.

Industrial hygiene consulting was about construction and maintenance of workplaces, like wearing the right kind of respirator, wearing your right kind of gloves—basically to keep the regular guys in the trenches safe. I helped the contractors in building, maintenance, or cleaning, such as for a construction firm that might build a new lab. The business client would hire me to go to a site and check it out.

I consulted with clients who often were associates of mine through running and had their various smaller businesses inside Kodak; I was like a subcontractor and thought it odd when I sometimes found myself working right back within the very walls of Kodak though not employed directly by the decrepit Old Man. Although Kodak had failed me, I had not failed it. As an independent safety engineer, I used the knowledge I learned at Kodak to turn right around and give it back but to also branch out. Specific skill sets were communication, project management, observational skills, and OSHA compliance understandings (I used to teach OSHA certification and an OSHA Ten course).

One year stands out as a particularly different and difficult one in this phase of my professional life. I was to work on a new building going up at our Ivy League college in Ithaca, New York—Cornell University. I was asked to be a safety project manager for the construction company that was erecting the Life Sciences building there. This story stands out to me because it was my first extended out-of-town stint for Postler & Jaekle, the company for whom I consulted. I stayed at a hotel. I also worked for them in Corning, New York, to renovate old research and development labs. I was a rock star there because I knew all kinds of things about chemicals that the regular construction guys didn't. I loved the work, but I missed my family. I wasn't running. I was playing golf, starting to pick up the bottle again, and generally having a hard life. So, when those particular projects were done, I simply decided that I would take no more out-of-town projects. And the rest of my years working for myself were just great.

Surprisingly, I found my Plan B to be just as good or better than my Kodak years. This consulting business—it was a good thing for me, my saving grace. Once again, God had provided a path forward, a moving brook of his infinitely wise design. Although I worked for a lot of high-powered companies on intense technical building projects, I guess I loved the consulting I did for races most of all. It was easier, and it was even more people-oriented, at least to me. The way I saw it, when a project was all said and done, I could look up at my work memorialized in a huge, brick-and-mortar structure, or I could look into the eyes and heart of a real person standing right in front of me, listening, about to run.

THERE NOW, RUN ALONG

Coaching Days

"The Bridge"

How many bridges have we seen?
(Opposing sides of them we've been.)
I'm here and sometimes you are there,
With only loneliness to bear.

What good is anything I do
If I can't do that thing with you?
If I am here and you are there,
How can the things I do we share?

When sharing is the only thing
That really has a full meaning,
Togetherness, then, is as well
The joy, beyond the task itself.

And once again, my friend, you're here,
And now the gulf is to the rear;
And evermore will it be spanned
By God, yes, through his loving hand.

Next, I'm going to discuss coaching I've done for both individuals and organizations and ways I've tried to build bridges to people in order to impart my knowledge of running to them.

Individuals I've Coached

I've trained hundreds of people, but I lost count (I'm not a counter, remember?). I liked them all, every single one. My coaching days were generally during the time I was attending that megachurch, Faith Temple in Rochester, New York. God showed me the way to helping many special people, and here are a few of the ones I remember best.

John Prohira was a mentee of mine many years ago. I didn't know how much I had influenced him until I discovered that he had become an ultramarathon runner. I know all this now about John because I reconnected with him recently at the hospital. He was in there for heart issues. I found out from Facebook. He hadn't called me, because he was too sick, but I went to visit anyway. He's doing better now. I'm glad I could be there for part of his recovery time and to watch this fantastic runner get back on his feet.

Jen Donahue was someone I coached in her high school years as well, and I had become friends with her after her secondary years. We connected again also through social media, and she told me about her desire to run an ultramarathon. I told her what she should do and what her goals should be. I told her, let me know when you're thinking about running.

The next thing I knew, she called back a couple days later and said, "I just signed up for an ultramarathon."

I said, "Let me know how you finish."

After she'd done it, we met to talk about it. "How'd you do?" I asked.

"I won it!" she beamed.

I asked what the distance was. She said, "One hundred miles, trail race."

"You gotta be kidding me!" I responded. "Nobody ever just jumps in with a hundred miles and wins it; that's insanity!" But she took me with a grain of salt, and I knew she could see how proud I was of her.

Fred Scott is a former Kodaker and runner. I coached him for the Boston Marathon. Now, at over sixty years old, he is an accomplished Hawaii Ironman triathlon finisher and coach for specifically triathlons. He lives in Tuscon.

Another person I coached is the well-known Christine Webb Batchelder. She was a local TV news anchor on Channel 13 and is a friend now. She ran the Rochester Marathon and competed in the Lake Placid Ironman Triathlon. When she left Rochester, she went to a TV job in Florida and was then moved by God to go to seminary for pastoral ministry and missions work, praise God! Her church is in the Orlando area. She blogs daily inspirational stories. I am sure she is another one who still calls me "Coach."

With this handful of individuals and so many, many more, when I hear of their accomplishments and the resulting accolades showered upon them by admirers young and old, it always gives me pause. Their success is my success.

Coaching Organizations

After I'd coached high school for twelve years and was deep into training for the Boston Marathon and ultra running during the late 90's, I found out about the National Arthritis Foundation's JIM (Joints in Motion), a marathon training team. If you have arthritis, you may have heard the phrase "motion is lotion." That means that walking, or running if you can, is good for your joints.

The Arthritis Foundation was initiating a fundraising concept fashioned after the successful Team in Training (TNT) group sponsored by the Leukemia Foundation. The TNT would train a group of interested individuals who had leukemia themselves or who had a friend or family member battling it. Cities who have a chapter in the Leukemia Foundation would hire a coach to train runners to do a specific marathon in some enticing location like Hawaii or Disney to raise money for leukemia. That model had turned out to be a very popular and lucrative venture.

The Rochester chapter of the AF caught on to this idea as running marathons gained popularity and hopped onto the bandwagon. Of course, they knew nothing about running marathons. Knowing of my marathon "fame," they approached me. They needed a coach and asked me if I would be interested. The coaches weren't paid a stipend but reaped the benefits of a free ride to the venues and camaraderie with a happy bunch of folks. Knowing their setup, it didn't take too much convincing for me to jump into the water as JIM Coach Greg.

I worked with our AF, and we developed a strategy to host informational meetings to present the plan to people who were keen to raise funds for an endeavor near and dear to their hearts. The planning committee and I, through my running connections, were successful in garnering lots of interest. Potential JIM members liked the idea of getting a highly experienced coach and the opportunity to run at exciting places. The participants would be doing it for a worthy cause and simultaneously increasing their health and perhaps reaching lifelong personal running goals.

It wasn't long before I discovered that most of the participants had never run a marathon before. I had only a year to train them. Was I up to the task? I knew I could coach kids, but adults might present a different challenge.

I set up individual training schedules based upon experience and ability. One of my "trainees" was Johnny S., who owned an Irish pub in Rochester. I chose a night midweek, Wednesday, for training runs a few miles away from Johnny's pub. The runners gathered at a park next to the Erie Canal path for a short, approximately one-hour, weekly run. All shapes and sizes showed up. Over time, I needed to evaluate their run logs, make any necessary adjustments in their schedules, and slowly increase mileage. Some weekends we scheduled group runs elsewhere. But it was the Wednesday night runs and the social activity which followed at the pub which bonded everyone together. (I drank soda.)

Our local AF staff sponsored many Dublin marathon teams over the ten-year association I had with them. Let me describe a typical team adventure. I got the team travel-ready (passports, hotel reservations, prerace registrations, appropriate run gear, etc.). I had to plan everything, and I mean *everything*, from packing to checking us all in at the airport. Then my eager team and I were ready to rock and roll! About a dozen would go. We all had team jackets with JIM logos. We traveled together as a team, flying to Dublin. The runners were excited to go to a foreign country and have some good old "American" fun.

When we would arrive in Dublin on a Friday, we'd be severely jet-lagged. I'd encourage the gang to remain awake until evening so as to reset their biological clocks for the race Sunday. After getting settled in the hotel, we'd stay awake by walking about our new destination. Ireland was a different world, and the inhabitants were just so friendly and inviting that they made us forget our fatigue from flying. It was a jolly good time, but I warned my runners not to overdo the sightseeing. One thing I learned the hard way at the Boston Marathon was that in doing the tourist thing and walking too much, you are taking an early withdrawal from your muscle bank.

Sunday would bring the long-awaited event. Nerves were on edge. Everyone was excited to get to the startling line and begin running. I had developed a starting strategy over the years. I would get the team situated at the start, find a start spot for myself near the front of the line, and run at my own pace. The team would run at a pace we practiced many times in training. What worked for me is that I could go accordingly to the pace I was trained to run in so many previous marathons—dozens of them—finishing the race somewhere in low three-hour, or maybe below three-hour range. I would wrap up my own race, grab some nourishment and water, then go back out on the course and pick up the next JIM team member and run them to the finish line, doing this over and over until all the team was back. Oh, the feeling of seeing their joy of accomplishment for all those weeks of hard training! So, how many miles would I put in that day? I dare say it was over ultramarathon distance!

Mind you, my wife and I were still both working full-time, raising our three kids, engaging in a substantial amount of church work, and I was running local races like ultramarathons and training myself for my annual Boston Marathon. Some of my friends would worry about me. I reassured them, "It's okay; marathoners can do this stuff!" I've discovered in life that being tired is relative to how much you do or do not enjoy the activity. People seem to feel more energized when they are participating in a pursuit that engrosses them and provides entertainment value. We in the JIM groups had just so much fun going to places like Alaska. There in Anchorage, we ran on a trail along the ocean, where we'd see sperm whales and have moose encounters. It sure was something to remember. We sent postcards back home.

As I said, I had lots of vim and vigor because the Joints in Motion experience was quite rewarding, especially in that I was teaching inexperienced people to train for and finish their first marathon. Some people were not only newbie marathoners but novice *runners* to boot. This was a fun challenge which I enjoyed as much as coaching high schoolers just discovering distance running. In most cases the JIM people were a ragtag crew of every shape, size, and adult age. To look at them you might think, "What? You want to run a marathon?" But appearances were deceiving. It was all about their hearts and willpower.

God is Calling You Too

So back to the bridges of my dad's poem. Do you know that you could be a bridge to someone? Possibly you're a bridge to multiple people right now. Believe that you exist for that reason. Know that God is using you as a conduit, a powerful role model for someone else. When you're down, stop focusing on yourself and know that you're vitally important for those other people. You are a thread in their developmental tapestry, without which there would be a discernable hole. A simple compliment, a warm hello, whatever—just let your feelings show through to your pupil. You don't have to do anything heroic or fancy, just be yourself. God's got you there for a reason, and the lives with which you intersect are interdependent with yours. It's a divinely inspired, sacred network. So continue to be that bridge, a section of that strong weave. You are a structural support in God's vast design.

My senior quote in the high school yearbook was as follows: "He is the greatest whose strength carries up the most hearts by the attractions of his own." The quotation is by Henry Ward Beecher, social reformer and minister, a brother of Harriet Beecher Stowe, the famous Christian abolitionist and early feminist. The funny thing is, I don't ever remember selecting that quotation for my picture. I think at the time that the secretaries may have just chosen quotes for us; I don't really know. But it seems apropos now looking back at all the coaching I later did. The quotation means "Do unto others as you would have done unto you." Be someone standing in their corner. More than that, be a cheerleader of people. You don't even have to be acting in the official capacity of a coach or teacher or even mentor. Like a faithful disciple, just be a good follower of Jesus Christ. Your informal daily example will result in better teaching than if you stood up at a podium and formally lectured for a century.

Anyone can mentor, assist, or help develop someone else. Anyone can be someone's ally. There are so very many opportunities, both formally and informally. You just have to have the know-how, ability to articulate your skills, time, patience, and kindness, or some good partial combination of those attributes, to want to teach or reach someone. Is there anyone in your sphere of life who might benefit by your support and instruction? Go on, share some of yourself. You might want to start the conversation with "You've been on my mind. How can I help?"

BLIND FAITH

Beep Ball and Blind Runners

"The Gift (To Be a Friend)"

The Lord was good to me today,
He let me help a friend.
I could extend a hand to him,
Whose troubles knew no end.

It really didn't cost me much,
Was just a thought or two
To offer him an open heart
To tell his problems to.

We tarried by a tranquil stream—
Its gentle currents flowed.
To offer up a friendly ear
Can help though you not know.

It doesn't take your sage advice
Or well-intentioned prayers.
The only thing he really needs:
To know that someone cares.

Let's think for a moment about people who, for whatever reason, might not be able to run. I always wanted everyone to experience that thrill, that joy. But think of the faculties necessary to run. It takes a lot of body power—and brain power. It takes all kinds of coordination and spatial processing skills that are primarily governed by sight.

As my coaching days went on, I wanted to help people who might not be able to run because of visual impairment. So, I became associated with blind runners. This is a fascinating concept to me. Did you know that people who are blind can run? And that they can run in a race, safely? It's true, and I had the privilege of being involved with them to facilitate events.

85

This story begins about ten years ago, with the Sunset House, an outreach mission of my second church. I should tell you a little bit about it. It is a non-profit hospice that I've volunteered at. It has helped comfort countless families as they usher their loved ones out of this world and into the next. Sunset is a fitting visual symbol for the end of life. Some people may say it's just a euphemism, but I think it's appropriate for the setting of one's life. Anyway, the church wanted to raise money for the Sunset House and decided that they could do it through a race. I wasn't going to that sponsoring church yet. My good friend Ward Abbett, who went there and knew I was a race director, asked me if I could help them get started. I wouldn't direct the race myself, but I would show them how to set it up.

They ran it for ten years themselves, but then they lost their race director. I found out that they didn't have the race that year, and intervened. I said, "Oh my gosh! You didn't have the race this year?! Why not?" It bothered me because I knew this had caused the church to lose thousands of dollars of income just for that. So, I worked to reinvigorate the run. It has now become a big-in-quality and big-in-participation event in the neighborhood. Runners are young and old, and all different levels of ability, from the everyday gal or guy to the more seasoned competitor.

A Special New Friend Who Plays Ball

After casually checking out the church, I decided it might be a place that Donna and I could fit after a change from my first church. I met my blind friend, Leah, through that new (very old) church. She's a close friend now. As I got to know her, I wondered, what must it be like to be blind? Apparently, it's doable, somehow. Leah does so well in moving through her environment.

Making small talk on Sunday after church one day, I asked her, "What did you do yesterday?"

She remarked, "I had practice."

"What kind of practice?" I asked.

She said baseball practice.

"What do you mean by baseball? How can a blind person play baseball?" I candidly inquired.

She answered, "It's called 'beep ball.' It's baseball for the blind. It's played with a ball that has a beeper in it. We hear the sounds and navigate to the ball that way."

Wow, I thought. *I've never heard of such a thing! I can't fathom it.* From there, I told her how intrigued I was, and asked her if I could observe sometime. She said of course.

So, we were off to the beep ball field for me to see what it was all about. Leah invited me out to Cobb's Hill where they do their thing. I drove out there, and of course here I went walking up with my old legs and unsteady gait, and I got some slightly strange looks from some of the sighted players. I had to laugh to myself. I knew what they were thinking: *Oh boy, here comes a lame guy! Hope he's not going to be on our team!*

As she said, beep ball features a ball that beeps. It has an electronic beeper inside it. The game requires a fined-tuned sense of hearing, great individual spatial and coordination skills, and super teamwork. A fun and competitive spirit also applies!

Now let me explain to you the dynamics I saw out on the field. It's a little different than baseball. The catcher, the pitcher, and the batter are all on the same team, not opposites as normal. So instead of being an adversarial relationship between pitcher and batter, the pitcher is trying to help the batter. The pitcher is trying to lob the ball so that when the batter goes to swing it, it's likely to hit, not strike out.

You have to understand that the pitcher and the catcher are sighted. The batter is the only one who is visually impaired in this special three-person arrangement. If the blind person has some ability to see, they actually have to wear a blindfold so as to put them on an even ability level with other batters.

Surprisingly, the beep is not real loud. Since the batter can't hear the beep so well as it is being thrown from far away, the pitcher tries to throw the ball right in the batter's strike zone. Imagine an invisible ball coming right at your face! The pitcher says, "Ready, set, pitch!" and then suddenly it's there! Needless to say, the batter and pitcher must be very well synchronized and trusting.

Now let's look at the other team. The opposite team is in the outfield. Each one of them is blind and trying to catch the ball out there after it's hit by the batter. Mind you, with auditory commotion going on around them, these players are trying to hear the ball and scrambling for it in the huge area of the baseball diamond and outfield. It's hard. These players have assistants. They are called spotters and are sighted people. They are verbally signaling to the outfielders where the ball is, although they can't physically lead them. The spotters are calling out section numbers, like "Area 4!" or "Area 7!" If the outfielders can control and secure that ball, they get the run point. The outfielders never have to throw it back to the base.

If the fielders dive on the ball and can control it before the batter gets to first base (there are only two bases, first and third), then it's an out. On the other hand, it's considered a run if the batter gets to base number one. As you can imagine, it's a bit tricky to find that base. But there is another beeper set up, inside a cone that resembles a little lighthouse made out of foam. The batter can hear first base where that marker is. And yes, you have to be able to discriminate between the beeper in the ball and the beeper that is leading you to the base. Difficult! Exciting!

Once I learned the rules, which are fairly simple, and had seen the team practicing, I told Leah, "Gee, it's really cool that you can do that. I'd like to go see you in a game someday."

Running Blindly Ahead

After observing these players at a few games, I was so impressed with them and their dexterity and athleticism that I suggested something more. I said, "How would you all like to run a race?"

Well, dear reader, you now understand beep ball, but can you wrap your mind around the logistics of marathon running for people with the disability of blindness? In this case, I could envision it right away, because this was *my* area now.

Running a race for a person with blindness works just fine, believe it or not. Each runner is tethered to a sighted one, a guide. But the guide is not in the front with the blind runner following. They run together side by side, each holding an end of the tether which is about three feet apart. They coordinate speed; their pace must correspond with one another. It's an issue only if a blind runner is running faster than his or her guide or vice versa. They have to talk a lot and practice to know each other's cadence.

That's one problem solved. Next, tripping hazards are more of a problem for a person who cannot see, of course. Since blind people are more likely to trip, they must be agile and quick to catch themselves if they do. Most of them are, especially if they have played beep ball. To deal with glitches in the pavement, like say potholes, a manhole cover, a curb, or a curve in the route, the team talks through them. The sighted person can touch the blind person to guide them around a hazard but probably won't because that could slow things down. Some of these unsighted runners are pretty fast! It floored me how rapidly they can move!

I'm extremely proud to say that this beep ball team of Leah's boldly took on the challenge, once they learned of such a thing. None of these people had ever done an event like this before, so I had to give them a lot of credit. I invited them to run, and the whole fabulous, positive team came over to the Sunset House race to try something completely new, to branch out with their athletic talents, to be esteemed by sighted people with far less ability.

You may ask, can the blind runners try the route out first, so they get some familiarity with it? Yes, they could, but there wasn't time for it in our case. This was going to be all new to them, right down to their first few steps. No time for a dress rehearsal here! My gang ran through my Irondequoit neighborhood where the race was located—on the side streets raw.

This Sunset House race featuring the blind runners that year was quite an official production. There was a lot of publicity for our little race. We had prominent political officials from the city and suburbs, TV cameras—all that good stuff. Not many people in Rochester ever knew about this activity of blind running until we acquainted them with it. A hundred spectators or more stood in awe and watched a dozen blind people run with a dozen guides and all the regular contestants. The function of the road marshals (guards that stop the cars from going onto the course) was even more important at this race, as you may imagine.

I was just absolutely glowing when everyone finished their first 5K. I was over-the-moon happy with that. It was a tremendous thing with that team, that they could do that. Moreover, it led to a special relationship between me and my newfound friends, a bridge God had formed.

My pal Leah ran; I was so proud of her. She was one of the top-line finishers. She's quite a runner, really. After this adventure, I took her to a Thanksgiving race, the "Turkey Trot" in another one of our suburbs, Webster. It's for sighted people, a little over 5K. I set her up with one of my friends who's a runner, Chris McAllister. Leah was the only blind person who ran among hundreds of seeing people. Again, she finished strong, and we were all humbled. Leah and Chris, her guide—those two women are formidable competitors, I'll say.

"Play [Beep] Ball!"

From there, the beep ball folks asked me to be the director of a big beep ball tournament. They invited other teams to come to Rochester to compete in it. Of course, I gladly accepted. And so, we had teams from Boston, Toronto, New York City, etc. participating. They have a very organized league of beep ball teams and games, including a World Series. As the organizer of the whole shebang, I got the players set up, the field marked, the dugouts arranged—everything. We had to hire sighted umpires to help us for the tournament. They had to learn the rules of beep ball. We had a little rule book they had to memorize although it isn't complicated. It was so much fun, a huge success. It was at the Grace and Truth Sports Park in Greece, New York, a ministry of First Bible Baptist Church, a megachurch in a suburb of our metropolitan area. This tournament was a blast.

After that event, one of the sighted volunteers who had some connections around town wanted to promote the beep ball team so that more locals would attend the yearly tournament. Our Rochester promotional game would be called "The Pioneers Versus the Politicians." The *Pioneers* name refers to their founders. The New York Telephone Company's service group is called the Pioneers. They have been friends of the blind and generous for many decades in helping raise funds for equipment and initiating programs for them. Their advocacy and financial support have been greatly appreciated by many. In this Pioneer-sponsored event, the blind baseball team was playing beep ball against the sighted politicians—the judges of Rochester, town supervisors from surrounding suburbs, and other bigwigs.

So, what happened? The blind team beat the *heck* out of the politicians, of course! Hey, playing beep ball is not an easy thing, and the politicians in this case were clueless. They had absolutely no idea of what they were doing! That's even though we told them the rules! Remember I said that if you can see, you have to wear a blindfold when you bat and when you are out in the field. Well, those people were awful. Those politicians got creamed. It was hilarious. Everyone was in hysterics because they were so, so very bad. Inept to say the least.

When I was racing the Old Dominion trail, you'll remember from an earlier chapter that I was naïve and didn't prepare correctly. My battery in the flashlight died, and my friend and I were stranded when we became without light. I was running blind and trepidatiously, how it must feel for visually-impaired runners. I had to try to pay attention to every tactile clue in the path. It was largely impossible. I was reduced to desperation, begging God to rescue me from my exasperating and dangerous situation. I even bargained to get out of it, just so long as I and my accompanying friend were alive.

Although hindsight is twenty-twenty as they say, I had had no practical foresight. Thank God I *did* have the *spiritual* foresight, though, to immediately realize that I was in over my head, was nothing without my Maker, and needed him to guide me if I were going to make it through. I had temporarily lost only a flashlight, luckily not my permanent vision. But that little taste of the deprivation of light was all it took in my case to paradoxically *see* the light, to get my priorities straight. My reliance on God for races was thenceforth forefront in my mind.

We can learn a lot from blind people, wouldn't you say?

ORGANIZING ROCHESTER

My Days as a Designer, Director, and Certifier

"Chaos"

I have a very special place.
Where chaos does abound.
It seems to gather all my stuff,
And nothing can be found.

I organize my desk so well.
Each thing does have a place.
I file each sheet and stack each note,
Of clutter there's no trace.

But if I leave it for a day,
When I come back, I find
Some jerk has come and stirred it up
And left a mess behind!

So I look 'round to see what's wrong.
A gremlin there I see.
But when I try to chase him out,
I find that he is me.

Getting organized takes hard work. Some people are naturally better at it than others. On the other hand, some people are inherently "messier" than others, and there's some brain research that points to different cognitive styles concerning this. The "random-abstract" personality, your classic messy person, actually prefers what we call "organized clutter"—an oxymoron, of course. They prefer that to the perplexity or consternation of the "concrete-sequential" person, who detests disorganization and clutter. Whether you are an Oscar or a Felix (a slob or a neatnik), I think we can all agree that some people were born to organize, and some were not.

I never thought of myself as a button-up sort of guy. I had to be organized for my job and as a parent, of course, but as I told you, I was mainly a "Type B" personality. I went with the flow, until that flow led me into dark waters and I had to clean up my life, as I've explained. Then when Kodak went under, I had to change again, to reinvent myself, as I've explained as well. So I had some experience in adaptability. It always led me to becoming a more organized person.

God presented me with a number of situations in which people were desperately seeking someone who would be willing to come to the forefront, sometimes as a volunteer. That person could help out and perform some very needed organizational jobs—race designer, race director, and race certifier.

Once I'd been a coach for a while, I stepped up to being a race director. That's a person who arranges everything, from planning out the course long before the race, to marketing it, to signing up runners and staff, to executing the actual race on event day and making sure everyone's healthy and safe (again, the industrial hygienist coming out in me).

Road Rallies and Family Fun

But first, I want to tell you about experiences that spurred on my course designing. I will explain to you where I got my skills and passion for planning out my most successful running courses.

My love of doing that began a long, long time ago, when I was just a kid. Mom and Dad were sports car enthusiasts. I'm not sure how they got interested in them, but in the 1950's Dad bought a mini Renault as a second car. I think for the next car he traded up to a TR3 convertible. He joined the sports car club SCCA here in Rochester. I wasn't old enough to drive, but I definitely was interested.

There was a family event that the kids could participate in too. The Rochester club scheduled road rallies, which were fun treasure hunts on wheels. Each course was designed to follow country roads in the Southern Tier of our state, with clever clues you had to follow in the family car, Mom or Dad driving, of course. For example, you were told to proceed on your route until you saw the big orange vegetables. Then you were instructed to turn right and go for ten minutes until you saw a creek by a green barn. The average speed was determined by those who designed the course. Drivers had to watch their speed, and navigators watched for clues when to change direction. Each car in the competition was timed at the start and finish. The team who finished closest to the designed time would win a trophy.

The rally would usually end at some country eating establishment where trophies were given and conversations were had about who got lost or missed a clue and ended up in Pennsylvania or Ohio. The whole thing was a ball even for us kids. I met some fine folks. Mom and Dad had many trophies and eventually were road rally course designers themselves.

Later, when I got out of the service in 1970, I bought a used red MGB, a little rough around the edges. It was fun to ride the roads of Irondequoit. My "race course" was the twisty, hilly road towards Durand Park and Kings Highway. Most young drivers in Irondequoit know this road well. I'm sure there were many drunk driver accidents on that road and still are, sadly. But for me, it was lighthearted abandon.

When I joined the Postal Service in 1970, my walking route traveled around the city. I went around my mail routes with my bag of delivery mail, the top of my buggy down, long hair flowing in the wind. So, recalling these three formative experiences (the rallies, joyrides, and postal routes), I guess I associate the actual layout and design of racecourses with a lot of happiness—good times.

The Big-Time

So, this is what happened when I tried to redesign and organize my first big race. I first wanted to reinstate the defunct Rochester City Marathon. Our city's only big race, a 26.2-mile marathon, was begun in 1972 by the Rochester Track Club. In the early eighties, I ran it in 2:50 (placing somewhere in the top 20) as my best time. But then there had been a moratorium on it starting in 1989, and that caused an emptiness felt by a lot of people. So, in keeping with that and my desire to always advance to yet another personal goal, in 2005 I tried to revive this race from its sixteen-year hiatus. I was hoping the Arthritis Foundation would work with me and co-sponsor a new Rochester City Marathon, as I said I had coached their JIM teams. I floated the idea to them. But no, they couldn't see putting that kind of money up. So, I had to make them believers that it could still be a big deal for them.

After more talks and knowing I still wasn't getting anywhere, I hatched another plan. I would design another event, but this one would not be in the city, so it would be less costly. It would be along Lake Ontario, like the first marathon I ever ran. I did some research about the logistics of putting on a marathon, designing a course, etc. and presented the Arthritis Foundation with a second plan. Birth of a new-old marathon! We proceeded to bring a marathon event back to our area after lying dormant for several years. It was a challenge for Coach Greg. But with much prayer and planning we pulled it off. It was small, but it was mine and I learned much as a race director. The benefit for the Arthritis Foundation was several thousand dollars. I think I had their attention then. They figured out that to make money, you had to spend money.

So, this small start gave us hope for that bigger, city marathon. We could have a five-year financial plan to bring Rochester Marathon home again permanently. And we did it! Today, the Rochester Marathon brings tens of thousands of dollars to its sponsors. So let me tell you about being the race director of Rochester's only marathon, the one in which I had participated as a contestant and the one I brought back to life.

The Erie Canal

It all began with course design, or in this case, redesign. For the first seventeen years, until 1989, the race had started from downtown Rochester, went out to Fairport, and looped back to end on Main Street in the city. To try to incorporate more points of interest, I changed the course but didn't add onto the distance. I took out most of the sections that ran through the city, because the cost of the necessary police force was exorbitant. After I redesigned it, it still started in the city but went from the scenic Erie Canal in that eastern suburb of Fairport out to Genesee Valley Park, back to downtown through just a little bit of the city, over the Genesee River on the bridge, by the University of Rochester, and then to Frontier Field, our major stadium.

Besides the financial benefit, the route was now so much more enjoyable and doable, I like to think. It was easy on the canal portion. At least half the path there was cinders, which are softer on the legs than pavement, and runners really liked it. The route went through our historic village of Pittsford by lock 62 and meandered around to lock 63 in the city (locks are exciting to see working). It was in all a beautiful design, if I do say so myself. It was done by someone (me) who knew running, knew the Rochester area, and had consulted other runners and clubs for feedback. Serious runners were attracted to it because it would help them to get a good time to qualify for larger races like the Boston Marathon.

But we kept an element of hometown feel. It was nice because not everyone who wanted to run had to do the full marathon. I had also designed it so that we had a secondary race, a half-marathon, going on simultaneously. It began downtown just a few minutes after the full marathoners left. It departed from the regular marathon route so as to bypass much of it farther to the east, rejoined it at mile twenty along the canal, and ended at the shared finish line.

I should stop for a moment and elaborate on Fairport and the Erie Canal. Fairport is one of a few quaint little "ports" in our area, which is interesting because of course we are near no oceans on which to have seaports. Instead, we are near the major waterway of the Erie Canal. A history of Rochester would be remiss if lacking in some explanation of our grand Erie Canal.

It goes right through the heart of Rochester and has touched the lives of millions over for about two hundred years now. It is a living, breathing place that is much greater than the sum of its parts. For those of you not familiar with New York's geography, there are quite a few towns with the suffix of *port* that are dotted along the long, long Erie Canal. Around here, we have Fairport on the east side of the city, as I mentioned, and Spencerport and Brockport on the west side. The Erie Canal was a massive mecca and a cutting-edge piece of technology in its day. It was opened to the world in 1825, second in size at that time only to China's Grand Canal.

It took thousands of workers eight years to build, and that was at a frenetic pace. It was quite an accomplishment of civil engineering and remains one of the most impressive historical artifacts of infrastructural ingenuity in our nation's history. This vast manmade waterway covered over 368 miles and ran east to west in its numbering of ports intended to link the Atlantic Ocean with the Great Lakes. The Great Lakes were the major commercial trade route to destinations away from the coast, going into the heartland of the country (thus the canal being named after one of those Great Lakes, Erie, the one it would touch). The politicians actually had a ceremony called "The Wedding of the Waters" in which a jug of water from Lake Erie was emptied into the Atlantic Ocean, therefore uniting them and celebrating the canal's completion. The expansive route would indelibly transform the state's geographical, political, economic, and cultural landscapes for the rest of history.

Donkeys with ropes on towpaths along the side of the canal pulled barges transporting goods and supplies. The waterway had to be at a consistently flat elevation so that 1) the water wouldn't tend to run in one certain direction if the idea was for vessels to move in both ways, eastward and westward and 2) because flat barges need very calm, level waters. But since there were different natural elevations along the route and waterfalls had to be eliminated so as not to interfere with smooth transit, a series of small dams had to be set up, called locks.

These intricate locks were mechanisms of iron enclosures big enough to hold a ship or two. They would take in the ship or barge between their two walls, shut or "lock" it in a temporary pool, and then, using a system of smaller side streams, raise or lower the level of the water inside that isolated pool chamber. In that way, a ship could be transitioned through to the other side at a different level. The ship would go higher or lower depending on which direction it was headed.

Some locks are still in use today. It is very interesting to watch a vessel go into a lock and see the water rush in or out of the monstrous mechanism. In fact, many school children are taken on science and history field trips to watch the process in action, even though the Erie Canal is used only for recreational, not trade, vehicles today. It's an awesome sight to watch a yacht go through a lock.

As the New York state government website reminds us, all the state's major cities fall along this canal route, and "nearly 80% of upstate New York's population lives within twenty-five miles of the Erie Canal." Because transportation on water avoided the ruts and mud of roads before paving was available, it was generally more convenient and faster in the old days. This gave the canal in New York immediate and unrivaled economic success in its early epoch and is the reason why New York is called "The Empire State." To give you the full extent of the canal's significance, the New York State Canal Corporation's website explains: "The iconic waterway established settlement patterns for most of the United States during the nineteenth century, made New York the financial capital of the world, provided a critical supply line which helped the North win the Civil War, and precipitated a series of social and economic changes throughout a young America." It was instrumental in the making of New York City and instigated a major thrust westward undertaken by American pioneers.

The rest stops, or *ports* (meaning *doorway* in Latin), were very "happening" places as you can imagine, entrances into exciting little worlds of gambling, drinking, entertainment, etc… Music, art, and literature were infused with stories and legends from the canal. As a matter of fact, there are quite a few folk songs written about our "little ditch," and anyone my age can remember being made to learn these catchy little tunes in elementary music class.

Because over time commercial vehicles had to get larger and the canal could not accommodate them, engineers tried enlarging the canal a few times, but after the turn of the twentieth century, it largely fell out of favor and really went out of commission by 1960. In vogue for only a short time considering the massive effort that went into it (it was largely hand-dug), the Erie Canal today is an important time capsule of American history. When it was built, it was an acute period of greatness. Thomas Jefferson had described the proposal to construct it as "a little short of madness," and in hindsight, maybe he was right. Although the canal had an amazing run, just like Kodak, it lasted only so long because other forms of transportation, such as the railroad and highways, came in and beat it. The traffic dwindled dramatically, and now the Erie Canal is still somewhat operational but more of a landmark. So again, it's part of the mystique of these port towns like Fairport. You get the idea.

The word *fair* in our language didn't use to mean average to poor as it does today. Just like waterways are constantly changing, so is language. *Fair* in the nineteenth century used to mean *beautiful*, actually. Just drink up the imagery of *fair port* for a moment, and you will understand the ambiance of the location of this part of our city's race. In designing the race, I wanted to celebrate that beauty and pay homage to the Erie Canal, such a force that made my state and hometown great. See, designing courses is not always only about optimizing athletic prowess. It's sometimes about honoring the past and the men and women who trod the same memory-laden ground in yesteryear.

The first year of our new race we had sixty entries, and forty-five finished. It was a great experience. We subsequently grew year after year. I did have lots of help from other people while I was organizing, for which I'm very thankful. I did it for several years, until the end of 2013. It was at that time that the Arthritis Foundation quit doing it; then the owners of Fleet Feet (a national organization of franchises) and Yellow Jacket Racing took over, and it has been going strong ever since. One of the current directors was my timer for about six years.

I'd now like to tell you a story about my most challenging time as director of this race, and of *any* race I directed, in fact.

Dropping Like Flies

My time with this race program of the Arthritis Foundation was important to myself and many others. Being the race director, one is responsible for how the race is going to work in all aspects. Unexpected things can crop up, and you have to problem-solve to deal with them. It can be super stressful. For example, you need to understand that if there is going to be a thunder and lightning storm, you should cancel the race—call the race off—and that can be a hard call. It can make lots of people disappointed, even angry. Yet you are responsible for all runners, and your organization that is sponsoring the race will be on the hook for a lawsuit if something goes wrong. So you have all kinds of major and minor concerns. Most of all, of course, you don't want anyone to get killed in your race. Yes, the anecdote I'm going to share with you now concerns my most nerve-wracking time ever directing a race.

So, it was very, very hot in the beginning of this particular AF race. If you're a race organizer, you know that there will be people on the course for hours, so if you start the race in the morning, it's only going to get hotter and muggier as the day goes on. That day I had a meter, a device that could measure relative humidity and ambient and radiant temperature, and a wet-bulb, measuring how much the ambient temperature sucks moisture away from something; it's another instrument for air quality measurement. If it's really muggy out, the situation is more dangerous for runners; it affects the runner's body temperature because their sweat, which is designed to lift heat away from the body, can't be absorbed into the air as readily as if it's dry outside.

I had a whole medical team that was associated with the marathon. There was a medical triage unit at the finish line. Dr. Doug Jones, a runner and my medical director, soon alarmingly reported that we had a big problem that day. I had dozens, maybe fifty people, with heatstroke, going to the hospital. The hospitals that day, in fact, were getting full. I never had a guy die in one of my races, and it's normal for a race to have several runners go to the hospital for various reasons. This day, however, had many more than normal, so at that point, something drastic had to be done. (I never had this problem in any of the dozen races I'd done before as a race director). My medical director and I were conferring the whole time, trying to develop an action plan, to do damage control.

After about three hours, people were dropping like flies, being dragged into the medical tent, so we called the race off at the twenty-mile mark. As individuals came through, we'd pull all of them off the course at that point. We cancelled the race for those people still far behind on the course; they didn't have a chance to finish the race. We still had a bunch of people come through and win the race, the fast folks finishing in 2:50, when there were still hundreds of people out on the course in various stages of dehydration. There were about three hundred people total. I'm not sure exactly how many people didn't finish the race; if I had to guess, I'd say about a quarter of the people didn't, which is for an average race considered a lot. It is most often semi-chaos managing that many people and the crowd, trying to get the awards ceremony set up. But on this day, it was nutso. My worst weather story ever. My most anxiety. Poor people. Poor me. But no one died!

From a Journalist's Point of View

For publicity, I had worked these nine years of the AF's race with Assistant Sports Editor/Night Journalist Jim Castor of the *Democrat and Chronicle*, our city newspaper. He was very action-oriented and reported on things play by play. When he wanted to see the lead runner, our driver would take him out to different points in the course. He would also immediately interview the top winner and cover the awards ceremony. He did a commendable job.

And we became great pals. Our association was all about serendipity, he says. One day talking, we discovered that far away up in the Thousand Islands we both had summer cottages, about a mile apart, reachable by each other with just a twenty-minute boat ride. On the same island, in fact! He's on the northeast end of Grindstone Island, and I'm on the southwest end of it. "It's a small world!" as they say. Apart from fraternizing at the race, after that discovery, we'd always visit each other up there during the summers.

Jim has always spoken highly of me regarding our working relationship, as I of him. I was Jim's primary source for answers provided to the people of the city. He has said that I knew my stuff and had "a lifetime of knowledge," was a dedicated and good runner, and, "as an engineer and a safety inspector, had a way of thinking that is always good for an organizer to have." I think he means that "The Devil is in the details," as they say, and I'm a perfectionist when it comes to courses. He also tells everybody that I'm easy to know and like, not demanding, and so have worked well with volunteers. He says I'm a "good businessman" who functioned in step with time constraints of the daily media. I also helped him capture the true spirit of the race in his writing. I would share my perspective with him, off-the-record confidential things that would give him more holistic insight though not be reported verbatim.

And he would share his perspectives with me and his readers. I met with him the other day to talk about bygone days. The following section contains some of the things that Jim would comment on when he wrote every year about the AF race. These were things I didn't or couldn't necessarily see, due to my attention on so many of the race's other details. What he saw was mainly the emotional experiences of the contestants themselves and the public viewing. The aspects I concentrated on pertained mostly to health and safety of my runners, their physical welfare. But here are some fine points that the community itself and other readers of a wider audience were interested in and so Jim reported.

Although this was Rochester's cornerstone athletic event, it was on the small side, with usually about five hundred men and women. It was planned for early Sunday morning (although that was typically my church day and day of rest), so as there were very few people out on roads—no heavy traffic; that time was specifically chosen to keep it as low-key and family-friendly as possible.

Moreover, the race didn't offer significant prize money. By 2008, we were giving away only $6000 in total, to be divided (unequally) for all awards. The award categories included: raw speed of anyone regardless of sex or age, also fastest in age group or sex, plus a few others. The highest amount was $750, for the fastest person period. The least amount was $50 for the third-place wheelchair entry. Why was that money the least? Most people think that competing in a foot race in a wheelchair would be difficult. However, wheelchairs actually have the advantage. Wheelchair athletes come in first always; with their wheels, they can go faster than a runner's legs! The fastest finishing time of anyone, 2:18, belonged to the only wheelchair entry in our race of 2007. The man who won that year on foot came in after that, at 2:33. An incredible comparison! Anyway, our prizes were small. If the race had offered more prize money, it would have attracted national and international racers who were professional athletes, drawing more people, more traffic, more chaos. But that's not what our community wanted. The original organizers and I chose to keep it small for this reason.

Although we didn't want the spotlight so much, we did want the fun, celebratory feel. To help his newspaper readers envision what it was like from the sidelines if they hadn't been able to attend, Jim would describe the setting—the day's weather and the actual spectators. He'd write that there were many people attending, all involved to some degree. There was a great deal of joyous noise—clapping, cheering, and cowbells ringing as contestants ran by. There were lots and lots of volunteers with paper cups of water, stretching their arms out into the street, pinching their fingers over the top edge of each cup so the runner could get one without it all being spilled in the transfer. The runner would gulp it down or throw it over their head to cool off as they ran by, since there was no time to stop. The lead runners know how to do a pick-up really well and don't slow down very much. It's not like a true pit stop.

Timing Is Everything
As far as what it looks like at the finish line for spectators, such an excellent place to be, the runners in most races come through like a bell curve. Most are in the middle, with a few at the front, and a few in the back. In our race, after three hours and fifteen minutes, most of the pack was arriving. Mind you, there's the gun time and there's computer chip time. The gun time is for the event itself, while the chip time is for the individual runner. When the gun goes off at the beginning of the race, people at the front of the group obviously start earlier than the people running at the back, so the start time for that latter group doesn't register yet even though the gun time does. It's about a minute in our Rochester race with five hundred runners before all contestants, from front to back, have gone through the start line. That gun time to full start component is what every organizer, like me, cares about.

Chip time, on the other hand, is what every runner and the public care about. I was race director at the time when computer chips, not stop watches like in the old days, would automatically record each runner's time. You as the runner wore the chip around your ankle. There was a miniature radio transmitter that sent a signal, and when you crossed the finish line, it gave a little beep, transmitted to a nearby computer as organizers watched. Most people finish a marathon in four to five hours. Their average is a nine to eleven and a half minutes-per-mile pace. A finishing time that's under four hours is a real accomplishment for everyone other than elite runners, who today finish in around two hours (this time keeps going down year after year, as winners are running smarter).

Breaking this down between the sexes, according to Jeff Necessary, RRCA-certified running coach, "In 2016, the average finishing time for men of all ages in U.S. marathons was 4 hours, 22 minutes. That's almost exactly 6 miles per hour, or a 10-minute mile. The female average time was 4:48, or almost exactly 11 minutes per mile, which works out to roughly 5.5 mph." It is interesting to note that over the recent two decades, average times (not individual win times) have been slowing. It's because more and more average runners are joining the game. Anyway, it was Jim's job to gather and report all these statistics then, back in the day.

Issues

Jim and I were recently talking about some of the problems that I handled back then. He reminded me that we'd have to go out some years as late as the night before to frantically set up or reset cones in preparation for the race. Usually, these cones to mark the race were set up well in advance. But sometimes I had to do an emergency change of the course because of construction—part of a road dug up, or paving, lane changes, or other city street things. So, I had to deal with some last-minute, urgent modifications with my partner Rich DiMarco, that's for sure.

Also, once there was cheating. I handled it as gracefully as I could. The USA Track and Field organization has rules for runners, one being that you are not allowed to be "aided or abetted" by someone running alongside you. This would be a pacing person or someone riding a bike or running along with you yelling instructions to you or letting you know about competitors' times. In one incident a participant had someone helping them, telling them their pace and standing at various points, getting there with a bike. I got lots of complaints, because the person who cheated was one of those who got one of the more sizeable prizes, and if we had been able to rescind their prize, it would have gone to another runner.

Upon investigation, we believe this cheating wasn't due to ignorance of the rules; it was intentional cheating, though a gray area because it was hard to prove, since the age of cell phones and ubiquitous picture-taking hadn't arrived yet. We didn't have any evidence, just verbal reports from other runners. So, during my race directing the next year, I asked Jim to write a story in the paper reminding everyone of the expectations, cautioning runners to follow the rules. Things have come a long way since then in terms of cameras and accountability.

For another year's race I organized, there was a guy who had won the Master's division of the Rochester Marathon and others, like the Las Vegas Marathon, etc. He had a record of being a cheater; the word got out to watch him. In our Rochester Marathon, they got photos of this guy at different places in the race, and there were a bunch of telltale signs that he was up to his old tricks. For instance, he had different uniforms on, so we know he cheated. No one knew if it was cheating by bike, car, or something else, but we were sure he was taking shortcuts of some sort. Did this make other runners angry? Maybe, but they never acted on it. I never heard of runners getting in fights during a race. I've heard about runners fighting *after* races about someone cutting someone else off, but usually runners are gentle people. They just want to run.

Certifying

There was one more pursuit in addition to directing. I eventually got into certifying races, a whole other level. This was totally different. I had this new goal of becoming a master certifier for the USATF. Ontario Shore Race was my first one. To certify a race is quite an involved, official process. The route someone else has designed has to be re-measured extremely accurately, basically down to the centimeter, just like a surveyor would measure a tract of land. As the race official who was often both the organizer and the certifier in one, I'd decide on the race directions over the city and then measure them just so, to make sure they followed regulations. Sometimes I did just one of those roles, and sometimes I did both. Most of the time when I was a race director, I was the designer and the certifier both. I did this multiple times for the Ontario Shore races, Rochester Marathons, and Sunset House runs.

Sunset House

As I briefly explained, in a less professional capacity, I was asked to be a race director and certifier for my second church, the Irondequoit United Church of Christ. It was in my connection with the body of Christ that they had seen my experience as a runner and an official and thought I might be useful.

As of 2020, the race is in its seventeenth year, generally raising over $15,000 each time—more than most golf tournaments! Now, I have lots of Sunset House 5K fundraiser tee-shirts; they're my favorite thing to wear, and when you see me these days, I'm most likely dressed in one of them. It's kind of a ubiquitous fashion statement by me.

At the time I was approached, I didn't know much about the IUCC. While being asked to help them design and direct, I decided to check them out for myself as a visitor and was pleasantly surprised. I began going there and soon became a member. I enjoyed being back to a house of God. I had had several years of respite from being burned out by my sizeable amount of work at Faith Temple. I found it refreshing to get back to a church family, and I soon would reintegrate myself into fellowship and service.

I'd like to ask you now, could you take your skills and be a facilitator of some sort? Is there any local, county- or state-wide, national or global organization or cause you could become a part of to increase visibility of that entity's mission? Or might you lead any groups, such as Scouts, church youth groups, sports teams, or clubs? If you're the shyer sort, can you volunteer in a supporting role to help someone who's attempting to lead? I bet you'll get just as much back as you put forward. But whether you do or not, go ahead, "be good for nothing." Great-granddad Edward would love that.

Part II

A FALL

Nobody's Perfect

"Peace and Quiet"

I oft'times long for rest and bliss,
A little peace of mind—
If it weren't for that voice inside
That's talking all the time.

I think sometimes it would be nice
To have some solitude.
But there's an ever-present nag—
He's one you can't elude.

There is no peace or quiet there,
No tranquil time within.
He's always yakking in my ear,
Creating quite a din.

There's no escape in it for me;
I'll run but cannot hide.
He's always there inside my head;
He's always deep inside.

Someday I'm going to fool him, though,
Right then I won't be home.
I'll go and run and find a friend,
With whom to be alone.

Have you ever told yourself stupid stuff? Been your own worst enemy? I mean of seismic proportions here...
We cringe when we think of the concept of a fall—dishonor happening to real people. Someone in the spotlight takes a big hit, and it's pitiful. We have the saying "fall from grace." It's always about loss of something great and the humiliation and remorse that go along with it. If we've been unfortunate enough to experience such a fall, the scripts we play

in our head afterwards can be self-sabotaging, mercilessly browbeating, and further defeating. In an earlier chapter, I discussed the classic conflict of person versus self (my drug use). While it started out as fun, it eventually led me to feeling demoralized and less-than. This forthcoming chapter is again about man versus self, the worst type of conflict—because self-inflicted wounds seem so dumb, so pointless, so illogical. Counterintuitive.

Nobody likes to fall, and the *fall*out isn't pretty. After we do, we shake our heads and say, "I shudda seen it coming!" Cudda, shudda, wudda. My experience was no exception to that rationalization after what happened to me in my fifties. But the fact is, there were so many little things piling up at this time in my life, little red flags on the way that didn't seem so red. Orange maybe, but not red. I got inured to them because they were so prevalent on a daily basis and didn't seem to be an issue at the time. Then, instead of a catastrophic fall from grace everybody knew about (or, to express it in a more updated way, public *dis*grace), it was a private thing that happened. It was no less painful, though.

My disaster was something I did that I wish I never had. I'm ashamed of it, but to protect certain people, I'm not going to discuss it very much. Let's just say that the demands of church leadership on Donna and me were the orange flags eventually overwhelming us and taking their toll. I was feeling burned out from my duties as an elder and Kodaker and runner. So, I dropped out of the church and left my problem behind. Or so I thought…

Because I believe in karma, I look back now and know the ego-related problem put me on a one-way collision course with the failure of a major bodily organ, with a physiological breakdown as we shall see in the following chapter. As they say, payback is…well, you know. Although I had become only misguided, not fully lost, and it wasn't the end of the world, it *was* clear that I needed to learn a lesson. My moral fall and resulting punishment were about the universe's stern leveling of my good-old-fashioned pride. We live in a fallen world, full of iniquity, but a higher force has got to keep all that in check.

Or should I say "bad old-fashioned pride"? I think my pride was twofold, that is, physical and emotional. Part of it was that I thought my body owed me something more than a mere mortal might possess. It was the kind of pride that makes you imprudently think you're "invincible" so that you make stupid decisions and take unwise risks. That was part of the physical piece.

Then the emotional…Pride in accomplishments is good. Confidence and courage, its cousins, are great! But I mean PRIDE. You know, the kind that could make you think you're more important than others and cause you to conduct yourself not as respectfully as you should, the kind that makes you walk about with a disconnected demeanor, with your "I-don't-care" blinders on. That kind. But beware—it has repercussions. They involve the suffering of others and your own guilty rumination lasting for years afterward, like in my father's poem.

And that's all I have to say about this episode in my life. Take it for what it's worth.

DEALBREAKER OF THE HEART

Coronaries

"Vacancy"

A presence in our self lives,
Besides the one that shows.
There's the one that's in the mirror
And one that no one knows.

They are in constant conflict,
An everlasting fight.
One speaks of evil concepts,
The other only right.

They speak with little voices
That only you can hear.
They talk where no one else can,
They whisper in your ear.

Some people call one conscience,
So deep within the heart.
No matter what you call them,
You must tell them apart.

Sometimes it isn't easy
To choose from what they say.
One tells you what it wants to,
The other one says, "Nay."

God gives you all the answers,
Allows you to decide.
So put your trust in Jesus,
And with him you'll abide.

But if you're indecisive,
Can't think through all your doubt
Of how to send sin packing,

Just kick the demon OUT.

Once you are done evicting,
Have freed yourself from sin,
You'd better fill his spot, or
He'll find his way back in.

Y ou see that in my chapter title I've foreshadowed a love affair gone bad. The term *dealbreaker* is a useful word, especially in the dating world's past couple decades when its application to romantic relationships was born. It means an unacceptable situation or factor that comes along as part and parcel of the world of a potential new love interest. It means a roadblock to someone's requirements for a viable partnership. This unhappy discovery is abortive and renders the relationship over before it even really started.

But this chapter's not about that; it's not about the uncomfortable feelings of having to stand one's ground to get one's romantic needs met, or the disappointing feelings when the other person can't bend a little so the relationship can take flight. It's not about emotion at all, in fact. This chapter is about the real, physical thing. A physical "dealbreaker" of the heart.

My life was almost prematurely taken. The dealbreaker was a near-fatal heart attack. I almost died from a massive coronary. At this point, you may recall the Greek runner Pheidippides I discussed earlier on—the guy who had a heart attack after a big, momentous run in service to his country. Pheidippides was true-blue and ran to fulfill an admirable mission. His death enabled him to go out in a blaze of glory and just added to his whole amazingness. However, here I want to talk about my fate, the wages of sin, and irony. Like I told you in the preceding chapter, in later years I had an ongoing sin that was impairing my life, and I believed that the coronary was just punishment.

Do you think I'm being too hard on myself? We all make mistakes from time to time, right? Even whoppers. But does God really want to punish us? Or do we punish ourselves, because we can't live with what we've done? I tried to take it "like a man." I tried to power through it. Did I even know I was having a heart attack when the crushing pain started? Yes, I certainly did. But even more than the pain, I was experiencing, as I said, what I thought was the divine justice of the whole thing, the payback. *That figures*, I said to myself. I immediately got the message and felt sorry for all I had done. I had caused my family emotional heartache, so it seemed fitting that I should receive a physical heartache in return.

Progression of a Heart Attack

I guess my poor little heart had done a good job up until that point in my life, which was age fifty-eight. It had beaten literally billions of times! My body had unbeknownst to me been headed for a coronary event for a while, though. I survived only because I was so physically fit otherwise. My "lightning" struck in the aftermath of a Boston Marathon race, only minutes after I'd finished. Of the total number of Boston Marathons I ever ran, it happened at the nineteenth one.

Having been a race organizer, I was familiar with the signs of a heart attack. I did all of the AHA's (American Heart Association's) recommendations for addressing the situation if you think you're having one. I observed chest discomfort and shortness of breath, went to the medical tent, and then they transferred me. The physicians patched me up at Boston General Hospital. I was in there a few days.

Reviewing the cause, I had started developing heart disease in my fifties although I didn't know it. But then again, I wasn't ever "listening" to my body. I know that sounds terribly ironic, and everybody says something about it when they hear of my story—because as a serious athlete, my heart should have been in top condition, with my instincts and bodily intuition also clear.

You know, we often have a medical family history that is a harbinger to our problem. My paternal grandmother died in the hospital of a massive brain hemorrhage the result of atherosclerosis (part of heart disease). The Hematology Clinic at the University of Rochester, New York, has an autopsy report on this. She is buried in the Dano family plot on Grindstone Island. So why wasn't I thinking about her? Would you have thought about your long-dead relative's medical history had you been me?

After I got back from Boston, over the heart attack, I was back on my training regime again. I started having some difficulty in my breathing and getting pains. I thought, this isn't right. It got to the point that the pains were so bad I couldn't even run down the street. So, I went to the doctor. He gave me an EKG; they found nothing wrong. Then I was scheduled to see a cardiologist, and for each patient, they'd put you on a treadmill, get your heart rate up to a certain level, and then see what would happen. So, they said, after a few minutes with me, "Okay, you can get off the treadmill now." Surreptitiously in their minds, they must have said, *If we kept anybody over fifty years old on the treadmill and he died, we'd be negligent.* So, to avoid a lawsuit, I would guess, they took me off before I got symptoms.

So, I told them, "You have to let me stay on this thing long enough so I can feel the symptoms." Reluctantly, they did, and they saw them.

Then I had to wait. This went on for two months, I'm not sure why. Finally, they got me in for an angiogram. They said, "We see that you've got some blockages. Here are your choices: we could try to cure them with some drugs, or we could do a transplant, or we could put some stents in." They wouldn't tell me what to do; they merely gave me choices.

I had a running friend, a famous cardiologist in Rochester. I said, "Joan, this is what's going on…"

When I had finished explaining, she replied, "You'd probably be okay if you had some stents put in." So, they put one or two stents in the majorly clogged-up arteries. In a month or two I was back running again. I felt good. I felt like I had dodged a bullet. Stents, for your information, are tiny tubular implants that go into your heart, with little balloon thingies that open up into arteries; they're wire-mesh devices that stay inside your body. They are in my ticker today, doing their thing, ballooning away. It wasn't smooth sailing even after those stents were put in, however. The medical director in downtown Rochester on Andrew Street told me it wouldn't be.

That guy still sees me regularly, Dr. Varon. He's a big wheel in the cardiology world. He's been with me from the beginning…I'm sure I was his first marathon patient. He's been good to me. He's a kind and genteel doctor who appreciates the chance to study someone like me. I'm sure he could have written many of my chapters.

Round Two?

There was another incident, which happened during a race when it was really cold. With those stents in my heart, I attempted the Dublin, Ireland, marathon. At that time, I really did have a second heart attack, or maybe you'd call it a mini one. So here goes my heart attack in a foreign country, an ocean away from home. I had been over there six or seven times before and nothing. After the heart attack, I had coached people and also run myself. I had been happily running and still training at this part of my life, although I couldn't run as fast. Then I felt those familiar, crushing pains.

That marathon where I had my second round of heart pains made me believe I might both forfeit my second race ever and maybe even kill myself. I was stubborn and ran through to the finish line anyway. I know, I know…I'm bad. I finished the race strong and was able to stave the onslaught off for the time being. But I sought immediate medical attention after that. Fire and police were there; my body was telling me "You better stop right now, or you're going to be dead!" I had my nitroglycerine with me, popped a couple of those pills, and asked my medical director, Doug, if he would keep an eye on me. (Nitro slows your heart *right* down—you'd better believe it!) After being seen at the hospital, they determined that it was just another blockage. Chalk it up to bad genetics.

So, you guessed it—again, I had another couple stents put in. Wake-up call! If you don't have a heart, you don't have a life. And I mean that in a couple different ways. The heart is an engine; a symbol of love, of loyalty, of vitality, of self; but it's also a symbol of introspection.

MIRACLE MATE

My Wife, Donna

"My Partner"

My love has come to my own house,
Says just to live with me.
But why she'd want to do it, that
Is quite a mystery.

She puts up with my messes great.
For this I do not see
Why kindly she would live with it,
My eccentricity.

All things must be done in my way
In order to be right.
As long as she agrees with me,
There'll never be a fight.

Someday she'll find me out, my traits—
See me for what I am.
Though I can't really blame her much,
She'll take it on the lam.

I don't bode that much happening;
It's plain for me to see.
The reason that she sticks around:
She's just in love with me.

Our Early Life Together

Now I want to tell you about Donna, Donna Meisenzahl. At this point in my life, when I was really quite scared about my health, I relied on her, my mate, as most married couples do when a crisis strikes. As of 2020, I've been with my one and only, Donna, for five decades. We celebrated our fiftieth wedding anniversary a little while back.

(Today, not many couples can say this.) She has truly been "my rock." Donna, in many ways, along with the famous runners before me and my fabulous, nurturing dad, is one of my most significant heroes. She's run this crazy race with me, all these fifty years as husband and wife.

I met her upon being discharged from the army, in 1970, at a bar. Our first, unofficial date was at a biker bar downtown, the patrons there with hammers on their belts. They were real bikers, like those of Hell's Angels. I went with a good friend, Dick, who was meeting his girlfriend, Loretta, who brought Donna with her. Afterwards we all retired to Dick's apartment. Donna and I talked all night long. There was an immediate attraction.

The next morning Donna and I could say we were a couple. We have been together since that night. The next day I went back home to Irondequoit, gathered my speakers and stereo equipment, stuffed everything and some clothes into my MG (car), and moved in with her. From there we found another apartment in the Park Ave area on Merriman Street. Fifty years ago, that was the beginning.

Donna was raised Catholic with strong Catholic values and educated in Catholic schools her whole school life. Unlike my parents, Glenn and Lucille Meisenzahl were regular churchgoers. Donna's family didn't disapprove of her having a relationship with a non-Catholic, but I'm sure they weren't too happy when I moved in with her before marriage.

Donna and I were the whole nine yards of hippiness—the flowers in the hair, the beads. And the love. Our wedding was a hippie wedding. We got married down by a creek in the back of a justice of the peace's house in Webster. We called him the "marrying judge," Judge Van Ingan. We were truly happy and since then have enjoyed every minute we have spent together. Plus, I think Donna's parents approved after a time when we weren't living in sin anymore.

Then we moved to our first house, on Winfield Road in East Irondequoit. I couldn't have asked for a sweeter, happier time with the love of my life in that home. She and it were my havens. My wife got pregnant there with the boys, twins we would name Zak and Jesse. I left Rowe photos when Donna was expecting. I knew I had to make some real money, so I tried my hand at Kodak. I don't think that the MG went there to Winfield with us. It was sick, so I sold it. Donna had her first VW, and I can picture it there in that driveway. To this day she drives a VW Bug.

When we entered our faith experience together attending the first church, Faith Temple, we encountered a bit more resistance from Donna's parents. As committed Catholics, Glenn and Lucille weren't too up on this "born again" stuff and thought we were involved with some type of cult. Glenn actually did some checking and found out Faith was for real—just not

Catholic, nor any denomination for that matter. I'm quite sure they were even more surprised when we both were water baptized together. We were real Bible believers, walking, talking, praising, and dancing with God and our new spiritual family.

Interestingly, when my kids were in junior high, my dad retired, and he was going to sell his house, the one that I had lived in during high school, on Oakridge Drive. So instead of him selling it to someone, I bought it from him. My family continued to live in my father's house, the house of my youth in Irondequoit, and my wife and I still live there now.

Number-One Fan

Donna has been my greatest supporter of all my races. She was a fan, and she took care of the kids while I was out running and racing. Today, I can say that together we've raised three beautiful children (our identical twins are in their forties, and Ashley is in her late thirties). Donna didn't go to a lot of the races that I was in; it wasn't really her interest. But she knew that it was important to me, so she was always there for me emotionally. She was there physically too for my first road race, which I remember gratefully to this day.

When a race came up and we had the opportunity to go there together, she'd sometimes go. It was really important that she showed me support for the biggest race of my life as far as repetitions go. I'm talking about the Boston Marathon, of course. About thirty or forty thousand people run it, and all of them are amazing, accomplished runners. It's awesome to be running in a pack like that, and I know Donna was proud of me. First, even to qualify for that race was tremendous, and Donna knew how much it meant to me. I had heard so much about it. Every time with these Bostons, it was so high level that only the best of the best were there. Donna truly believed I was that type of person who fit in with them. I was just so ecstatic to be part of that arena. Understand me: I wasn't a great marathon runner, but I was good. I'm more of the long-distance runner, the ultramarathon man. But Donna always believed that I was the best at everything.

The time she was there that I remember her most vividly is when I ran my first Boston, when she was pregnant for our daughter, Ashley. Even pregnant, she was there to support me. She stood there at the finish line with that look in her eye of "I know you, Greg Brooks." You can imagine how excited I was just to be there, to run in it, and especially to have family with me. And you can imagine how excited I was to be a father again too!

Health Issues

Besides all she did for me to raise our kids and back me on the racing, Donna is a story in herself. She's not just *my* rock; she's a rock for *herself.* You see, she physically has had a very challenging life.

As a young teen, she was diagnosed with severe scoliosis (a sixty-seven-degree curve of the spine), and at age fourteen she was operated on. From there, she was placed in a full body cast for a year. It was very incapacitating. She had several vertebrae fused, and the cast helped straighten her out. So, she was flat on her back, recovering from the surgery at home for an entire year. She received tutoring instead of going to school. Then she got back to a normal, functioning life. I have a favorite picture of her in a yellow bikini, sitting poolside with feet in the water, her very straight, slim physique bending around to show the side of her face. She's flashing a cute little smile framed by her long auburn hair. It's a classic Kodak moment of innocent feminine beauty.

However, she continued to suffer with the progressive condition the rest of her life. She's always had some back pain. Me—never. I've been blessed with a sound, healthy backbone, one that has served me well. Inside the well-oiled machine of my athlete's body, it has withstood real abuse all those years of pounding the pavement. I have no idea why Donna didn't have the same strong spine. Since the causes of scoliosis are mysterious but believed to have a genetic component, when we saw the telltale signs in our children, we knew that they would experience the insidious condition as well. All three of our children have scoliosis. One has had a brace, one has had a rod placed through the entire length of the spine, and one has escaped any operations and major problems. They are doing okay, considering.

Scoliosis didn't stop Donna, however. At the other major industry besides Kodak in Rochester, the U of R, Donna became a phlebotomist. She gradually became a hematology research technician there, a leading teaching and research hospital.

...But then something even more devastating than pronounced scoliosis happened to my love. Donna had two cerebral aneurisms. Not one, but TWO! How could anybody survive one, let alone two?! These aneurisms each sent me into a tailspin. These were very traumatic times in our lives, as you can surmise. What's more, she wasn't even old. The twins were juniors in high school, and I was working my job at Kodak. I was in undergrad school for her first one.

Then I went into my graduate work to obtain that master's degree the boss man was saying I'd better get, and she had her second one. Most of those Kodak guys in my role had graduate degrees, as I said. They encouraged me to go get my grad program done. So, I enrolled in that program, Industrial Hygiene, at the University of Rochester and got 95 percent of the way through it. All I had to do to get the degree was write a thesis, but I couldn't do it. I had no motivation. So, I never really did get that master's degree, although I had done all the coursework for it. My advisors knew, but they couldn't get me over the hump. I just couldn't put it together. Everything was just too scrambled, too jumbled.

Yes, Donna is a resilient trooper. I adore her, and I look up to her. She has taught me so much about life and about being positive. As a result of her health problems, she and I decided to make hospital visits to other people. We give prayer, hope, and encouragement to the sick and aged. Our empathy has moved us in that direction. Donna has been loving not only to me, but to all those around her. Because of all the setbacks Donna and I have had in life, both physical and spiritual, we now look at ourselves as victors, not victims. We are conquerors. We have strengthened each other. We have gratitude toward our God as well. We "can do everything [including ultramarathons, scoliosis, heart attacks, and aneurysms!] through Christ, who gives [us] strength" (Philippians 4:13).

WELCOME TO THE CLUB!

Social Running Groups

"All Alone"

How shallow is the victory
When no one's there your win to see.

What pleasure does the sunset give
If no one's there to share it with?

The moon is but a lifeless light
When no one shares that special sight.

So he is destined to be blue
Without someone to tell it to.

Can one enjoy the times alone
While he has no one of his own?

Sharing our good times with others is wonderful, a great big perk of this life. And with running groups being so friendly and receptive, it seems like the idea is "the more, the merrier."

Although running isn't a team sport, it is one that brings lots of people together through social circles based on their common interest. People feed off the energy of each other, train together, ask for advice, share experiences, and root for one another in races. Research shows that working out in a setting with others increases one's endorphin output more than working out alone. The workout gets done, and a good time is had by all.

Many young and old people have set their sights not so much on competing but on enjoying the social aspect of the running culture. So, clubs rather than races are what they participate in. The clubs feel like big families. Runners hang out together and just enjoy each other's being there. Even some of the closest lifelong friendships are forged there.

I'm so uplifted by my running friends. In addition to my wife, my friends in the track groups around here gave me excellent psychological therapy after I had my heart problems. Staying connected to them has been beneficial.

Greater Rochester Track Club is the premiere running group in Rochester. It welcomes runners of all sizes and shapes, from teens on up, and their membership is in the thousands now. I do remember that when I joined I was #75. Trent Jackson and a lot of famous runners who were track (short-distance) people have come through there. This group morphed into more distance running with the likes of Dick Berkley, a Hall of Fame runner who was a world-record holder in the indoor two-mile race category. I was not only a member but also on their board of directors and inducted into their Hall of Fame. They sponsored many road races including the Rochester Marathon as well as a winter race series called the Freezeroo. Just about every weekend there was some type of race in our area because of them.

Although GRTC is the primary club of the area, there are other small breakout clubs. Out of the organization grew several unofficial neighborhood running groups like Oven Door Runners (ODR), Cats AC, and the Gold Rush Runners (GRR). I was in all of them, at one time or another. They trained on weekends in any kind of weather. Chris Boshnack and Don Curran started Gold Rush in Irondequoit in January of 2001 for the sole purpose of getting runners ready for the return of the Ontario Shore Marathon. Yours truly was the race director. I would move the marathon to downtown Rochester a few years later. Together all three of us would groom contestants for destination marathons in Ireland and Tanzania. Gold Rush is still going strong today. Chris Boshnack has remained a friend who actually was very instrumental in me writing this book, but you'll have to read the Acknowledgments to see how.

Later a more formal club was formed, Genesee Valley Harriers (GVH), which has claimed national recognition for quality coaching and for runners of all age groups, both male and female. Many of these people were training for the Boston Marathon when I knew them. That race is in the spring, so preparation happens in the winter. The months of December through March here in the Northeast make it difficult to get quality long runs in as necessary. Rochester runners are tough, though, enduring sometimes subzero temperatures on snowy and icy roads.

I did most of my Boston prep with ODR, which was founded by my good friends and fellow Kodakers Bill Hearne and Craig Litt. Some seriously long training runs were accomplished with them. I learned the art of "negative split running," which served me well running the Boston. To develop the negative split training mentality, I would start twenty-mile runs in the back of the pack socializing and then work my way up to the lead part of the pack. This was my special secret that I perfected as a go-to strategy in various distance races. By starting at an easy pace, you meter your energy better, so that when you get close to the end of a long race you're not running on empty like everybody else. It feels good to have that kind of leverage during the hardest part; it gives you that little extra surge that makes winning possible.

Being in the ODR club was fun. I remember one such race in Mendon (a half-marathon), where I decided that as a warm-up I was going to show off and run from home (Irondequoit) to the race's start location twenty miles away—and *then* run the race. Although beat from that dumb long warm-up, I still came in first in my age group, which amazed the men in my club. They thought it was funny, too. They still are great friends of mine, though my antics are few and far between now.

HIGH PLACES

Mt. Kilimanjaro

"View from the Top"

You stand at the base of the mountain tall,
Surveying the lofty peak
Because that is where your dream has gone,
The goal of which you seek.

The path is long and tortuous
And strewn with many a test.
Each twist and turn, each angle sharp,
More difficult than the rest.

When finally the summit's reached,
Your quest is thus obtained;
Alas another peak is there,
More lofty than whence you came.

It seems that is the way with life
For those who dare to dream.
You're off again on another trek
Because yet others remain.

The nature of challenges in this life is that they just keep coming. When we surmount them, we feel great. We've earned it. Needless to say, you can't get "a view from the top" if you don't legitimately get there yourself in the first place. Nothing and nobody's going to carry you up to the world's highest mountaintops; you are on your own two feet to do it.

I was a hiker and adventurer, so I always conceived of myself getting to the top of anything. Now, as someone who had experienced not one but nearly two heart attacks, I was afraid of losing the life I had always lived, yet my mind said I wasn't done achieving yet. One of the highest places in the world is Mount Kilimanjaro. I felt a calling in my heart to do one more big thing in my life, perhaps the biggest thing I would ever do. Nobody was going to drag me up there. I'd get up there the old-fashioned way. I'd climb.

But things were far different now with my body. I was damaged, a participant in not only races but heart disease. Was it too late? Facing sixty, I was more cognizant that my running, racing, and climbing skills were waning. I realized that if I didn't take advantage of opportunities at that point, I'd soon be sitting around saying, "I wish I had done this; I wish I had done that." Regret is a merciless mistress, even a silent killer of some. This trip would be my facing off with myself, more youthful aspirations fulfilled. If I attempted this improbability, I had to stretch my capabilities. This expedition was going to be purely for that aspect. It involved the challenge of the intimidating mountain and the challenge of proving myself.

According to Joe Friel, who wrote *The Triathlete's Training Bible*, "Most of us go through life never coming close to our limits and living only on wishes. But wishes are important; they are the start of great feats. Wishes grow into dreams when you are able to mentally 'see' yourself accomplish the wish. Dreams turn into goals when a plan for attaining them is defined. Goals become a mission when unwavering self-belief and purposeful zeal are realized. Big challenges require mission status. The difference between a goal and a mission is attitude. Passionate commitment is self-evident in successful missions. With the proper attitude, almost anything is possible. What you believe, you will achieve." Well, I had the wish, the dream, the goal, a mission, and zeal. I was mostly good with the self-belief, but time was ticking on; my biological clock was running low on years.

Peaks or summits are not necessarily our biggest obstacles. Some people would never want to conquer those, because they are not interested in climbing and that sort of thing anyway. We are all not wired the same. For most people, though, including runners and climbers, the hardest challenge may be the conquest of the self. But self-discipline gives you power. In life, we all have problems, circumstances that need beating. I have had many: personal, physical, and spiritual.

I have continuously scaled challenges. Sometimes I am doing it for fun (Can I finish this giant ice cream cone?), sometimes for momentary gain (Can I finish this week's project?), or sometimes for broader life goals (Can I develop my ministry?). Those are work I choose for myself, and they can come whenever I desire. There are others that I do not choose, and those keep on coming intermittently, thrown at me by life. Somehow, my tests, trials, and roadblocks are always tougher than previous ones. So tomorrow, what else will I face? I will talk about current challenges in the final chapters of this book, but this chapter speaks to an earlier time in my life. It's from a younger-older man's perspective. It was adventurous, fun, and stimulating. It was demanding, rough, and gratifying.

A Crazy Dream

So, you know my crazily ambitious—perhaps foolhardy—goal, but how did it form? The exact goal was to climb the highest peak in Africa and run the nearby Kilimanjaro marathon as a bonus (not that Africa was so special and a place that I always wanted to go, oh no!). I wonder, what gave me the strong desire to do what I did?

To recap my formative childhood running, climbing, and exploring exploits, was it those times I mentioned of racing around Irondequoit on our bikes, discovering new woods, and swinging on vines in them like Tarzan of the Jungle? Was it the early years up on Grindstone Island bushwhacking across the terrain for the whole day, finding new cliffs to climb? Was it our expanding command of the Thousand Islands, betting ourselves to make it all the way around our isle in just twenty-four hours and then go on to the next? Was it camping with the formality of the Boy Scouts and the official way they groomed us to investigate and voyage around everywhere? Their Camp Barton? Algonquin Park? How about the spelunking we did? Or perhaps it was our all-day, arduous journeys rowing in canoes? I also think about the weekend trips in college in the forests and rivers of Missouri on field trips for my ecology and botany classes.

I remember my first Adirondack experience with my college girlfriend's father and little sister. (Where was that girlfriend? Not with us!) I had climbed my first peak (not so high a peak, just about four kilometers), and it was awesome. We canoed and camped in the summer of '66. It's funny that a much-later canoe trip took me to the same lake and peak in Saranac. Mount Ampersand is not a wimpy climb. There was a reward, though. The view was fabulous both times.

So, decades later, this grandest African expedition happened after I had been retired from Kodak not even a year. I was going with two running friends, two guys who had been in my social running groups. We would be climbing to the top of Mount Kilimanjaro in Tanzania, Africa, *and* running their village's marathon. To do both of those together was going to be a great thing, an accomplishment of a lifetime using all the skills and stamina in my personal toolbox—and hopefully I'd live to tell about it, despite having heart disease. And that was a huge *despite*. Yet this kernel of a dream, this positive potentiality, rose to the top of my bucket list. I was determined. Yes, I had several cardiac stents in place for a weakened heart, but that didn't matter so much to me.

I guess it mattered to my friends and family, though. People who were worried about me had visions of my failure. Not because they wanted me to fail, but because they foresaw danger. "What will you do if you have another heart attack while up there, so remote?" they'd ask, almost pleading with me to see my poor judgment—or insanity. Their visions of doom and gloom seemed somewhat justified. But I never let myself be dragged down by what-ifs. If a helicopter had to come and rescue me, so be it. I hoped, of course, that that would never happen. Like a little child without any inhibitions, I just wanted to get to the highest place in the world, and I wasn't going to listen to reason.

The "high places" spoken of in the Bible were originally the spots of notable elevation where the ancient Israelites would go to be nearer to their God. They made sacrifices there to acknowledge their sin, ask for forgiveness, and be redeemed in the eyes of their creator. Moses received the Ten Commandments on a mountaintop, and the ark of the covenant that held the stone tablets upon which they were written was often brought to temples established in other high places. These were holy, venerated locations. There is something about elevated places, where we feel closer to God, in communion. Standing there up high gives us a bird's-eye view where the insignificant things fade into the distance. As we are surveying the surrounding vast expanses, rippling gently many miles into the horizon, immense feathery clouds are now strangely in our grasp, sometimes even *below* us. We feel above life; we feel "above" all that's temporal. We feel more spiritually in tune and forget everything else. We feel only God in the rare, thin atmosphere.

Now to describe Kilimanjaro, majestic beast and dormant volcano that it is, with some numbers and factoids. It towers at about 16,000 feet above its plateau base. But you've got to remember that that plateau is way up high in the first place, about 3,000 feet. At a total of 19,341 feet above sea level, it is the highest mountain in Africa and the highest free-standing mountain on earth. Tremendous! (The Himalayas in Asia are the only mountains higher, but those are conjoined). The first reported hikers to have reached the Kili summit, not until 1889, were Ludwig Purtscheller and Hans Meyer. Today, it's the climbing destination, along with Everest, of course, that is considered the Holy Grail by courageous and stalwart hiking enthusiasts.

We Train

Can someone ascend Kili and not train? Surely you jest. No way. We knew we had our work cut out for us. How to prepare? Research, research, research. Foresight. Uncompromising training. As they say, practice makes perfect.

We chose a long, steep hill at the Bristol Mountain ski resort in New York. We loaded the backpacks we were going to use on Kili with the weight of two heavy one-gallon water jugs, went to the location, scaled it, and did repeats—up and down, up and down for an hour once a week, half a year. In the early fall it was pretty and pleasantly cool. In the late fall, it was quite manageable as long as it wasn't snowing. The closer it got to December, the closer it was to snowmaking by Mother Nature and the snow machines. In February with full snow conditions we found a road next to Bristol and repeated the same routine, getting used to wearing heavier clothes as well as breaking in our hiking boots. It was a profitable effort, testing our gear as well as our bodies. But we knew that once we got to the real thing, conditions would be far, far harder. We crossed our fingers and hoped for the best.

We Leave

It was go time! Bill Hearne and Craig Litt, compadres from my running group, were ready. To commence this amazing journey, we boarded the plane and left snowy Rochester on February 14th, 2006 (Valentine's Day—again, I had Donna's unwavering support). We were leaving the USA in the dead of winter, yet going to Tanzania during their dog days of summer. (Our February is their August.) Our flight from Rochester to JFK was to leave at 11:15 a.m. We would land in Amsterdam in Europe at 12:30 a.m. EST (that's 7:30 *a.m.* European time, being they are seven hours ahead). Then we would hang out for half a day. Instead of going to the red light district there, we went on a tour of the Anne Frank house.

Then we had another flight, eight hours to Moshi, Africa. Touchdown in the world's largest continent! We had a nice finish to our flight, arriving just after 9 p.m. in their time zone on the fifteenth, right on schedule, looking at a nearly full moon. I said to myself, *I wonder what it will be like under this moon on the mountain tomorrow night...*)

It felt hot as we disembarked and headed into customs, maybe mid-eighty degrees and quite windy. There we picked up our bus drive to the hotel, taking an unpaved, very bumpy road. My ankles and feet were swollen from sitting so long—not good. This concerned me because of my cardiac issues.

We checked in and started the process of organizing our packs for the following day. This was a complicated job. Although I was exhausted and feeling jet-lagged, I scientifically packed and repacked stuff that we would take—stuff that we would need. We would carry our own packs but also prepare extra bags of our things for others to carry, professional porters. I had to get to sleep, though. Our beds at the hotel had these funky green mosquito nets over them. I had strange dreams that night. Do you think we were nervous? You bet.

The next morning, we had to measure the weight of our extra bags. Each was to be no more than thirty pounds. The bags containing the equipment we would be giving to the porters to take up included sleeping bags, tents, clothing, flashlights, headlamps, first aid supplies, etc., and there is a strict limit on how much they can carry. I got frustrated about this measuring, trying to be exact with the scale I was using to weigh my gear. I pulled stuff out of my bags, stuff I thought I could do without. I'd repack and repeat. Finally, perfect! I was ready! Then we met with our guide, Mohamed. He walked over to my extra bag, hefted it up, and walked away. No scale was used; what a waste of time and effort having stressed about this! So what was all our fuss about? Our American engineer mentality.

We piled into the big vehicle (Land Rover) at 9 a.m. and drove into the heart of Moshi. We got our first view of downtown on a bustling business day. Most people were walking or working in front of shops on the street. One worker was cutting rubber from tires to make sandals, and we got a snapshot of that. My buddy Bill wanted to take some interesting pictures, here and there.

Across the street was this military-type policeman at a checkpoint into the city. "Hey that's cool!" I exclaimed about something on him that caught my eye. Snap, snap! In less than a few minutes, this guy with an automatic machine gun who just had his picture taken came over to our vehicle, and a huge argument ensued. Ah, the *polisi* were not happy, and we weren't really catching on why. This went on and on, back and forth, with phone calls made. From the tone of it all I didn't feel it was a warm-and-fuzzy; in fact, I wondered if we weren't headed for jail. I think Bill, Craig, and I eventually figured out what the problem was through some very broken English translations of the Swahili. (Our guides weren't the best with our language.) No pictures of police!!!! Bill ("Mr. Kodak") showed the officer the image on the display of the digital camera and then proceeded to delete it while they both watched. Thank God the guy understood what we did. We were off and running with that behind us. After a little bit we all laughed.

The Kili views from here on the highway were breathtaking. The grassy green terrain was changing to vivid red dirt, very rough. What impressed me was the colorful clothing of the people against the barren terrain. Contrast. . .all over. Rich/poor, black/white, have- and have-not. We were to understand more of this new culture as the moments passed by.

The paved road now climbed into the highlands through banana and coffee bean groves, and the road got even choppier. We passed through many very poor villages but saw fairly well-established Christian churches and schools with little kids in uniforms. This was the really rural agrarian area where you still see a bit of western influence, with little touristy sheds selling "African stuff" to the folks coming into the trailhead.

We Begin on Foot

We finally reached the main gate for Machame trailhead. It's a fortress. A huge barbed wire fence greets explorers at the gate, and many hawkers were barraging us. They are always waiting to get chosen as porters or just simply trying to sell shirts, hats, bandanas, junky souvenirs, or whatever. Once inside the gate we were safe from the disturbances. We stopped by the ranger station. (Those are desks at various campsites along the climb where you check in with the park police.) After signing in, we observed one of the people who would be our cook choosing and packing up the fresh vegetables we would need for our week on the mountain. We were eager to sample the local fare.

We left. The trail was cool and very well groomed, with impatiens and passion flowers all along the way. The sereneness of the trails was refreshing, with many different birds singing. We reached the halfway mark of the trail about 1:30 p.m. under full sun. About this time we met up with a couple from Germany and chatted a bit. I was already huffing and puffing getting to this point because we were still severely jet lagged.

The trail continued up through dense trees, but then they began to thin out as the way inclined. The pace for me started to slow a bit. Our guide regulated our pace. Bill and Craig were strong climbers. I was content to lag behind them and take my own pace, enjoy the solitude. I was really not interested in hearing American politics here in Africa. Something that quite upset me whenever we came upon travelers from other countries was that somehow the conversation had to swing around to Bush bashing.

We reached Machame Camp (at 9,996 feet) late afternoon. Just after our arrival, the skies opened up, and it rained hard. It was a messy and crowded site—especially with the mud from the rain. Thank goodness it wasn't long-lived. The sun came out to present some incredible views of Kili and surrounding mountains. I knew I got some good shots. We spent time meeting other hikers from France and Australia.

Our dinner was by candlelight in our mess (dining) tent. It was an interesting vegetable mix with local flair and spices. Juma, our assistant cook, served us. She knew little English and just nodded a lot, especially if we tried some very coarse Swahili. After we finished dinner, we went out to see the stars. We zipped into the tents.

Since I couldn't sleep due to the jet lag, I went for a walk in the moonlight. It was awesome! I was the only one in camp awake at this hour. I have no idea what time I finally hit the pillow. I had some crazy dreams, like the night before. I was awake at six o'clock, and it was only thirty-five degrees out.

The next day's goal was progressing from 9966' to 12,590', Shira camp. My group was the first up the trail from camp. The climb was steep and strenuous because of elevation compounded by sleep deprivation. But we enjoyed the scenery; the many changes in flora were interesting. We had some good views of Mount Meru before the clouds rolled in and the temps dropped more. I felt good at this point but put on more layers for the cold. The steep cliffs had some hand-over-hand with lots of panoramic views, caves, and volcanic debris with obsidian rock leading up to the Shira plateau, where our next campsite would be.

We arrived at that campsite in the clouds around one o'clock in the afternoon with the terrain looking much like a moonscape. Our tents were already up and ready for us, having been arranged by workers who would stay at each camp from now on (stewards and cooks continuing to go with hikers and moving between camps would have been much too impractical physically for them). I walked around scoping the place out and fixated on these huge birds hanging around. They were called white-necked ravens and seemed to be everywhere, looking for handouts or scraps of food. Rains came quickly but only sprinkled, then cleared. This weather pattern would be consistent with our entire climbing experience. My night's dreams were foreboding again.

The next day, on the eighteenth, we proceeded from the Shira station to the Barranco one. The two points were at 12,590' and 13,055', respectively. Inside the tent it was only forty degrees; the temps outside were in the low twenties. I could hear Bill snoring in the other tent and our African team talking and laughing. I was moved by how jovial these guys, the porters, were among themselves.

The land was very frosty. We all started to get our equipment organized and dried out as the sun appeared. We wanted to get an early start out of camp. The ravens arrived, squawking for breakfast. These were funny birds, big and fearless, and they seemed to take ownership of the camp.

Today we would head along a ridge towards Lava Tower, which is a unique geological formation that is a minor peak within Kilimanjaro, a three-hundred-foot straight-up-and-down mini challenge above the regular trail. This is an incredibly tall, jagged cliff that juts out of nowhere into the sky. It is difficult but is considered a non-technical climb because it doesn't require any ropes.

The trail going there was well worn, so we didn't have any fear of going off course at that point or any other. But Bill accidentally did take us off trail at one fork, because he wasn't paying attention. (We sometimes refused to use the guides provided, as we prided ourselves in our autonomy, and there were no trail markers like one might have in the Adirondacks). Before long, someone yelled, telling us we went the wrong way. "Bill, you're fired!" I joked.

As we climbed easily, many porters were flying by us with huge loads on their heads. There was hardly any vegetation now. Sometimes other climbing parties passed us. We couldn't wait to get to our "little" tower.

We reached a fork in the trail, where the Lava Tower side trail began. The way split at 14,757' as that's what was registering on my GPS. The sun was out, but the clouds were rolling in again, enveloping us and creating a surreal setting. We looked up as we approached and saw these little colorful dots, parkas of climbers ahead of us. That started my group's climbing juices flowing.

I didn't realize that Craig had some climbing fears until we were headed up the Lava Tower. We dropped our packs at the base, and Mohamed, our porter, led all three of us to the top. For Bill and me it was a decent climb, and there were many good hand and foot holds with lots of crevasse grips. It was clouded, so our views weren't that great. GPS told me we were at 15,200'. We were elated for this part of the adventure.

We arrived at the Barranco camp at 3:10 p.m., tired and sore, worn. I'm not sure if it was the elevation, lack of sleep, climbing for three days, or all the above. The camp had some protea flowers and giant groundsels. That night I couldn't sleep well either and woke at four-thirty in the morning. It was so light because of the moon and stars that a flashlight wasn't needed to get around.

I was up at six a.m. for good and got all my medicines ready: Cipro and Imodium (to prevent diarrhea due to impure African water), CeraLyte (to prevent potassium/sodium imbalance due to dehydration during strenuous activity), Diamox (to prevent high altitude sickness), plus my normal pills for heart disease. As you can see, there were a lot of deadly circumstances we wanted to prevent. Today we were going from the Barranco to Karanga camps, from 13,055' to 13,260'. We got to the base of Breakfast Hill three hours after waking up. On February eighteenth, the previous night, we had looked at this steep incline, and now, again, it looked insurmountable. Eight hundred feet of hand-over-hand.

At 10:10 in the morning we indeed did make the summit of Breakfast Hill, registering at 13,865' by GPS. It had been very difficult, but I took it real easy. The very fit porters also took it easily with packs on their heads as they ascended. It was hard to believe how they moved up the mountain, but I'm sure they had done it many times before.

The next eighteen hours went quickly. Morning evaporated into day, which faded into evening. The moon was fantastic, lighting up the whole camp as we viewed the lights of Moshi miles below us. Later that night, at four-thirty a.m., as I was trying to sleep in my tent, I heard something ominous—it sounded like thunder. Come to find out, it was rockslides careening down the mountain. We later witnessed one during the day. Indescribable, the force and vision of it! A bit scary, too. We knew from before that rockslides had recently taken the lives of several climbers at the Western Breach campsite.

We Continue to Climb

The next day would have us moving from Karanga Camp to Barufu Camp. The elevations were 13,260' to 15,325', a simple climb of only two thousand feet, with Kili's top finally looming to the left. We climbed up a short, rocky face to a very interesting campsite. Large rocks were all over in a very exposed location on top of this short peak. The tents were tucked in behind the rocks as much as possible to get them out of the ferocious wind. (It was blowing good!) The sun seemed very high and direct. It was a place not meant for people! Up in the sky we saw this huge, ominous eagle-like bird soaring around in circles. We identified it as a Verreaux's eagle being pestered by two ravens.

Hopping into the tent after lunch to rest was weird. As on the planet Mercury with its two different sides having two vastly different temperatures, when the sun came out of the clouds, the tent was like a sauna; when the sun went under, it was cold and windy. It weighed heavily on us that we were now higher than we had ever been before in our lives yet still had another four thousand feet to the summit, not to mention that we faced a fifteen-hour hike to our next bed.

It started during dinner. Snow! Hence the name *barufu (ice* or *snow*). Temps were falling even more drastically, and the wind picked up again. I was wondering at this point how my scant quantity of only poor-quality sleep would pan out for a very long, hard period of climbing coming up. Ironically, I was wishing we could go right then, during dinner. We knew that if the snow would lift like it usually does at night, we would have some moonlight to enable us to see our path. The nights are usually calm and clear; conversely, as the sun warms the day, the wind and clouds increase in intensity, decreasing visibility though it is light. Not good timing for travelers—kind of backwards of what you'd expect.

Okay, so this was it. From the summit of Barufu to Kili! That time would be one of the toughest spans I can remember in my entire life. As I contemplate some of my twenty-four-hour or hundred-mile runs, this might run a close second.

The temp didn't seem too cold. I was quite comfortable with only a short-sleeve shirt under my long-sleeve Duofold (like a heavy Coolmax), running tights under my waterproof nylon pants with gators, and my System 3 shell running cap with a fleece headband. Our plan was to leave before midnight. We headed out at 11:50 p.m. with our headlamps illuminating our path, hoping to make the summit by sunrise. Mohamed was in the lead, followed by myself, Bill, Craig, and another porter pulling up the rear. We kept this order the entire way up, because it was too dangerous to switch. The path up was snow covered and treacherously steep, taking us up a rocky rise then across a short, flat stretch, then up another very long, steep climb. It was extremely dark, and we could see only a few feet in front of us. The wind picked up as we chanted "polé, polé" [Swahili for "slowly, slowly"] while going up the trail, and it got much colder. Our leader was reminding us not to take it too fast, as doing so could cause us to burn out.

My body was doing okay. We took small steps, one at a time, with a water rest every hour or so. My lungs and breathing were unexpectedly fine. It felt frigid, but after putting on my extra down jacket under my shell, I was toasty warm. That garment was special to me; my Tucson friend, Fred, mentioned in the coaching chapter, had loaned it to me with the intention that I bring it along for good luck.

Up to this time I had had two layers on my hands (wool gloves and the Gortex shell). On our first stop the hand warmers went in. It is odd that they really didn't seem effective at this elevation. I was wondering if the thin air prevented the chemical reaction that produces the heating. So, I put one more layer on my hands (my red wool mittens). I had worried about my hands before the trip (I have Raynaud's Syndrome, a disorder of blood vessel constriction in the appendages), but now I was quite comfortable. Looking back now, I wonder to myself, *How the heck did I ever deal with that?*

I thought our pace was perfect. My recollection is that Craig was complaining that we needed more rests, and Bill was laboring a bit with his asthma and had to take some puffs from his inhaler. But it was really neat to look down at our rest stops and see the string of lights below us from the climbers who had left after us. All their headlamps lighting the trail looked like a long, luminous ribbon snaking around.

As we climbed, we came upon a man and woman who were maybe in trouble, lying down and keeping each other warm off the trail. I say maybe, because obviously people die from hypothermia by staying still, but in this case, they could have been just taking a well-earned rest and/or trying to get warmer by close proximity. We pushed on, knowing that anyone ascending would have a responsible guide to handle them. Later, we came upon a guide and a man in a similar situation, but there was also nothing we could do except go on, continuing with our mission. The guide knew what he was doing; he knew best. If we had tried to assist the people, it would have been just interfering. Also, we ourselves may also have mis-apportioned our finite energy reserves, compromised core body temperatures, and broken down. We could not take a risk like that and endanger ourselves even more.

We trucked on and on for hours and hours, and then some more hours, up and up with only a few trails of footprints to follow in front of us. Mohamed had a good handle on the trail. I wondered how many times he had climbed this exact same route. Probably quite a few, just in that year alone.

At 4:37 a.m., the twenty-first of February, we reached Stellar Point, which is the rim of the crater on the top of the mountain but not the technical peak. It's called Stellar Point because of all the millions of stars in the sky above that are shining brightly, waving their hands and saying "Look at me!" Yet we still had a one-hour hike to the Uhuru (Kibo) peak, which was said to be an easy climb. We were dragging rather badly by this leg of it, so it seemed anything but "easy."

As we headed for the peak, we encountered one small group of lucky and accomplished climbers who were headed back after having made it to the final, extreme destination everyone strives for. *Wow*, I thought. *I'd give anything to be in their shoes right now.*

Shortly after seeing them, we attained the welcomed summit (Uhuru) at 5:37 a.m. We were agape. We had made it! How astounding! We collapsed in happy exhaustion. . .momentarily.

We wanted to take in and savor each square foot, to own this place and moment and brand them in our memories. But no. Time to rise again! All set with a new shot of adrenaline pumping up some fresh exhilaration, soon we made it over to where there is a big wooden sign. How was a sign like that, in that location, ever even built, we wondered? Some poor devil, a superiorly muscled and brave porter or mountaineer perhaps, had to carry all those wood pieces, augers, and hand tools and then assemble that thing one day in a freezing, unpleasant, inhospitable wind. There was only one other group there as we took the customary pictures for those who overcome the majestic mountain.

I got out my thermometer and GPS to get some readings. Result: they read five degrees Fahrenheit at 19,333' on this barren peak. Not bad for instrumentation, as I knew the exact elevation is 19,341' above sea level. We were at the highest steps anyone can go—except for about seven tiny ones more.

Now, before I get to my mountaintop experience, I want to stop a moment and give some advice you might want in case you ever attempt Kilimanjaro or any other ridiculously high mountain. To my fellow climbing enthusiasts... I am sure you are wondering about my overall physical experience. What was the hardest part of making the summit, overall, you ask? Well, it wasn't the actual climbing or getting super out of breath, we found out. It was simply the whiplash weather. Here, within a matter of days, I was dealing with extreme temperatures on both ends of the spectrum. You've got to realize: the base of the mountain is a jungle environment near the equator, in the eighty-degree range, very humid. The top of the mountain, on the other hand, is sub-zero and very dry, like a whole other, arctic world. This is an assault on the human body, the sudden change. It's very bad. A barrage on the senses, a major sense of discomfort, if you let it go that far. You had to adjust as quickly as you could. Withstanding just the radically different temperatures on that trip will push a human being to their limit.

We Apex

And that limit coincided with my final seven steps. Wow, was it worth it, though. So rewarding. A nickname for Mount Kilimanjaro is "the Ceiling of Africa." I saw why. As we reached the very highest summit of the summit, the ultimate landing, I sensed I had reached the ceiling of the earth, as far as a person could go on foot. From there, maybe borne on angels' wings, we might have been at the doorstep and threshold to the heavens. In fact, Ernest Hemingway, in his short story "The Snows of Kilimanjaro," called this place "The House of God."

The sky was showing signs of a pink sunrise. The song in my soul blended with the moment. Like a mother looking at her newborn as her memory of pain dissolves, my arrival at the summit made every skinned knee, side cramp, and turned ankle I ever had in my long life go away. For that reason, had not it been bitter cold, my eyes would have been tearing up. Having made the summit gave one a feeling of wholeness. It was the fruition of a plan I had been so disciplined with. That stringency had paid off. Mind over matter. Man versus nature, with man winning. How often does that actually happen?

"Let's stay here a while, guys, so we can experience more and get some great sunrise pictures," one of us suggested. My comrades felt the emotion of this time and place too. Standing there motionless, feeling so personally confident, I'm sure my buddies would agree with me when I say we felt so very close to God. We wanted to bottle up and store those priceless feelings for safe keeping. We wanted to capture and preserve that magnificent tableau that had put us so clearly in the presence of the Lord.

Standing there like tiny specks on the face of the earth, yet specks firmly positioned, we wanted to make our little mark on the timeline of existence somehow permanent. In the fresh light of dawn we could see the images of the ancient glaciers, scintillating and sloping in natural grandeur. These were the Creator's permanent marks on the landscape. The elegance of the smooth lines was boldly enchanting, and the sheer beauty reverberated through our beings. It was no less than transcendent, ethereal. It was a reminder that God had done all this. *All* this. God is like a mountain—strong, immovable, lofty. What a wonderful view and experience—something I can hardly describe to this day.

And I knew it was even more than that. It was an imparting of messages. Those were about personal humility and God's sometimes inscrutable love.

Way-Up Lesson #1

First, the lesson about personal humility. In cultures worldwide, there are many sayings about mountains, especially about moving a mountain, which means to do the impossible. Although this sounds ridiculous, it seems as though there *are* times in life when we are called upon to do just that. It happens only if God is behind us, though, orchestrating a miracle. Without God's permission, it just won't happen. It can't be about unreasoned desires operating within a full-blown ego. The person who aspires to moving a mountain needs to first admit to a limit of their puny strength before God can enter and fill them with his pure intention and omnipotent power.

And so it dawned on me. God, in his infinite wisdom, had a plan for me. I was a flawed man. I was broken in body and fallen in spirit. God didn't want me to run full throttle anymore; that was certain, as all the signs were there. I wasn't about to ignore the medical science he had provided me with, through the doctors and the testing. I had to put that stupid notion about still being a competitive runner aside—for good, or I was surely going to get seriously hurt. Because of the intense exertion needed for a marathon, I'd have another heart attack. I just knew it. I'd die right here in Africa, thousands of miles away from home, if I ran the way I always had. I obviously didn't want to experience that metaphorical crushing "rockslide" like the real one had just foreshadowed; I didn't think that my being close enough to witness the rockslide had been random. In fact, I felt strongly that it had been designed for my instruction, so I obeyed God's directive and prepared to seriously change my tune. I decided then and there to "run" but not to "race" in the upcoming Tanzanian marathon and all others after that.

But God also knew I had wanted to do one last big thing—one final hurrah, one glorious swan song—to restore a bit of my wounded confidence and prove to myself that I was still some kind of athlete. That had been the most important, defining piece of myself, Greg Brooks. The quest to achieve one big final physical feat was the "mountain" that needed "moving." I had worried *How could I be an athlete on this adventure and not worry about my heart?* Turns out that that was a wrong concept. With a simple paradigm shift, the miracle presented itself to me like a snap of the fingers. Instead of trying to "move the mountain" myself, God and I had worked with it together. I accepted it and myself right where we were. I went up the mountain, and it was a perfect fit. I was doing something equally as demanding as my former pursuits, but in a different way. Climbing that mountain was an athletic challenge that I was able to take at a slower pace and preserve my heart. It was safer than running, believe it or not. It turned out great, because God had granted my wish, and the price I had to pay of agreeing to end my racing days was worth it. Once again, the message that

God always knows better than we do came through, and I was grateful that he had given me a viable alternative. Not that I'd climb any more mountains or have a new sport. This single act of completion was enough. That was my first spiritual lesson up there, trusting God.

Way-Up Lesson #2

The other lesson at the summit of Kilimanjaro was in regard to God's mysterious love for us—all of us as humans. While I was up there, it seemed as though the mountain was resounding with some wordless message. It was as if my consciousness, my whole being, was melding with the mountain. I didn't know exactly what that was, what the mountain was trying to tell me, but it was speaking. I have since reflected more on the moment, and I put two and two together. I would find out what all this really meant only years later, when we were writing this book.

Mount Kilimanjaro had been hiding some special facts for millennia, geologists say. The mighty mountain had guarded those secrets undisturbed for many thousands of years. Then in 2000 it would finally give them up to some very motivated and intelligent researchers. Our technology today is incredible. Some creative thought, a diligent eye, and scientific equipment can shed light on the events of human history and bring forward evidence for ancient legends. This includes Bible stories that some may question. After millennia, the silent, cold, forbidding mountain spoke in reference to one of these. Its story is written right in its ice, indelibly, open now to anyone who wants to read it. How? According to the *Magellan Times*, "Scientists extract [ice] cores by drilling into glaciers and ice sheets around the world...—either by hand or with special machinery. And as power-drilled cores can travel to depths in excess of two miles, elements of that ice may have been on the planet for as long as 800,000 years."

The secret I mentioned was a literally "ground-breaking" scientific discovery made about Mount Kilimanjaro. Over the decades, there has been much thought devoted to the controversial theory of global warming. Originally there to try to find a reason why Kilimanjaro's glaciers are melting, researchers from Ohio State University had ninety-two native porters drag equipment up the landmark. The scientists drilled into the mountain at nineteen thousand feet and retrieved frozen cylindrical samples, each about one hundred seventy feet long, of the ice, ground, and rock beneath. Through these, researchers could see the layers added onto the terrain over thousands of years. "Each layer of ice that is added creates a record of the climate during that time. They provide key information about former climatic conditions on our planet," states *Magellan Times*. These layers and their varied sedimentation told stories about sizeable ecological events, almost how rings in a tree trunk show us the age of the tree and environmental hardships the tree may have endured over time.

The most pertinent stories recorded in the ice and rock of Kilimanjaro were the occurrence of three major droughts of a distant past versus the existence of a very watery environment at some point. Indeed, says *Magellan Times*, the last drought is written about in Genesis, and this modern scientific documentation lends credibility to that book and the story of the Old Testament Joseph. The Joseph who supposedly had a coat of many colors in fact predicted a drought and ensuing famine. The latter of the significant ages apparent in the ice core samples coincided perfectly with what biblical historians believe was the time the Egyptian pharaohs were struggling with that situation. The information that the mountain had been holding is scientific proof of an event that indeed did happen and is chronicled in the Bible. This further proves the Bible's authenticity. God's Word is true, and even science bears it out for the skeptics. There is, moreover, a finding presented in the Ohio State research about the area being extensively covered probably by a super-expanded Lake Chad at one time, so all you people seeking theories about Noah's flood may want to check that out too in the original scholarly publication, though it doesn't make conjectures relating to biblical stories (Thompson et al. 2002).

Standing at the apex, I was privy to all this—the beauty so ostensible and the truth I intuited in my heart. As a man of the twenty-first century, I was sharing in a vast history of my forefathers. The people had survived this terrible event, this famine. And I began thinking about another story from Genesis—Noah and the ark. God had told Noah his will, and Noah with his free will obeyed. God instructed him to build an ark, because a flood would fill up all the low places and kill everyone there. Safety would be in the high ground of a mountain, but no mountain was going to come to Noah. He had to go to the mountain.

His ark eventually came to rest on a high outcropping, Mount Ararat, which some researchers claim is in Turkey. We don't know for sure where Noah's ark came to rest, but that particular location is a compelling theory. It seems obvious that a mountain would have been an excellent, logical place to survive until the waters calmed down and receded. I know now that the picture in my mind's eye of the Kili mountaintop is like what Noah saw when he looked out of the ark and saw dry land. The first piece of earth that Noah ever stepped onto after the flood was probably a towering, majestic mountaintop. In terms of being at a place like that to see it all, Noah and I seemed to share our humanity. Knowing now that I was surely standing on God's evidence for part of the Bible (the massive drought), quite literally written in stone, was ineffable. And thinking about Noah told me the story of God's ultimate forgiveness and love for us as sinners, his promise that he'd save the human race and never send such a deluge of apocalyptic proportions again.

We Descend

I could have stayed there for hours, being pensive, soaking it all in, marveling at our days-long deed and at God's hand in all of it, but Bill wanted to return, and Mohamed was pushing us to go down. I remember Bill was clearly having a hard time with his lungs and impatient, but I was dragging my feet. The sunrise and the glaciers (which I had heard so much about) above the clouds were a true sight to behold, and we were some of the few human beings to ever see them. We were tired, but that realization lit us up. I was trying to take a big volume of pictures, as many as I could to preserve the moment and our marvelous view, but it was so cold and sparkling, surfaces glinting off each other randomly, that I wasn't sure how many, if any, would come out clear.

Now comes the bad part. As we carefully descended, our minds still swirling about where we had just been and what we had just seen, we got horrible news from other climbers—reports of a death on the mountain, just below us. On the crater rim we came upon a body partially wrapped in a space blanket (head and shoulders) with a lonely guide standing next to him. Bill and Craig got close to him, but I couldn't approach. All I could see was a late-age man, with stomach skin exposed, looking very grayish. I knew he was dead. It was so very unsettling of a sight. Our guide chatted with his guide, who kept his post by the body. The guide knew he was American and speculated that it was a heart attack from pulmonary edema. He told us the guy was fifty-eight years old, the same age as Bill and I were. I worried about the pandemonium if this had ever been misreported to our Rochester newspaper.

It's common knowledge for climbers that Kilimanjaro's overall summit success rates have been around only fifty percent. The reason why summit candidates do not succeed is not usually because of lack of strength or inability to climb the treacherous peaks with the required coordination, although those are true for some people. Rather, it is most often about the inability to acclimate to the environment mostly in terms of decreasing pressure and, as we said, harsh temperatures. You have to be patient and take it slow; that is the trick. Most unsuccessful climbs have failed because the person has tried to make a faster climb and they developed high altitude sickness. Your success also depends on which route you take up. There are several. We were advised to take the route with the slowest, most gradual incline, the one called Machame. In certain sections this route is steeper than some of the others and so more difficult, but it is easier overall. So don't rush it, and *do* take your Diamox! On your way down, you don't have to worry about any of this, as air concentration is a nonfactor.

There are many who attempt Kili's arctic peak who are not mentally prepared or physically conditioned adequately. I feel sorry for those people, because I know that many of them do train for the best possible outcome. Even if they do, however, the hidden inherent risks of nature and fate can wreak havoc with one's best intentions. It's scary to think about the half who don't make it—as well as how many deaths that could be covered up because of the fear of negative publicity taking away from the Africans' potential income. I guess that is a whole other story, though.

Anyway, after seeing the man's body and saying silent prayers, we tried to go back to thinking about the good things of the summit experience. It had been pure rapture. The widening brook of my life had carried me away with waves of overwhelming emotion. Standing up there was more than fulfilling my wish list's highest item. I was more than a poster child conquering my heart disease and age. I'd be back home for my "fifteen minutes of fame" in the New York state running community. Those things would be nice, but what I really prized it for was the mystical experience in which the spirit of God had exalted itself in my brain. It had been enthralling, engrossing—and more. I had somehow felt included in the knowledge of divine things. Nothing and no one could rob me of this feeling now, no matter what negative things might happen to me from here on out in my life. I made a pact with myself over that. Nothing bad could touch me after this. (Wow, would I ever be challenged in keeping that promise, though, later on, as you will see in upcoming chapters.)

Here in "la-la land," entranced by the triangle of God, nature, and myself, one foot was going in front of the other, mindlessly. I wasn't thinking in my normal mode of rational calculation, judiciousness, and prudence. I wasn't thinking about how hard it would be to get down, or about my survival on the descent. In many ways, the descent of a mountain is worse. More hazardous, more menacing, as you can relate to what you saw in my earlier chapter explaining the downhill aspect of races. So, basically, I wasn't taking it real seriously, and God might have been protecting me from falling.

At this point, we didn't retrace our steps. We went a different way, so things looked and felt very different. That was interesting and refreshing. The way was shorter and more direct, called the Mweka route. First stop on that was Camp Mweka, just over 10,000'. The decline is very pretty. We saw views that we missed coming up in the dark. The sun was peaking over Mawenzi (Kibo and Shira's sister volcanic cone).

The trail was loose scree, formed as the sun melts the hard-packed snow. According to Wikipedia, scree is "a collection of broken rock fragments at the base of crags, mountain cliffs, volcanoes or valley shoulders that has accumulated through periodic rockfall from adjacent cliff faces." It's gravel. It felt like we were skating downhill on sand! Fun, not dangerous. No firm footing—just sliding down like on skis or a snowboard.

It was like a giant slide for kids at the playground. What a blast! This would have been murder climbing up, though! With that great scree at our disposal, it took us less than three hours to get back to Barufu. It took so much of the return time off us. That scree was the best thing ever!

My legs weren't too bad after that, but again, it felt like we were being pushed to get back. I didn't want to feel that rushed. We passed many porters who were positioning themselves to bring down the body of the "fallen soldier," the dead hiker we'd seen earlier, in a slow relay sort of fashion. It was a practical yet eerie affair. Each guide was to provide two porters to transport the dead body back down the mountain. I guess there wasn't any real rush. It was a done deal.

We followed the trail down through terrains which reminded me of a wasteland. Our legs were getting so tired around then. We reached a part of the trail which I would think you might see in a southwestern American desert, with unique, vividly hued flowers I hadn't noticed before. My legs were really trashed, and downhill walking was terrifically hard. It was difficult to appreciate the beauty.

We arrived in camp, warm and sunny Mweka, at 1:45 p.m., where we donned shorts. It was over twelve hours since we had headed for the summit from the last camp. It had been a total of five nights going up and one night going down. As we signed in at the ranger station, the party started! A celebration of a mission finished. Veggies, rice, meat, and smiling native people welcoming us back and congratulating us. Bed by seven p.m. and the best sleep so far. I got up early, before sunrise, under a crescent moon. Looking up ten thousand feet at Kili, I saw the Big Dipper appearing as though it were dumping radiant moonlight on the summit.

On Wednesday, February twenty-second, leaving the Mweka Camp to return to the hotel, again we descended and walked through yet another terrain. This was more of what I would describe as a jungle again, complete with the smells and sounds you would expect in a zoo or botanical gardens. The trees were huge, and we spotted a large colobus monkey. It was black and white with shaggy fur. I wasn't able to get a picture because it was frenetically jumping around high up in the trees, where it defied capture from our lenses. It's like it wanted to engage us, to play hide and seek. It was as though he didn't want us to leave. I knew this whole experience would be over too soon.

When we arrived at the ranger station to check out, we saw how attractive the flowers were in the garden surrounding the buildings. My legs now were returning to normal, and this time I was able to really appreciate the beauty. I felt so full of joy and bighearted that I wanted to give our guide something extra. I noticed that Mohamed had been admiring my trekking poles. I thanked him for taking such good care of us and gave them to him.

We took a different route back to Moshi, passing through a pretty rural area rich with bananas and a huge coffee plantation again, continuing past a large teaching medical center and a university. Later we would come to understand that this road we were on was part of the marathon route, and the race registration hotel was there.

You can't imagine how good a hot shower and shave felt. Our room looked like a war zone with all our stuff scattered about as we were trying to organize for our next adventure. Tomorrow morning we would be off on safari for three days. After lunch we headed over to the hotel's internet room. I had already set up a distribution list of people I wanted to notify that we made it back safe and sound and that I was not the same fifty-eight-year-old American guy who died on the mountain! I was stronger than I thought.

SAFARI

Animals of God's Great Basin

"Teach Me to Play a New Love Song"

Teach me to play a new love song,
One exciting and new.
Not to replace the song we once had,
But let it enrich all we do.

Life is for us now to savor,
Not to worship the past.
Don't lock the pain away in your heart
Our treasures aren't certain to last.

Teach me to play a new love song.
Fresh and vibrant and free.
Move on with life that you now have left,
Be grateful whatever might be.

Isn't God's presence in our lives just one big love song? God's love is a melody we can hear if we pay attention. Every time God gives us a new adventure, it's like a symphony of that love in motion. All is in active harmony. We haven't heard it before, so we don't really know where it's going, but it will be beautiful with its crescendos and decrescendos, its ups and downs. Like a great composer's work is his or her music, God's greatest work is us and our spiritual progression. He wants to stay connected to his work through his relationship with us. It is for us to listen to his communication, his "music" in our lives, as it unfolds.

Another amazing part of creation is our four-footed friends, the animals. They share so much of our DNA. Did you know that we are 98 percent genetically the same as a pig, and even closer to a chimpanzee? Our likeness cannot be minimized. And we should be living in consonance, in harmony, with all God's creatures.

An unexpected, new "love song" for me that year was going on safari and communing with nature and animals. Like I said, I hadn't gone to

141

Africa to go to Africa per se. I had gone with the one-track mind of wanting to scale the mountain and run a race, period. As far as I was concerned, safari was going to be maybe a pleasant side trip my friends would enjoy as we waited out the time between the climbing and the running. Needless to say, I didn't really know what I was in for, what gorgeous musical notes God would send to my ear. Over that safari, I can say I felt something primal, primordial, stirring deep within my soul. It was my heart connecting to Africa.

Other than our connection with domesticated animals, our pets, we Americans don't really have the opportunity for much interaction with wild animals, not the way that many Africans do. Unless we go to the zoo or look at pictures, we quite literally never see them. Within the volcanic basin where these observations of mine would start brewing and the lava of my feelings would rise to the surface, I would have another epiphany. We are all part of God's creation, person and beast. We should treat every life form with dignity and respect. Humans can learn things from animals. They can "teach us to play a new love song." Their song is indeed "fresh, and vibrant, and free," as Dad's poem says.

For one thing, animals are in continual motion, and they don't hold onto the past, as the poem cautions against. Every day is a new day for an animal. And Thursday, February twenty-third, was a new day for me! New day, never been used! Like a little kid all excited for another adventure, my heart sang: "This is the day that the Lord has made! Let us rejoice and be glad in it!"

In the Thick of It
So, this was the day we were officially on safari. We threw our gear into the vehicle, and off we went. Our vehicle was a bus, which seated seven and had a huge luggage rack and a pop-up top through which we would stand to shoot pictures—many pictures. We hit the road and headed into the center of Moshi for an ATM, gas, and some groceries.

The road to our first park (Tarangire) was paved, the same one we came into town on from the airport. We passed through a much bigger city called Arusha, more modern than Moshi, with a lot of hustle and congestion. It also happens to be the geo-center of Africa. It was a hot ride, and we all had several liters of bottled water to guzzle.

On down the road we went, passing barren plains with Maasai tribes herding skinny cattle and goats to few-and-far-between ponds for watering. Not a lot could survive out in these torrid stretches. But nature has a way of overcoming. The guide showed us an anthill taller than me! And the sporadic trees were unbelievably tall and vast in girth—quite striking, particularly the very old baobab. These trees are an important symbol of Africa. They are called the "Tree of Life" because they live a very long time, up to five thousand years, in these arid, scorching conditions. In that time, they can grow to exceptional proportions—one hundred feet high and thirty-three feet in diameter! It is believed that they can survive very dry spells through storing water in their trunks. We also saw dust devils (dust storms) swirling in the distance. These areas had not had any appreciable rain for two months, but the rainy season was approaching.

Along the way, we stopped again. I think our driver was addicted to Coca-Cola and cigarettes; those are what he stopped for a lot—a quick break. We might not have liked the breaks so much, but he was so very likable. While we paused, our vehicle was mobbed by similarly likable women and children trying to sell us souvenirs. They were excited, practically jumping into the vehicle to pressure us to buy. One woman said to me, "Oh come on, Papa, help a Maasai woman!" I learned early to say no in Swahili (*hapana*). If you say this emphatically enough, they back away. Still, it is hard to refuse them. They are so poor, and the trinkets are so cheap.

Not long after that stop we turned off the main highway (A104) onto a gravel road. It would take us to the park entrance past many Maasai villages with all these little kids roadside just sitting there waving to us as we powered past. The conditions they live in looked very impoverished, and I'm sure that they are dependent on the tourist dollar.

We soon arrived at the park entrance, and I was thinking, "Man, it's hot." It was probably in the nineties, dry. As we entered the park, eager to see what this whole safari thing was all about, we were then bumping and jumping on the dirt roads, kicking up as much dust as a tornado when we went. We would be passing by many other vehicles creating dust trails like ours, and the windows went up every time we saw one approaching. As the dust cleared, the windows went back down.

It wasn't long before our guide, Dousan, led us to the wildlife. I'm sure he's been there many times before. We spotted birds, waterbucks, water buffalo, wildebeests, baboons, antelope, zebra, giraffes, and warthogs—a whole panoply of enormous and/or swift African animals. When we drove along the roads and encountered drivers of vehicles coming in the opposite direction, once in a while our driver stopped, and they conversed in their language to see if they had spotted anything unusual that would thrill us or make the "book" for the Big Five (lion, rhino, elephant, leopard, hippo). We had seen many big animals and had pictures galore. "Oh, another zebra, another giraffe—no big deal!" They were everywhere.

Then, we got a report that there were LIONS nearby! Our driver picked up the pace, and we made a turn onto a road swinging us by a river. There were a half dozen Rovers parked there as we approached, all with excited people just like us. Lions! Up close and personal. We got close to a male and female in the shade of this hot day. How close? Twenty feet maybe! We got our fill of camera opportunities as our guide told us it was mating season and they had probably just mated. They were docile. We made jokes about cigarettes. These amazing animals were in their own world, not bothered by our presence at all. We actually spotted six in this location. I guess we had a very opportune sighting. We never saw another lion on any other legs of our journey.

We left the park and returned to the hotel. The town of Moshi reminded me of some in Korea: very busy, very tight, and poor. That night, there were some birds still chirping and crickets sounding off, with faraway dogs barking in some village. Tomorrow would be another new day and new adventure. We would be headed to Ngorongoro conservation area and the Maasai village. I understood that they are in a crater. I was told that in the first place there would be new animals we hadn't seen yet. It is a very interesting destination because the animals stay in there and can't migrate. In the second place, I would see an authentic, centuries-old African culture.

Ngorongoro: God's Basin

Friday the twenty-fourth brought us to the Ngorongoro Conservation Preserve. It's not a national park but a *preserve*, and because of that level of respect towards animals, the Maasai and the animals coexist together. We drove past herds of baboons on the road in town and wound our way up a steep escarpment rising from the plains to a spectacular view of Lake Manyara, to be visited on our last day. **The views were wide, and all life felt free and noble.**

We continued to drive through hilly country, encountering many villages, still with the Maasai prevalent along the roads and the terrain changing yet again. The hills were reddish brown, contrasted by verdant fields and vegetation. Very pretty! Every detail of the visual impression was soothing.

After signing in at the park office, we again embarked on a very choppy, dusty road. We climbed up and up, winding around sharp curves with many dips, to the rim of the volcano crater. Ngorongoro has an immediate and overwhelming initial aspect, like any great natural sculpture. Its stature is gigantic. The crater was formed some eight million years ago when the cone of an active volcano estimated to be larger than Kilimanjaro collapsed. Its dimensions are two thousand feet deep and twelve miles wide. The rich soils and plentiful water supply create a zoological sanctuary for the many species of wild game and birds that inhabit it today. Designated as a World Heritage Site, this African crater has one of the largest concentrations of wildlife in Africa. An estimated 25,000 large mammals make it, along with the Serengeti, the principal attraction on the Northern Tanzanian safari circuit. Its cross-section of wildlife is as diverse as you will find, dispersed among an amazing array of ecosystems within this natural amphitheater. It is home to one of the few remaining populations of black rhinos in Tanzania and just about every other East African animal.

We traveled maybe a quarter of the way around the rim before we could get to a road to take us down inside the basin below. Again, we were on a very steep, rough, and winding road. Once at the bottom, on the plains, you get a whole different perspective on how vast this area really is. Our driver, Dousan, seemed to know his way around the many, many roads inside the crater. We drove around seeing the strange foliage and large prey. Checking with other drivers paid off. Bingo! We caught wind of a black rhino sighting and went off and running to find him. There were only fifteen in the entire park, so to see one is rare and extraordinary.

We then headed off to the hippo pool, where people had driven up to observe their behavior and take photos. A hippo just lazes in a big muddy pool doing absolutely nothing. You are lucky to see them even yawn. Perhaps that makes us laugh, but there's another side to it, too. They are actually temperamental, surly, aggressive, and very dangerous creatures when provoked. Yet their usual extreme stillness causes one to ponder. Just what are they thinking? I got some good faraway shots of one grazing in a field with some birds hanging around but not disturbing it.

The sky changed suddenly, and we could see a sheet of rain coming across the plain. We heard thunder, and it seemed that we were in the path of a large storm, but it only sprinkled, defying our expectation. So we went in search of another rhino or the leopard which we needed for the Big Five—finding one was rather unlikely.

The Maasai Village

Eventually, we were headed out of the crater. It took us a full thirty minutes to ascend in four-wheel drive up maybe two thousand feet of switchbacks on a one-way rocky highway. After the rim, we had to descend again to get back to the Maasai village.

The sun was breaking out. We drove up to the gate of the village, which is in a lonely expanse of valley, and I was glad we had Dousan to translate for us. But we wouldn't need him for that. We were greeted by the chief, Joseph, who spoke English like he was Harvard educated, better than my own. (Some of the Maasai speak both languages.) He was extremely personable. He, in fact, said he would give us a guided tour of his village.

Note: I had heard that the Maasai do not like to have their pictures taken. They are a very beautiful people, and from what I understand when you take their picture, they believe it takes something from their soul. So I didn't, but I really wanted to get some great pictures of real people so I could better remember them. Here is what I recall: the young men and women came out of the gate of the village singing and dancing to greet us and welcome us into their village. This was awesome, and we were so entertained. I didn't care if it was a bit staged; it was the real deal for me. Their colorful, distinctive garb and jewelry lit up everything. The young men were wearing their red capes that symbolize strength, holding spears and jumping high in the air, chanting. The women were doing a similar routine—laughing, jumping in royal blue robes that signify they are married, with very large white beaded tribal collars like discs resting atop their shoulders. Those were stunning, elaborate, huge flat necklaces about twenty inches in diameter, worn horizontally. There were several small toddlers around, watching, taking it all in— barefoot and dusty, carefree.

The chief took us into one of the huts. He explained the design which has a pen inside for goats or calves on one side of the hearth. The small pot on the fire had milk all skimmed over, full of flies. This would be their meal. They depend on milk as their main diet. Okay, all you athletes, think about that! Not very substantial…On the other side of the fire were two spaces separated by some sticks: the adult bedroom and the kids' room. It was all dirt floors and windowless mud walls with only a tiny peephole in the ceiling for light and exhaust.

The interior of the village had a communal walled pen for their cattle, a very prized structure. Surrounded by the pen was also a huge display of the villagers' dazzling crafts. I heard more African music in the distance. People were watching a show of young African boys and girls performing music and traditional dance in costume. Very cool! They were incredible athletes doing acrobatics and balancing acts with a background of invigorating African drumming. Wow, these kids were good!

It is important to reflect that while these were the images I saw of the people on our tour, which are customary when we think of Africa, I do not mean to tokenize their culture based on white American expectations. They are not all the images of Africa. Africa is a huge continent with many countries and diversity in all respects. This is simply the slice of it I saw, one place in Tanzania, one part of the old cultures that seems so foreign and exotic to us, that most people want to see and learn about, among others. We are fortunate on a vacation if we are able to step outside ourselves and discover ways of life truly different from our own. But to reduce the nuances of the people into a monolithic representation would be not to give Africa justice. What we nowadays call the "single story" is never true. The famous, internationally award-winning African novelist Chimamanda Ngozi Adichie has taught me that.

Lake Manyara

The next day would be our last safari before the marathon. The morning greeted us with a fresh, benevolent face. I breathed in easily. Here is where

I was supposed to be. I was mindful of that going against the grain of my earlier false expectation. I felt a sense of vital assurance in God's itinerary.

So on the twenty-fifth, Saturday, we left MtoWaMbu (means *mosquito river*) near our hotel at 7:50 a.m. and went to Lake Manyara. As we entered the park, the first thing we noticed was how suddenly the vegetation became tropical and how tall the trees were. We immediately glimpsed a waterbuck, and there were also three elephants, including one baby, just precious. They were very near to us on the road, but they didn't seem to mind us being so close. Besides the animals we had seen before, we also spotted impala, ostrich, antelope, dick-dick, saddle-back storks, and a Goliath heron. Needless to say, we got some good pictures of them.

We packed up and hit the road to return to Moshi at 12:40 p.m. We continued to see interesting fauna we'd never seen in the United States before and were enjoying ourselves. There was a very disturbing scene we came upon at that time, however. A donkey was recently hurt by a hit-and-run and was trying to get up from the road, but because of broken bones couldn't. Its struggling motions deeply bothered me. The incident wasn't surprising to the area's inhabitants, I suspect. The Maasai keep their cattle and donkeys along the highway, and I wonder how many of their livestock fall victim to the tourist vehicles—those of foreigners who have not attuned themselves respectfully to the close proximity of animals.

Off to our left, we got some great views of Kili and her sister Mawenzi (17,000') covered with snow. Many more than we had seen before. As we came into Moshi we ran into a wedding party. What a kick this was because the party was parading around one of the town traffic circles (roundabouts) in a caravan of vehicles—trucks filled with lively musicians playing wedding tunes with the wedding party in a convertible. This must have been two relatively affluent families because the women were dressed in gowns of designs like you might see here at home, and the men were in coats and ties. It seemed so out of place in this poor country, but that was the final image we saw. It was pretty, like so many of the other things I'd seen, and I'll always remember it.

We had an errand to run before returning to our hotel—that is, to pick up our marathon race packs. Oh, yes, tomorrow we would run 26.2 miles. The expo had our orientation packs. After getting our numbers and papers, we joined our driver to return us to the hotel. We were supposed to meet with our safari guides again so we could give them some leftover gear and clothing we were going to donate. Plus, we had to sleep. We still had a big day ahead of us tomorrow and lots of miles to go on legs already hammered by the rough Rover rides. Would we be ready?

"KILLIN' IT"

Kilimanjaro Race

"Vintage Day"

Like wisps of light smoke from a smoldering fire,
The sun's beams rise up for the day,
They're drifting now out of the deep-green marsh mouth,
And smudging the soft, mirrored bay.

The whispering breeze in the fluttering leaves
Will soon sweep the dense fog away.
The people come out for the pleasant, clear view,
The morning is daytime now gay.

The sun shows you all a most special, warm hue,
An image of beauty and grace.
A nice, vintage day that's reluctant to stay,
Is one that you'll never replace.

That poem of my dad's represents perfect felicity to me, the warmth of a memory of a happy time and place that can't really be duplicated or recaptured. It's the peace that comes from experiencing anything beautiful, pure, and comforting, something that makes all right with the world.

I had run a lot of races, and as I explained before, they were always done by me in a mode of inner competitiveness. But for this race, my first and last African race and my first anywhere minus a competitive mindset, I made it my goal just to enjoy the day. I had no desire to play the hero and win some big award. I had won enough races. After all I'd done on the mountain, the athletic training of a lifetime, and all the many race experiences I had in my quiver, this was going to be purely for pleasure. Now I'd be more or less along for the "ride." I wanted to make it a "vintage day," one with few distractions, because I wanted to implant it firmly in my memory for years and years to come. Because—right—as the poem goes, I knew I'd never be able to replace it with something else.

148

So here we were in the very early morning hours of marathon day, Sunday, February twenty-sixth. Whatever else would happen today in the village around the base of Kili, the normal vagaries of life and Murphy's Law events included, I knew I'd be "killin' it" at Kili! Meaning I would own this experience on special spiritual terms. I had no qualms, no anxieties, no bad portents; I was well rested from sleeping deeply the night before. I knew I was on the right track with God. Come to find out, some of our party of three were a wee bit nervous, but how many times had I been down this "road" before? This would be a light adventure (did I just say "light"?!), not a true race. I would bask in a swath of good feelings. It would be the dandy final event of my African journey, the cherry on top.

Besides, you and I both know that if I had tried to really run, like I used to, I probably would have had a heart attack and died... I wanted to go home alive to tell of my wonderful experiences in Africa.

The shuttle to the venue was on "Africa time" (meaning thirty minutes late—relaxed). As we assembled in the starting area, we tried to estimate the number of runners. We were thinking maybe one hundred to a hundred and fifty. Quite small by our norms. It was still dark, but the sky was starting to lighten up when the sun greeted us from Mt. Kilimanjaro. As our surroundings became more visible, we began to get a better picture of the start/finish area. We met other runners from all over the world.

The gun, or whatever it was that made that loud sound, went off, and we were officially in competition with these elite athletes. Under the banner on a dirt track heading out of the stadium, the mass of runners turned onto a paved yet uneven, irregular street going up a gentle hill. I had my nifty Garmin GPS on my wrist so I could get time/distance/elevation of the entire race.

It was warm. It felt humid. I noticed that even at a slow ten-minute pace, I was struggling and out of breath. Was it the elevation? Had it been premature to think this would be a cinch? Had I not truly learned my lesson about limitations?

It was getting light enough now to see the neighborhoods we ran through. The canopy of trees over us was very brilliant, with reds and purples in the morning sunrise. I have no idea what these trees were, but they were eye-catching. The neighborhood we were traveling through then seemed to be wealthy. We ran to a roundabout. You know, come to think of it, I hadn't seen a single traffic light our entire trip.

The course took us through the downtown area of Moshi and out of town on a fairly substantial highway going east, on towards Dar Es Salaam, downhill. At the roadsides were cheering people who were there waiting for a bus to go who knows where, also kids and parents who were waiting for the race to finish so they could get to church (remember this was a Sunday).

There were several really good cheering sections; most of all, Kilimanjaro itself in the background seemed to be cheering us on.

The turnaround back to Moshi was about eight miles. As we approached within a mile or two of the turn, here came the leaders running in the opposite direction as us. This was an astonishing mental picture—seeing tall and short runners, people with various skin tones, all the sizes and colors of humanity flowing together. They were up on their toes, flying back towards Moshi, all the different competition numbers on paper bibs waving on their chests. It was a sight to behold for sure, especially watching them float by with not a word among them. Soundless because this is a very staid race, as it involves millions of shillings. There were some of the best Kenyan and Tanzanian marathoners there, hands down. And for once I wasn't in the leading pack with them.

Makoi

As we left Moshi, I just hung back, content to let Bill and Craig run ahead. All I really wanted to do was finish and have a good time doing it, with no heart problems, and in that spirit, I struck up conversations with fellow runners who at this far back were mostly stout white tourist types, with the exception of one elderly African with whom I started to settle in. His name is Makoi Bonaventura, a surgeon born in Moshi who had returned home to run in his third marathon ever. He seemed to have some type of magical affinity for the people along the roadside. He was always getting the crowd revved up (I'm sure he knew many of the onlookers). The kids were calling him Ba-Bu, which means *grandpa* in Swahili.

I settled into his pace, which was ten to eleven minutes per mile. We quickly became friends, and then I decided to stay with him the entire race—which in the end was a wise, wise move. He was going very slowly, and if I took a medical turn for the worse, well, I had a physician in him to look after me.

We engaged in small talk as we ran. It turns out that this physician Makoi was educated in Germany. Upon returning to Africa (Moshi) to practice, the government had dictated to him where he was to go and what field of medicine they wanted him for (not surgery, but public health administration). However, he opted to stay in Germany to practice medicine in his specialization and raise a family. He ran his first marathon in Berlin. We both quite enjoyed each other's company, and I found myself having great fun calling out to the crowds too, practicing my Swahili. I think the most remarkable thing of the conversation in running alongside this man was that it was really so *un*remarkable. Not that he wasn't a most interesting man! It was more the *tone* of it all, the relaxed feeling that floated between us.

The water stops were frequent, with ample bottled water and with Coke (not electrolyte drinks, however). The first loop came back ten kilometers into Moshi, climbing uphill through the town, which was now starting to awaken. Not a really fancy (politely said) part of Moshi, but as I passed through the streets, all of a sudden I spotted Joseph, one of our cooks from the mountain. He had come to cheer us on! I slowed down and we had a passing hug, and he shouted out in excitement, which gave me a well-needed boost. Then soon after this I saw our safari driver, Dousan, sitting inside his Rover (which we had push-started several times) off to the side of the road. No, he wasn't broken down this time. He too was there for our support. How special it was to see him as well and realize that these two guys had taken the time to come and see us run. My new friend Makoi was very impressed.

As we ran through some rural sections of Moshi, we turned back towards the college and the well-to-do neighborhood where we had started. Makoi and I kept chatting. As you can imagine, we had hours to talk together. He was pleased with my diction and told me I spoke like a native. Perhaps he was just being kind. Over my years I have always tried to learn the language of the country where I was (Mexico, Korea). I had kept a small notebook during my trip with some common phrases in Swahili to practice. Most Africans spoke a little English, but the language barrier was ever present, unless you had a guide, or in my case a marathon friend, who could tell you what the folks along the side were saying or yelling about. They were still smiling great big, beautiful smiles and chanting "Ba-Bu, Ba-Bu, Ba-Bu!" as we shuffled along, making a bond with each other, yet poignantly realizing that we would probably never meet each other ever again.

Gazelles, and Mr. Price Too

The marathon course took us back past the starting area and climbed up towards Kilimanjaro and the Mweka route that we had come down several days before. The landscape looked familiar. Although I was way behind and still had about twelve kilometers to go, because of the looping of the course, here is where we saw the faster runners coming down to the exciting last stages of the race. They were still on their toes like the gazelles they were and looking strong and graceful, finishing at around only three hours. Quite a few women were in this pack. The winner had come in earlier, at 2:18.

The other observation I made then is that the marathoners and the half-marathoners were mixed together. At this point we got an idea of how many half-marathoners there were in the race. I was guesstimating maybe twice the number of marathoners. The half-marathoners we saw were very much like what I would deem as the "first-timer" kind of American runners. Many looked very inexperienced. As you can see, there was a wide spectrum of running ability in this race.

The last section was a killer, because it kept rising, along with the temps of the day. It was oppressively hot and hazy by this time. In this last part were water stops sponsored by local businesses, appearing with advertisements like a water stop you might see stateside. One sponsor which seemed especially well organized was Tanzanite Mining. They are the only exporters of a gem found there exclusively, near the airport in Moshi. This is a stunning, precious stone, competing in price per carat with diamonds.

The other big water stop sponsor which stole the show was Mr. Price, a big grocery store chain which had staked out the premier location of turn-around at the highest elevation. After that, we would then be going downhill for ten kilometers to the finish line (if you had the legs for it). But our legs were jello. We were running on fumes. Did I say this was a taxing course? Absolutely!

So, the actual Mr. Price, the owner, the mogul, was up front, all his employees behind him dressed in red tees and hats with their logos, the station very well staffed. Mr. Price's is their local Wegman's, or if you come from the north country of New York, the Big M, so we knew they'd have something good to offer. We had a tip that they had ice-water sponges and cold water. Being that it was a scorcher, we were looking for any advantage to survive the day. But it was to be even better than our expectations. As I approached the turn, I saw this worker with a Kili beer. I jokingly asked him if it was some kind of a beer stop; he replied seriously, "Want a cold one?" Oh, man! I told him I'd appreciate that (for this rare time). He reached into an ice-bath bucket and pulled out a can of Kili for me. Another photo-op was had there as I got my picture taken on my single break of this sweltering marathon.

All Good From Here

The elevation where we were was four thousand feet, but the race was all gently downhill from here. After my delay taking the beer photo, as I caught up with Makoi (Ba-Bu), who was slowing down but still moving forward downhill, we could see only a couple of runners behind us, so I knew we were the real "back of the pack" runners. I didn't care one bit! We were still chatting enjoyably away along the hot, dusty road, knowing that Bill and Craig were well ahead.

About the 30K mark on the course we came upon a lazy herd of cattle moving towards us on the road. Another Kodak moment! Did they think they were in the race? Maybe somebody should have pointed them in the right direction! Then it wasn't long before we were approaching the stadium again, still followed by troops of little kids skipping down the road, having some sort of conversation with Makoi, the town celebrity and magnetic Pied Piper. Some were running in flip-flops and others barefoot.

Coming into the stadium, Makoi and I crossed the finish line together. It was like a dream. Everyone was loving on us. I could tell my elderly friend was spent, wasted, although I was fine—minus the hammered quads and raw nipples that had constantly scratched against my shirt. (The latter of these and painful blisters on the heels happen if you forget to put Band-Aids over them before you race). Although I know I looked the worse for wear, I was just so very, very happy that I didn't really care about anything that was not part of the positive feeling. It had been a "vintage" race.

Ease of Heart

Then at the conclusion of the event, we ambled along, me with a bit of blood stain on my shirt and sneakers, to get our finish medals and hats (no shirts given here). I didn't need another shirt for my runner's collection anyway, but a hat…man, that was me! This little memento was special. I put it right on. Bill, having come in way earlier, was there to capture the wonderful moment of me and my African brother on film, standing together with our matching hats. I will never forget that man or that portrait.

Now let's stop there for a moment, freezing the scene for examination. As I reminisce about this sparkling crystal of time, I think about the lightness of heart this run gave me. I had arrived in Africa to begin with and experienced sleepless night after sleepless night. Something hadn't been right, although I just couldn't put my finger on what it was—it went beyond even the fear that my heart might fail. But God had helped me break free, and I ended with a placid ecstasy. My dream had played out in real, splendid glory. Yes, somehow this day, this place, and my true participation in life had melded.

I certainly saw ease of heart within the African people, and it was the quiet strength that was now shaping me and would be mine to take home. I had seen that most notably in Ba-bu and his smiling, skipping entourage. His soul had grown out of those landscapes which I had never before seen nor heard of. His short intersection with my life nevertheless made me feel the special kind of happiness he exuded to all around him. I felt so calm and safe with him by my side. Ironically, I didn't feel as though any of this race had been work. For once, it was something I didn't have to make happen or engineer, nor did I have to prove myself to myself. The day had just unfurled itself, in surprising and delightful ways. My reverie in slow-motion as the photo with Makoi was taken illuminated the true depth of simplicity.

I snapped to. After the regular finish line pictures, we were whisked away by a Mr.-Price-dressed guy in red and taken to the Kilimanjaro VIPs' tent. It was catered and had some rap stars performing. We enjoyed several beverages with "Freddie," a local celebrity, and his friend Frank after fetching Bill and Craig.

Then Monday the twenty-seventh was departure day. I left Africa with three experiences I had lived to tell about: Mount Kilimanjaro, safaris, and the marathon. I had filled my bucket before I kicked it. Yes, I had "killed" *it*; it hadn't killed *me*. But I had received so much more than I bargained for. I had deeply drunk of the beauty along the way.

"DADDY'S HOME!"

My Father Passes

"Silent Movies"

The memories that we have shared,
Are not so left behind.
They're here and quite available
In corners of our mind.

I shut my eyes and conjure up
An image from the past
To stay with me in retrospect—
And I can make it last.

So come with me and take a trip
To youth of long ago.
Enjoy the times that we once had;
Close eyes and watch the show.

Born in Rochester, New York, in 1921, Dad grew to be a multi-dimensional, well-rounded, interesting man, despite having at least three strikes against him. First, he was a sickly, maimed baby, yet he ended up a healthy and coordinated athlete. Second, he was also as a boy mostly silent, saddled with a great linguistic learning disability, yet he ended up a researcher and academic writer. Third, he was a medic and lost an eye in World War II, making him a disabled veteran, yet he obtained his pilot's license.

Professionally, he was eager to become an inventor in the field of biology, but he had to adjust his track a little and thereafter became a longtime, favorite dentist in town. He considered that artistry. Toward the end of his life he was also an amateur poet, as you can see by all his lovely poems in this book.

Dad raised four great kids (including yours truly). Through his great loves, he influenced me to appreciate family, biology, racing, and craftsmanship. Most of all, he loved me and I loved him. Before he died, he did see me go up Kili—well, that is, *know* about that. At the end, the death

155

of my father was due to cancer—painful and drawn out. It was kind of like the way he started.

That's a fair summary of my dad. But his experiences deserve more detail. To begin again with deeper illustration, let me say that my dad's life as an infant was painful. He had had a rare illness, called erysipelas, the scars of which he bore on his left thigh through life, where there was a drain threaded through his leg. It was ghastly. He almost died, since antibiotics were unknown in those days. We guess the Lord saved him for some purpose, which was, at that time, unknown to him, of course. Despite his unfortunate malady, he walked at ten months old—so early—and was apparently a happy baby, always smiling and singing to everyone.

Dad's name, as I told you, was Irving Loder Brooks, Jr. Our ancestors' ethnicities were basically British and German/Swiss. His name is kind of intriguing, as the first and last words mean essentially the same thing. *Irving* is a boy's name of Scottish origin meaning *green river* and simultaneously *sea friend*. You see the water imagery as also associated with the surname *Brooks*. In terms of the friend part, guess what?... You got it! He was not only my father, but my pal, my friend, in fact my *best* friend when I was growing up.

Loder comes from English origins and is an occupational name for a carter, from the ancient derivative word *lode* meaning *to load*; it also means *path, road,* or *watercourse*. I can't help but remember those magnificent porters who assisted me up the path of Mount Kilimanjaro, people whose job it was to bear the load of the equipment we'd need to survive the journey up the mountain. The watercourse part of the definition also corresponds to the water imagery of Brooks and reminds me of our Erie Canal. In German *Loder* is again an occupational surname, this time for a weaver of woolen cloth (*loden*). It makes some sense, then, that my father would be a craftsperson, in his case doing dentistry and poetry. That etymology ties everything together in a meaningful way.

But the symbolism of movement and doing and engagement with nature we've just seen in my dad's name isn't just for humans; it's for all creation. Anything that's moving is alive with energy! Heraclites, Greek father of history, is known for saying "You can't step in the same river twice," or something like that. We know what that means. Literally, if you dip your foot into the Genesee River in Rochester, then come back a week later to the same spot, the river is going to be different, changed. You'll never be able to keep things the way they were—because the river is in motion. A variety of things may be different. The physics of the water speed may be faster or more turbulent. The chemistry may be different in terms of the sediments, what the river is now carrying. The biology of the life forms there may have slightly changed, bearing different fish and amphibians.

That's the way life works, constantly in flux. And my dad would have liked that analogy, since he loved life sciences and began his post-retirement working years as a biological researcher at an oceanography institute.

Dad's Struggles with Language

We've spoken of water at various points throughout this book. Whether it was the Great Lake of Ontario, which Rochester borders, or the St. Lawrence Seaway, where my ancestors lived, or a simple babbling brook of my imagination, running, moving water has always been meaningful to me. I was happy, and it resonated with me, when Dad went to the west coast of Florida. He went there when he retired, and he volunteered to do research at Mote Marine Institute in Sarasota. They do a lot of scientific work on marine mammals and fish. He did research at the time on the dolphins that were washing up on shore and dying. He did autopsies, necropsies, and he was able to determine the age of dolphins by merely looking at their teeth. His best project materialized before the end of his life, better late than never, when he published a paper on that special kind of age detection. I think this was the closest my father felt that he had ever come to achieving his true potential as a scientist and communicator.

But I must back up a bit and tell you exactly why that academic achievement was so very significant to my father. You see, as a child, he had grappled with, as I said, a severe learning disability. I mentioned that in my early chapter where I talked about the sternness of my great-grandmother, who made him go to church. You will remember that he had an aversion to going there, a phobia, almost, because of its Sunday school curriculum requiring public speaking—reading aloud. My father, in his autobiography, related these declamation incidents as some of his "defining experiences, and certainly not the last which [he] would have during [his] long and tumultuous educational experience." I recall yet another anecdote here to show how much negative early scholastic experiences can mar us. He said this event had been branded into his mind, in fact.

"I remember it well," he wrote many years later as an elderly man. It had happened during one of those little theatrical productions put on for parents. It was a celebration play of the first Thanksgiving. His big moment, the one his parents and friends came to see, would occur when he spoke just one single line: "And now for the dance," which was a signal for the students to perform a fancy square dance. When the time came, he said it articulately and with great volume, and the dance was delivered flawlessly.

However, unfortunately, because of his reading difficulty, he had processed the script lines wrongly as he was following along and had mistakenly delivered the phrase two scenes too soon. This caused great confusion among the cast. The directors attempted to quell the turmoil on stage and behind the curtain in an effort to get the play back on schedule. As may be expected, this was Dad's last effort on stage and convinced him and others that he'd "never have a future on the stage as a thespian." He wrote that in his memoirs, and that it was a pivotal moment, "the first of many public embarrassments which were to stifle my self-confidence for the rest of my life."

So sad. He also had related troubles in composition, noting that whenever he tried to write a love note to a girl, he'd invariably embarrass himself because he "couldn't spell worth a nickel. I wonder how many girls I lost," he pondered, "because of my inability to communicate with the pen." I am glad, in the end, that he regained some of that self-confidence and self-published his poems. I think he would be pleased to know that we are making them known to a wider audience with this book.

My dad also believed that he had what we now know to be attention deficit disorder (ADD). "I wonder," he wrote, "how I learned anything in school." In reality, he may have had this problem, but he may also have been suffering from what we now, ironically, call giftedness. Like Albert Einstein, who failed grades in elementary school, my father always had inventions going on in his daily mental meanderings—daydreaming: "what project I was working on at home, what invention I had in progress, or was planning for the future." He never took notes in class; his notebooks were filled with doodles and drafts of wonderful future machines. Perhaps he is what educators today might call a "kinesthetic" or "hands-on learner." Physics and chemistry were classes in which he did especially well. "These gave me the first inkling that I wasn't the 'dummy' that my heretofore scholastic experiences would indicate," he later wrote.

Me Too

And there is a little twinge of discomfort, not only sympathy but empathy I have, that reaches beyond my dad's experience and directly into me. You see, I myself was always a hands-on learner, and I too inherited dyslexia, though stymied not as profoundly as Dad. To this day, I struggle and struggle with reading and writing, although I love them both. I see letters backwards and have a difficult time manipulating the written word, although I've always been intellectually curious and enjoyed thinking about new ideas.

Like father, like son, I gravitated towards the sciences and industrial arts classes because of my natural keenness for the subjects, but also because of my effort to avoid English. We both sought out sports opportunities as well, as they represented an avenue in which to develop the self-esteem that was lacking from language and literacy experiences; sports made us feel that we were special somebodies. While sports were about physical strength and natural talent the full extent of which neither of us was fully aware, language learning was our nemesis. I remember that freshman English at the college level was the most daunting course I ever had to take! It was a steep, uphill challenge.

At age seventy-three (would you believe it?!) I am overcoming my fear, the daunting prospect of writing a book. It has been tough for me, probably more so than for other writers, since I battle this strange and disorienting condition. Still today, little is known about dyslexia, other than that it runs in families, unfortunately. I have also thought that I might have a tad of ADD. It's sometimes hard for me to keep on one thought at a time, though running seemed to channel that.

A Joyride

I have a friend, Dick Giambra, who races his Alpha Romeo in the classic car division at world-famous Watkins Glen in New York each year. He's still doing this, even in his seventies. Sometimes he would get me a pit pass so I could get the inside scoop on having and driving a vintage race car.

Each time I watched the vintage car races at the glen, at noon they would allow street (non-racing) cars to do a few loops of "The Big Track" guided by a pace car. When Dad was still alive, I asked him if he wanted to go with me on one of my visits to Watkins Glen and watch, not telling him that I could take my MG out on the track.

When we drove there and got in line to do our practice run, he was surprised and overjoyed. Corvette in front of us, Mustang behind us. It was the first time I was able to really let it loose on a motor track such as The Glen. I really let it rip! The experience of the speed and the curves of the track was exhilarating.

After we finished, Dad said to me, "That was the thrill of a lifetime! Where did you learn to drive like that?"

Proudly, I said, "From you, of course, Dad."

Marie

I have said that my dad was a well-rounded person, and he was gifted not only intellectually but in an emotionally intuitive way as well. My father was a sensitive romantic. After Mom died, near the end of his life, he had more loving to do. My father entered into a romance with a woman named Marie. He had known her from before although there had been no attraction. She had been an island person, up at Grindstone, a neighbor. He somehow reconnected with her after my mother passed away, and things bloomed from there.

With his reawakening of his capacity for intimate feelings, that's when Dad really started writing poetry. I appreciate his poems and hold them very dear. Marie and her depth of feeling and own poetry writing inspired him. Marie and Dad were so in love, thriving in each other's arms, living each moment in utter bliss.

I've read some of her poems. What a muse she must have been. In one she wrote about a heavenly island and river that were "beyond the reach of trouble/ a place where peace rules every moment/ and nature is a friend/ nurturing the body and the spirit/ helping (me) to comprehend." Her quest to understand the afterlife was also filtered into him.

As I said, Marie completed Dad, and they enjoyed a wonderful relationship. But then, the unthinkable occurred. Unfortunately, they would be together only a few years. As you may predict, she died. As happens so often and so tragically, she developed cancer and passed away. In her memory, Dad composed this, one of many poems about her:

"She Sails Alone"

She's going away, this love of mine,
Across uncharted seas.
She's steered by unseen forces, not
By a compass familiar to me.

She's heading for his unknown place,
Wherever that may be,
And all I know of this journey of hers,
Is she's going there without me.

I watch her as she's slipping away,
Unable to alter her course.
In vigil by her confining bed,
I watch with tempered remorse.

I realize that this passing now
Is really God's natural plan.
It's not for me to change one bit.
I'll accept it as best I can.

I know someday I'll follow her
To a place where it all began.
I'll see the well-placed buoys she left,
Then we'll be together again.

Dad's Death
Loder lived another ten years, lonely, a broken, aloof shell devoid of Marie and her love. He had lived through Marie's cancer and then contracted

Lyme disease. He had some medical tests for that, and they discovered cancer, just as Marie had had. He then moved to assisted living, became sicker, fell down, and was moved into the hospital. It was obvious he was going to die a long, grueling death, just like his horrible birth. But he knew he didn't want to go down that road.

I was with him day and night at the end, and he finally said to me, "I don't want to live like this anymore." Of course, the sorrowful tears flowed freely on both sides. "If I stop eating, you're gonna know it's the end," he said, as if he could somehow pacify me with such a morbid and shocking indication. So, he was stubborn, and he stopped eating, all right. We put him in hospice across the street from Rochester General, at St. Ann's Home, and he lasted three days.

I woke up at three o'clock in the morning on that last day because I couldn't sleep. I got dressed, walked into the ward before dawn, and they said, "Oh, Mr. Brooks, we were just going to call you." They then moved him into a different room, which signaled his final, quick downward spiral. I was with him as he started his last section of the journey.

He had this little electronic, flameless candle next to his bedside always lit. I had been reading Psalm 139, which is a beautiful, life-affirming Scripture that's often used for people in hospice. It was at that moment that my dad's soul slipped away into paradise, and it was over...

But I was a little afraid. *Now what do I do?* I asked myself. I decided on the next course of action and went to the nurses. "I think Dad just died," I said in faltering tones. So, they said I could spend some time with him, saying goodbye.

When I went back to his room, the candle was not lit anymore. I looked, and the switch was still in the *on* position; I hadn't turned it off after reading to my father. I was flummoxed. I thought it might be the batteries, but before getting new ones, I decided to play with it for a second. I turned the switch off then on again, and it glowed. "Dad, you've got to be kidding me! You're playing with me now," I said, a little bit of anxiety about the whole death thing now leaving my body. I was relieved; his typical humor had done that for me. I had appreciated the good fortune to be there with him as he drew his last breath, because he was there for me when I took my first. Looking back, I realize that being able to be there with him lifted some of the sorrow of his parting.

My dad's spirit was finally free from cancer. "Free," in fact, is the title of one of the poems he wrote. It is about a dialogue between someone and nature, the latter of which is personified as a breeze. "The breeze whispered,/'Come with me—/there are such wondrous sights to see.'" Then the breeze indicates the way, and the narrator's spirit rises up to heaven.

"Oh Death, Where Is Thy Sting?"

When we think about powerful stories of life and death, we think of resurrections—people being raised from the dead. The central resurrection story, of course, is Jesus's. Here is the true miracle of miracles, on which our entire Christian doctrine of the afterlife rests. We can, like Jesus, transcend this world and experience an eternal existence just by believing in him.

Now, I want you to focus on the running aspect of the resurrection report we receive in the gospel of John. After Mary Magdalene had witnessed the arisen Christ and went back to the upper room to inform the disciples, there was a mixture of skepticism and excitement. One or two even went to see for themselves. In chapter 20, verse 4 we are told, "They were both running, but the other disciple outran Peter and reached the tomb first." (The Bible doesn't mention here who this "other disciple" is, other than to say "the one whom Jesus loved," and there has been much debate over the centuries about who that is.)

Anyway, as I said in my preface to the book, we can run *from* things like the past and run *toward* things like the future. This run certainly had everything to do with humanity's future, as Jesus's resurrection changed the course of history. We run away from things that scare us or things we want to get rid of and toward things that excite us or that we want to embrace or discover. Although many emotions may have been in play at the moment the disciples received Mary Magdalene's announcement, I venture to say that this running to the gravesite was a race of joy! Like for Christmas morning presents. The disciples lost track of themselves in this moment, in their pursuit to see the unbelievable, the miraculous, a gift from God. That day, they would see the greatest action of all time—victory over death with the promise of everlasting life!

So, I am comforted in my thought about my dad's passing, in that I feel reassured he has received new life—that is, eternal life with Jesus Christ. Daddy went "home" to be with his Savior and heavenly Father, and he's at peace. Loder is content, perhaps even watching us, looking down. He's being written about in this book. His memory has been revitalized on earth as well as in all my family members' hearts. And regardless of earthly concerns and his former inabilities, his spirit soars perfectly in the Great Beyond.

There are two cemetery plots in the enormous and historically significant Mount Hope Cemetery in Rochester, New York, where our ancestors are buried: the Brooks plot, where, naturally, many of the Brooks family members are interred—and the Loder plot, where Great-Granddad Edward Brooks and Great-Grandma Gertie Loder and many of her folks are. My mom and dad are also there. May they live in eternity.

STRICKEN

I Have a Stroke

"Oh, To Be Fifty"

If only I were only fifty again,
To be healthy, happy, the way I was then.

I'd do such things that once I tackled with ease,
Like touching the floor without bending my knees.

My footwear was stylish, but now don't you know,
My shoes don't have laces, they close with Velcro.

My pants have hip pockets with buttons and flaps.
But now these have turned to incredible traps.

The tight fit of clothing, the trousers I wear,
In order to don them, I must use a chair.

The spasms of pain with each step that I take—
One's scared with each movement that something will break.

But when I turn ninety, I 'spose I'll say then,
"Oh, how I wish that I were seventy again!"

Dad really was funny sometimes. He had a good sense of humor. After he retired and received the title of senior citizen, he was seeing the telltale signs of old age everyone eventually does. But he had a good attitude about it.

Various people see retirement and old age differently. Some people see them as a blessing, some a curse. I was in the first category for a while, but it altered. No longer in that joyous brook bounding with swift surety, I found myself in obvious stagnation, a funk. I was obsessing about it, but not because of my choices going into the golden years. It was because old age brought everything to a physical standstill.

They say that just when things can't get any worse, they *can*. Adversity. It sure can throw you for a loop! As if two heart attacks were not enough, something worse was coming. A stroke in my late sixties, seven years ago, 2013. Yes, there's that unlucky number. Dear reader, this was not just the rain when it poured. It was the torrential downpour, the tidal wave that really took me down. So now I have a cane, darn thing. Let me tell you exactly how I got it…to the best of my recollection. You'll have to bear with me while I retrace my steps.

Dizzy, Dizzy, Dizzy…

Donna and I were at the cottage, finishing up the summer. In fact, we had loaded our car with our luggage, ready to return home in Irondequoit the very next day. I hate to say it, but I was drinking again, depressed about my physical decline, not partaking to excess but still drinking moderately. Can you do this as a recovering alcoholic? The answer is no way.

I was out on the back deck getting the grill ready for dinner with a glass of port wine to help me. I wasn't loaded, but I'm sure I was buzzed. I bent over to adjust the coals, and when I stood back up, I blacked out and fell backwards, hitting my back on a bench, hard. I knew I had cracked something—like a major bone—because I was in quite a bit of pain. I could get around, but it was very painful walking.

I knew I was hurt and needed medical attention. I wasn't ready to call an emergency rescue boat, but I probably should have. We returned to the mainland in our own small boat and drove back to Rochester.

We stopped at urgent care for x-rays. "How did you fall?" the question was asked. "What happened?" I didn't remember. X-rays showed a cracked rib. "You'd better see your primary care doctor," they said. So, I made an appointment to see him a couple days later.

Meanwhile, round two: unbelievably, almost the very same thing occurred at home by our backyard grill a little while later. I didn't fall, but I had a dizzy spell. When I did see my primary, he suggested I schedule an MRI ASAP. I followed through with his orders, got the scan, and returned a few days later for the results. Dr. Rolls entered the room and said I had had a stroke. Not just one, but several. It was jaw-dropping news. I was stunned. Then he said something terrible, some of the worst words I could ever imagine. His "You'll never run again" rocked me big-time. "Go to the Emergency Department," he quickly said. "I'll call you in."

I'm not sure that I was there in the hospital more than a few days before I was released to home care. My balance was off-kilter. I was seen at home by a physical therapist and assigned my own personal old-person walker. Weeks turned into months of PT. I was getting somewhat better, but I resigned myself to the fact that I needed assistance walking with a walker or cane. I was not a happy camper, especially recalling the doctor's thunderous prognosis that would shut down my world. I kept saying to myself, *no sweat, you've heard those words before, after your heart dysfunctions, and always bounced back, running again.*

But this time I couldn't worm my way out of it. God really got my attention. He was loud and clear: *You'd better slow way, way down, OR I WILL STOP YOU.* I had to replay that one in my head. Notice he didn't say *Or I will slow you down.* The emphasis wasn't on the *you* versus the *I*; it was on the action words, the *slow* versus the *stop.* He had already slowed me down more than my liking. I realized more each day that I could not deny my new existence; I couldn't be so stubborn. There were plenty of warning signs screaming at me, and my confrontation with them wasn't nice. This time I would go off the rails.

Be F.A.S.T.

My best piece of advice: be aware. Know your medical history. As I mentioned earlier, doctors at the bedside of my paternal grandmother reported her cause of death as "a large hemorrhage of the right side of her brain"—in other words, a stroke. It was caused by heart disease. As far as family myths go, she claimed to be the seventh child of a seventh child, and that gives one special psychic powers not possessed by others, supposedly. She would seem to already know when she would hear of a birth or death of some close friend or relative. My father never did try to document her forecasts to test her "batting average," but simply based on the fact that she always seemed to know about my father's indiscretions, before or after the fact, we never doubted her intuitive gifts. I wonder if she ever had a knowing or premonition of her own death.

Although I can look back and see some precursors to my heart attack, I didn't anticipate my own stroke coming at all, even though I was vaguely aware of it having occurred in my family. Since I assume you are not psychic, you may not see yours (God forbid) approaching either. So, my second piece of advice is: know and recognize the signs of a stroke in order to save yourself.

According to the CDC's webpage "Stroke Signs and Symptoms," there are five things you need to watch out for: "sudden numbness or weakness in the face, arm, or leg, especially on one side of the body; sudden confusion, trouble speaking, or difficulty understanding speech; sudden trouble seeing in one or both eyes; sudden trouble walking, dizziness, loss of balance, or lack of coordination; [and] sudden severe headache with no known cause." Note the emphasis on *sudden*. You as the victim need to respond suddenly, too. And so does the person with you, if you are so lucky as to have one. So educate yourself and them.

The CDC recommends acting fast because "the stroke treatments that work best are available only if the stroke is recognized and diagnosed within three hours of the first symptoms. Stroke patients may not be eligible for these if they don't arrive at the hospital in time." The agency warns us not to hesitate, and they have an acronym, F.A.S.T., to illustrate just that. To act *fast*, what does a non-medical person do for someone who might be having a stroke? Do the following test: 1) Check the *face* (F). Ask the person to smile. Does one side of the face droop? 2) Check the *arms* (A). Ask the person to raise both arms. Does one arm drift downward? 3) Check the *speech* (S). Ask the person to repeat a simple phrase after you. Is the speech slurred or strange? Once you are done with these three tasks, remember that *time* (T) is key. If you see or experience any of these "off" behaviors, call 9-1-1 right away. If it's you who is affected, don't drive yourself to the hospital or even let someone else drive you. You are supposed to get an ambulance so that the proper medical treatment can begin right there on the way to the emergency room. I hope this information can make a difference for someone.

Aftermath of a Stroke

So yes, once upon a time, I had a stroke. Welcome to my life! I don't pretend to understand exactly what a stroke is. Sure, my doctors explained it. All I know is that one of the little brooks in my brain got plugged up, so the other little brooks, who were in a hurry, tried to get around it. They went outside the bounds, where they shouldn't have. They went over their levies. They left me with an entire side less movable, less responsive than it once was—basically confounding me at every step. *Why won't you work, legs?!* I would yell at myself. They left me a different person. Yes, I've made restorative progress, but it's never going to be the same as before. Today, the way in which it affects me is primarily through my balance. For that, I'll never run again. The doctor was right. Without the cane, I just can't balance.

The classic "Why me, Lord?" was eating away at my mind. But I couldn't fully utter it. I couldn't approach my God to communicate all my rage, hurt, pain, and disappointment. How could I "give it over to God," like they say, when God was the one who had apparently let it happen? I could never forgive him—no, not for this. We all must have our cross to bear—I realize that—but why did mine specifically have to steal away my forte, my highest talent, my enjoyment? It seemed so wrong. It was unfathomable, really. It's fair to say I went through all the well-known stages of grief in the loss of my physical ability to run: from denial, to anger, on and on. I'll tell you, it is hell to go from having the most conditioned, top-performing body to one that is damaged and dysfunctional. It's dreadful; it's humiliating; it's…it's…

(you fill in the blank if you're an athlete who has been permanently disabled due to an injury). It's a cliché to say that one shouldn't take things for granted before the career-ending event, that hindsight is twenty-twenty, but it's completely true.

Did I ever anticipate the stroke's complications and how much I would have to battle them? Of course not. My legs, their tight muscles and strong bones, had always served me in such good stead. Now, a new victim of another indifferent strike against me, struggling during the most basic physical therapy, the muscles were atrophying. Not of their own accord, but because of an injured brain that no longer knew how to give commands very well.

During workouts and training at the gymnasium, the ancient Greeks believed that athletes should not run on the stone floor but instead on sand. Have you ever tried to run on a beach? It's hard and frustrating, as the ever-shifting surface throws you off balance. But after you've trained this way for a while and go back to the flat, stable surface, you're amazed at how much more adept you are at running! It's called "overcompensation." The muscles and brain centers that naturally overcompensate to keep you from falling over are ultra-refined in runners to help them cope with uneven surfaces. Well, after you've had a stroke like mine, it feels like you are walking on uneven sand all the time, but there's no overcompensation happening to keep you steady and make you better afterwards. A cane is a poor substitute for a working leg—and an even worse one for a cerebellum.

My defective plumbing system was the heart attack; my defective electrical system was the stroke. The stroke is what really took me down. I've asked myself what caused the stroke, besides heredity, but I'm not really sure. I do have a theory, though. The plumbing and electrical systems are related and affect each other. They can alter and, in fact, irreversibly destroy each other, so I think that whatever started showing up with the clogged heart arteries was the same thing that caused the short circuiting in the brain. The circulatory and nervous systems are interdependent, but that's not all. The other systems are in turn dependent on them too.

"But Wait! There's More!"

So here's part two. Because I wasn't able to walk much, or perform my normal range of motion, my cardiovascular system was in a weakened state, and therefore my immune system probably was too. I was moving at two miles per hour tops. That was easy enough to see, but most people can't "see" their immune systems.

Several months later in the dead of winter I couldn't sit around anymore. I have a good friend I missed, a coach in Arizona I told you about named Fred. I really wanted to escape the Rochester doldrums, get out of Dodge and go see him. I booked a flight to Tucson for some warm, sunny weather by Fred's pool to decompress and rehab. The cacti were starting to bloom, and the weather was in the eighties each day. It was wonderful. I was even invited to lifeguard with Fred's training group for an open-water event at a local swim quarry. It hardly seemed like work as I cruised around on my paddleboard. *I sure could get used to this,* I said to myself with a smile.

Alas, my time there was up, and I had to return to the reality of gray, sleet-filled Rochester in early March. I booked a red-eye out of Phoenix back home, hoping to get into Buffalo without too much dread and denial on my part.

As we approached the Buffalo airport for landing, I started to feel sick to my stomach. My head was spinning. Something was wrong, more than the usual sensations you get while on a plane. When the vehicle came to a stop, I hailed a wheelchair to disembark and retrieve my luggage. They told me where baggage claim was. Some nice person wheeled me downstairs so I could complete my voyage and get my stuff. Chagrined and still feeling off, I waited for Donna to pick me up.

The baggage claim area was empty of people. I felt like everyone had just deserted me there, sick and disoriented, getting sicker, more nauseous and anxious by the minute. Shortly I was puking in garbage cans, wondering why there was no one to help me. Where was my wife? I tried calling Donna by cell. No pick up. I really felt alone and afraid, like *really* afraid. Like *panic attack* afraid. I didn't know it, but I was at the wrong baggage claim area.

I finally saw a sign of life and summoned that lone someone walking around the area. They figured the confusion out and directed me to the correct baggage claim to get my things. I was too ill to feel embarrassed. And then I was waiting again. But where was Donna??? I even had someone announce her name on the airport's PA system. Minutes, then parts of hours passed, I think. No Donna.

When I finally reached her, she was driving around the shuttle area pickup. She had had her phone turned off! I was too sick to be angry. Off to Rochester we rushed, no strange Buffalo ER for me. "Take me directly to Dr. Rolls," I barely vocalized.

He took one look at me and told Donna to take me directly to Emergency—AGAIN. An immediate blood test resulted in another surprising diagnosis…deadly sepsis. I was full of infection, in critical condition!

That definitely could have been my death blow, Rolls said, but I dodged another bullet. I was released from the hospital a few days later, only to suffer through weeks of daily self-administration of a powerful antibiotic drug that coursed through a PICC line, burning into an unfortunate vein, no remorse. Such is the life of a sick and tired, washed-up athlete. I don't know for sure how my sepsis got started, but to me, it seemed like this string of medical crises was related. I have an inkling about how the infection occurred. I had had an unattended sore on my leg that I believe I obtained from swimming around the quarry with Fred and his trainees. I had gone there, as you recall, as part of my recuperation for the stroke. That nasty little entrance wound is still there today, by now a thickened patch of flesh, and I can feel it right now, a battle scar on my right calf, behind me.

Long-term Prognosis

Did I already mention it this: I would never run again? Moreover, I would never even *walk* right again. Sometimes I still don't believe it myself. Would I somehow eventually be okay with those things? *Could* I ever be okay with them? This additional dealbreaker (the first one being my heart attacks) had to be mentally reckoned with. This new dealbreaker was now the brick wall, the thing I could not hide or temporarily shelve for later. My impairment would be obvious to the outside world. Everyone would see my unsure, clumsy movements. Everyone would see my cane, or walker, if it came to that again. What would they think? Nothing of it? Expected, considering my older age, no big deal? Sorrowful? Behind my back, or worse yet directly to my face, they might be piteous. ("He was a great runner, now he's *none* of that. He's a has-been, all used up!"). I hate to say it, but the parallel between great giant Kodak's decline and my own was all too palpable. Although I was only a man, not a vast empire, the running world had been the equivalent to me.

I tried not to think too much about all this. I didn't want to be against myself, to throw myself under the bus. In Galatians 5:7, Paul admonishes the congregation of the early church for backsliding. "You were running the race so well. Who has held you back from following the truth?" If I sat around feeling sorry for myself, I'd be that person who held me back, who cut in on me, unfairly. So I simply followed doctors' orders—did what had to be done. They put my recovery into motion; I merely complied. I've been doing physical therapy for a few years now. I've done all right. If you can find a decent therapist, they are worth their weight in gold.

I spent some time in physical therapy today thinking about how I got to this place. "The path is long and torturous and strewn with many a test." Remember that from my father's poem in the Kilimanjaro chapter? Well, this place (physical therapy) is where I have spent many a time getting patched up after one or another injury. Mostly my stroke, of course, and overuse stuff as a result of all the years of intense training and just plain going over the edge. The fact is that this body will not grow and repair like it did in my twenties and thirties. In your fifties, sixties, and seventies, the healing takes noticeably longer, and there's got to be patience. Athletic training and building yourself up are like that as well. Especially when you get older, knowing just when enough is enough and having the sense to back down or back off is imperative. As some people joke, "You're not a spring chicken anymore!" Right. Like it or not, you're an old man.

WHERE DID ALL THE GOOD TIMES GO?

I Get Depressed

"It's a Small World"

"The universe is expanding,"
I think I heard them say.
I think it's not that way at all;
It's just the other way.

Some say the world is shrinking
And getting rather small.
Now graced with understanding true,
I must these facts recall.

When I was young and helpless,
I was so very small.
I was contained within my crib;
I couldn't even crawl.

I learned to stand and run;
The walls I did escape.
The yard became my wonderment
With all that empty space.

One day that gate was opened,
And suddenly *I'm free*.
My world became forevermore—
All that, and more, to see.

Now that I've grown in years,
These paths I must retrace,
The yard, the house, the four plain walls,
Again my well-known place.

When I get old and die
In comfort of my bed,
My world will be diminished to

171

The confines of my head.

Well, isn't that description true to a life that's fully lived? I mean, we begin as babies—tiny, helpless beings. Then we grow and develop to our prime. We reach the proverbial "hill." Then we notice a pain here, a pain there. We tend to decline, growing weaker every day, until we're maddeningly feeble. Hey, it happens to the best of us. But what a moving testimony this simple poem brings forward—to a life, just an ordinary life, like most of us have. We rise and we fall. We live and we die. Is that sad?

Depression, whether in old age or any time before, pulls us down to our worst. It is very real, a situation that sometimes devolves into a chronic, debilitating mental and physical illness. It is caused primarily by two things, often in conjunction: a psycho-social stressor like a major, negative life event, and/or by the very chemicals we are composed of, if they are imbalanced.

Regardless of its source, depression hits you like a ton of bricks, figuratively, and quite physiologically too. There's no polite knock at the door. It's a dump truck loaded with a ton of emotional bricks, all two thousand pounds of them, ready to empty right at your front door when you go to see what's driven up on your lawn. Crushing your spirit and making you want to avoid life by staying listless on your couch. Trust me, I can attest. (I thought it was the guy from Amazon, but no such luck).

One of those stressors when you get older that's difficult to deal with is that you witness the passing of many of your friends. Even though I'm only seventy-three, several of my friends are now gone. It's happening at an increased frequency. Some guys have been ten years younger than me. Then again, I have some friends in their eighties and even nineties still alive and running. They're robust and impressive. Running, you must realize, takes years off your age. But when your number's up, it's up.

Bill, my fellow marathon runner and Kilimanjaro teammate (we had also climbed many Adirondack peaks together), unfortunately passed not too long ago. His wife never got an autopsy on him, but we all know what happened. I wasn't with him at the time. He was with one of my best hiking buddies and was on the way up Mount McKinley, in Alaska. He just dropped dead, and that was that. That climb was supposed to be no big thing for him, so his death was unexpected, shocking. The news was brittle, decimating our running world. For me, his passing also brought back bad memories of the dead Kilimanjaro hiker my age whom we'd seen. You just don't get that kind of image out of your head.

Good times? No way. Come on, sit down. Let Grandpa Brooks tell you a little bit about it. Maybe you can relate—or know someone who can. Like drug addiction, again, depression is a topic that is often taboo, but one that needs to be addressed. So many people suffer, unbeknownst to others. They don't want to say anything because it's hard to talk about, or they don't want to bring others down. Perhaps they don't want to deal with the inconvenience it poses, or a host of other possible reasons that could be known only to the person.

In my case, I've been fundamentally happy most of my life, so the dark moments, when they come, are confusing. I don't really get cranky or super (clinically) depressed—some people do when they get an injury; in fact, if they're serious athletes, these people can go a little haywire. Up until my stroke, I don't think I would have ever labeled myself as depressed. After it, yes, I think I was somewhat. I could have very easily fallen off the wagon permanently with the stroke, but I've been diligent not to go down that road. I know how easy it is to get onto binge drinking again. I had been a functional drunk, and I could do that again in a moment. But to my credit, I've been rational in my approach to the heart attack and stroke and the loss of my physical abilities. No longer Hermes, god of running, I had to put it all in perspective. I resolved to survive the knowledge of what my cane was telling me. I felt used up and irrelevant for a while, but it wasn't going to be the end of me. And now I'm declaring that openly, right here.

We need to remove the stigma of feeling bad and blue. It's bound to happen, statistically speaking, to most people sometime in their lives, but the elderly can be particularly vulnerable. (Remember, this is even coming from a former hippie, a happy-go-lucky—for the most part—kind of guy.) We have to do our part as individuals and society to fight against the collective uneasiness of conversation around depression, to educate ourselves more thoroughly, and to separate the illness from the person. This is my main message for you in your individual situation if you are depressed. Understand: you are worth something—worth something very special—and it's okay to talk about it if you don't think so sometimes.

WHAT NOW, LORD?

Healing and the IUCC

"My Guide"

Oh how does God have time for me,
With all he's got to do and see?
He guides and takes me everywhere.
He'll do the same for you; he cares!

And when this life I can't withstand
I sense his omnipresent hand.
I know I'm worth his special love.
He gives protection from above.

One never knows what is life's plan.
We do only the best we can.
To clasp the good and take the bad,
And marvel at the life we've had.

When viewing life in retrospect,
Propitious yet sometimes abject,
I praise him in his awesome grace
Allowing me to have a place.

Old age…the homestretch…the "cool down" part of the race. Heavy, deep reflection time. So, I begin by asking: why have I been here on this planet for this long? My father wrote in his late memoirs, "I am only now beginning to realize why the 'powers that be' have given me more than the allotted time…The reason being, I think, is because I have been a slow learner in life, and also the Lord has more things to teach me. I will fool him, though, and keep on learning."

A New Spiritual Haven

As I mentioned earlier, now I attend the Irondequoit United Church of Christ, and I'm very happy there. It's traditional. I got into it because of race people who attend there, like I told you. I enjoy my little church; it's much different than the huge church I formerly attended. This one "boasts" just about fifty people per week in attendance. But it is an animated and loving church family, just right for me at this point in my life.

Several years ago I was chosen by the IUCC leadership team to serve on a pastor search committee. The search team appointed me their spiritual chaplain. It was a two-year commitment for the process. I was able to lead and guide the group to the goal of finding and hiring a new pastor. That was ten years ago, in fact, and that pastor has since retired from IUCC. The church is now in the process again. I also serve as a liturgist on occasion for both early and late services.

Some have asked me why I'm involved with this small church as opposed to a vital and active, large church like Faith Temple in Brighton. First, I feel a local connection to IUCC, since it's in the town where my roots are. Also, I feel that it's my calling to help sustain and grow a longstanding denominational type of church. The engineer who's in my blood sees something that needs attention and wants to fix it. I have the imagination, skills, and spiritual drive to fill that hole and do whatever it takes to make a difference. I've done that with the Sunset Hospice's all-volunteer staff and as a former board member.

Besides the weekly services and involvement at church, even more importantly I'm daily connected to God in a personal relationship. I meditate on the Word of God every morning. I read a daily devotional, a publication of modern-day testimonies and Bible stories. It feeds my soul. It reminds me that God is my guide, and I should trust him. Each day brings blessings and learnings anew, like my dad said.

HEY, BY THE WAY, DO YOU NEED A CASKET?

The Memorial Woodshop

"Lost"

I feel so bad that you are lost
And you cannot be found,
So I just had to get involved.
I think I'll look around.

You're just not there, I truly swear.
How could this really be?
I do direct, we must inspect
A far vicinity.

I looked behind our every bush;
I peered below the stair;
I searched beneath the big pine tree,
But you weren't even there.

I thought I saw you down the road—
T'was just the other night,
But you seemed not the one I knew
Til you were out of sight.

Now since you are a friend of mine,
I'll tell you what I'll do.
I'll keep on looking everywhere,
Until I can find you.

That chapter title was a bit strange, wasn't it? Perhaps it caught you a little off guard? To contemplate death in our culture seems somewhat morbid. We shake our head in discomfort and dismay, and can only mumble the old aphorism from the burial service in The Book of Common Prayer: "Ashes to ashes, dust to dust..." The real answer to the titular question is, of course you need a casket (or some kind of burial container). Everyone will someday, unless their ashes are scattered.

Well, not so fast… The "you" in my question might mean the purchaser of a coffin for someone else. If you haven't already, there will come a day that you have to select a casket or urn for a loved one. You'll be there, sitting in the funeral director's office, considering what the deceased would have liked, what you can afford, etc., etc. I've got you thinking about it now, so when the time comes, you won't be "lost" like in Dad's poem.

Ishmael

In one of the finest works of American literature, *Moby Dick*, author Herman Melville writes about a baffling great white whale who has been terrorizing a sea captain. This guy really feeds into it with his own megalomania and an obsession to get even with this vicious whale. (You see, years back, the whale had bitten off the captain's leg.) The captain is named Ahab (an allusion to the wicked king in the Old Testament), and the white whale is named Moby Dick. This cat-and-mouse game, more of a whale-and-man game, is done at the expense of many surrounding collateral victims—Captain Ahab's former family, friends, and finally crew. In the end (spoiler alert!), crazy Ahab finds the elusive whale and harpoons it, but Ahab is no match for the mighty strength of this ocean king. The weapon is lodged in Moby Dick's flesh as tightly as can be, and the rope winds around the harpoon as the whale takes control. The creature pulls the entire ship down with tremendous force into a deep, watery grave—for everyone, except the sole survivor, a cabin boy now turned man by the name of Ishmael. (You got it: that's also no accidental name.) Melville presents him as the lone guy who makes it out alive. But he's totally lost then.

Remember Ishmael of the Bible? Jews, Christians, and Muslims all believe he was real. He was an important and interesting figure in the Old Testament. He seems to have been a mixed bag, not one dimensional. To make a long story short, because of him and the questionable circumstances of his birth, inevitable jealousies between people arose. Essentially a bastard son of Abraham brought into the world through conniving, he was ordained by God to forever be in conflict with his relatives.

Biblical Ishmael's unhappy fate had been infamously sealed. He was an ill-conceived child of wreckage like Captain Ahab's splintered ship. Yet he was blessed because he was the seed of Abraham, and his line would produce a great nation perpetuating into centuries. But that legacy wasn't good enough for him. Ishmael of the Bible, like his namesake in *Moby Dick*, was a man who found himself on the brink.

Melville's modern Ishmael is the Bible's Ishmael repackaged, and the white whale is the powerful God of the Old Testament. Both Ishmaels stand for all of us in their disinheritance, their loss, their separation from God. The modern Ishmael, in the very last part of the book, is seen floating on a coffin someone else made during idle time on the ship. The coffin is drifting along in the open ocean, just a piece of refuse from the takedown. Ironically, that coffin, a symbol of death, has saved his life.

Melville is saying that life, like the sea, has a way of swallowing us—of throwing us this way and that way, of being bizarre in its turns of events. Perhaps it's even being sarcastic, if you believe, like the ancient Greeks and Shakespeare did, that some nasty gods are up there in the heavens pulling all the strings. So like it or not, Ishmael finds himself very much alive but alone and disoriented on a vast, stark sea. The existential tone reminds us of that empty hole we can find if we look inside ourselves too deeply, without God.

How will Ishmael, a representative of humanity, go on? When Melville wrote the novel, it was an allegory for his concern about the decaying spirit and moral identity of modern Americans. We had had the Edenic, utopian vision the Puritans arrived with, slowly eroding into something different, and Melville, like a biblical prophet, had a disturbing prognostication for us.

Well, you see, this symbol of the coffin gives a person a lot to think about. How can these containers for discarded human flesh speak to us? What do they say? Rather than being the harbingers of doom, they might buoy us up in some strange way. I'm talking about potential. Not a fresh, new start or anything as simplistic as that, but an opening into a different chapter.

A New Work

Maybe I'm Ishmael gripping my empty box. Incidentally, I *am* him hanging onto a literal coffin. I'm him bracing myself up by it, and I'll explain why in a moment... It begins with a near nothingness, a blank staring out to sea like Ishmael of the novel does once he resurfaces and realizes it's just him there, and this is it. It was to be, once all the waves settled down for us, a meek resurgence of sorts.

Time to carry on! My medical problems were a bombshell, but it hasn't been a time to lay down and die. I'm talking about my woodworking hobby that has led to a calling. Maybe with my proverbial lemons I've made lemonade.

To begin with, I had had nothing to do, just bobbing along after retirement. I considered ways to occupy myself and be productive once again. I thought of my hobbies I had early in life. And then I hit upon it! I summoned my carpentry skills I had learned as a boy working on my family cabin (more on this later). I guess carpentry's in my blood too. And it was good enough for Jesus! I think anyone who is a carpenter has the potential to do good work to make other people's lives just a little bit more comfortable.

I find it captivating that my mother's ancestors were named Baumberger. This German surname means *tree dweller/woodworker.* Trees are living, breathing organisms with whom we share this earth. We use them, after we've seen to their death, to make things, such as the boxes we need for our bodies' remains. They disintegrate back into the soil with a body, entwining cells. It makes sense that there would be a thread in my ancestry like that, about trees and people who work with them, transforming them in a utilitarian way that comingles humanity and nature. Woodworkers. One day, as an older gentleman, I picked up my saw and wood, hammer and nails, and resumed the tradition.

In the last two years, my new goal (I've had a few) was to enjoy my old hobby as much as possible. As a kid, I had learned carpentry skills but never much used them. Since I reignited that old love, I've been filling up my house with furniture I've recently built. You can ask my wife: anything that's not already nailed down and resembles a piece of wood is fair game for me to use! Today as I write this, I'm working in my garage on the finishing touches for a cabinet. I'm putting on hinges and some other devices. It requires careful thinking and fine motor skills. Sometimes I'm not that good at some parts—you know, the stroke. But it's good therapy.

After making furniture for my wife and myself, I wanted to start another new business endeavor, and I have. It's not-for-profit, helps people, and occupies my time well. It's called The Memorial Woodshop, but it's not a business which produces furniture. I help a handful of men to make caskets. We rent a shop in downtown Rochester, at the Hungerford Building. It's a big, old warehouse where we tinker. I got the idea originally from a runner friend of mine who carves wooden statues for churches. I also had helped a homeless man make a large wooden cross he wanted to put up in our sanctuary as a prop for our Easter service. I guess that statues and crosses and wood and old age somehow led into me thinking about caskets; however, I think it was mostly God's direction.

The caskets we make are beautiful expressions. As each human being is unique, each casket has one-of-a-kind grains. Our caskets are simple yet elegant, constructed from Amish-milled wood. They are ordered typically for homeless people, but priests and nuns have recognized and commissioned our work for themselves as well. They are seeking something more modest than most modern caskets. They want a fairly plain wooden box. I am honored to have a hand in constructing these caskets for the deceased. This is my small way of giving back. For every casket that is ordered for someone, we make a second and donate it for another homeless person's burial.

And there's another purpose to this endeavor, another benefit. The program's artisans are local men whom are given a small stipend. I supervise them and teach them not only carpentry skills but practical workplace skills. It's similar to what I did being a coach; I'm coaching the men into developing employability skills. My craftsmen come from the Dorothy Day House at St. Joseph's in town here. I consider it my privilege to assist the men who work for our organization. Many are homeless, down on their luck, and just need a hand up. They've lived hard lives, lost on the street; life hasn't been very nice to them, in most cases. They are essentially looking for a friend or two—belonging—whether they know it or not. Really, it's my ministry. I once applied to Northeastern Seminary here in Rochester, but now, that woodshop and these men are my parish Monday through Friday. When someone extends their affection and friendship to another, neither person can truly ever be "lost." Just like the poem says.

History of Coffins, Dignity in Death

Coffins have two main practical functions—to serve as a container for viewing at a wake and at burial to slow decomposition of the body by keeping it away from insects and animals. Coffins give us peace of mind that we are preserving some measure of dignity for the deceased and give some aesthetic value to the funereal rite.

The casket industry traces its roots back to ancient Egypt and Mesopotamia, where wood, cloth, and paper were used to make sarcophagus-style burial boxes. In Europe, the Celts began making caskets out of flat stones around the year 700 AD. However, for centuries, caskets were used to bury only aristocrats and nobility. Believe it or not, the most common style of casket throughout human history has been nothing—the simple hole in the ground. Beyond that, it's been just a shroud (cloth covering). So having a casket, even the most basic kind, has been considered not a necessity but a luxury for most of history.

In the United States, casket manufacturing developed not until the nineteenth century. The casket industry evolved from local furniture and cabinet makers who doubled as undertakers. They originally built wooden caskets on an as-needed basis. However, during the Civil War, many thousands of coffins were needed to transport dead soldiers, marking the start of the mass-produced casket era. In the early twentieth century, companies began making metal caskets instead of wood, because the former were less costly in terms of materials and process. During World War II big companies made caskets out of only cardboard and cloth in an effort to conserve metal and wood. Things then returned to metal caskets. About fifty years ago, the nation's largest casket producer, Batesville, started to make hardwood ones again. Today there are wood, bronze, copper, and stainless steel products.

I'm not sure how many people actually pre-order their own caskets, but I suppose there are a few. Do they select an expensive one fit for royalty? A polished, gleaming structure with a thick white pillow and elaborate tufts to embrace the body and cushion its eternal rest? Since expense is generally determined by thickness of the walls, will the casket for a government figure lying in state be made in a hefty masculine style? Or would people want a feminine touch like that of Marilyn Monroe's delicate bronze bier with champagne-pink satin? There are also ultramodern caskets such as environmentally-responsible pods that disintegrate, growing a tree fed from one's remains. The National Museum of Funeral History in Houston features a display of "fantasy coffins," such as a car, a grand piano, and constructs that resemble a jet airliner and a fish.

Casket manufacturing in the United States is a billion-dollar industry. There are as many coffin styles as there are tastes in people. For the dead we service, a simple pine box filled with love and prayers is their last earthly place of rest. Again, when someone extends their affection and friendship to you, you can never truly be "lost" in death.

Contemplating Death

Returning to the idea I began the chapter with, yes, we are all sinners, and yes, we are going to die. As Albert Einstein said, evil is based on nothingness, the lack of goodness, like the disappearing white whale. Someday, our bodies will return to nothingness, but will our souls? Let's go back to my dad's poem for a moment. Loder's notes say that an old friend had emailed him that he once felt "just so lost," and that was the impetus for my dad writing this particular poem at the chapter's outset. I know my dad had empathy for the poor man, because he himself was feeling the same, to some degree. In their last days, some people find themselves standing on the brink of an unknown future, just as Ishmael did. They have an identity crisis or are extremely fearful of crossing over the veil. They feel cornered by the prospect of death.

Contemplating death is never easy, and you probably already have an insurance policy and maybe a will that will help your family legally and financially in the event of your death. But have you thought about the bigger questions for the end of your earthly life, like how your passing may affect others emotionally, how you want to be remembered, and if your legacy will go on? Most importantly, can you be sure of your entrance into heaven, having believed in Jesus Christ while you were alive? Although feeling apprehensive about any transition, especially this one, is natural, don't let it bother you. Work through it. Death is an inevitability for us all. Just get right with God, today. And then look forward to heaven tomorrow.

OAKIE COVE

My Happy Place

"The Skiff"

It glides on top the water,
Propelled by bending oar,
Along in ghostly silence,
Its track from down the shore.

Beyond where blade has touched it
Recedes the yonder wake.
Now fading in the distance,
Revealed—the path we've made.

The pools like craftsmen's markings,
Are left by dipping blade;
They seem to keep a tally
Of progress we have made.

The squeaking of the leathers,
The cadence of the sweep,
A movement in the water,
Their silence, then, to keep.

The skiff forgives your failings.
She'll serve your every need.
Don't try to pull too hard, now—
She'll give you no more speed.

The skiff is very trusty,
O'er rough or tranquil seas.
So if you treat her nicely,
She'll handle them with ease.

The skiff, it seems, is living.
Please use a tempered touch.
See, if you try to rush her,

You'll meet with no good luck.

So take this lesson from her,
Her secrets do consult,
Be soft, and strong, and you will
Produce the best result.

A h, a trusty skiff. If you're a sailor, you know the meaning. A small, casual nautical vessel that connects your soul to the land, sky, and water, so much so that it deserves the status of friend or guide. If you're *not* a sailor, I bet you can still think of an object that holds the same kind of sentiment—comfort, grounding, and wisdom—for you. It's valuable in that way.

My dad wrote this poem about the actual skiff he built and we used on Grindstone Island, our summer place in the Thousand Islands. Welcome. I'm taking you there now, to my "happy place"—my place to get away from it all, my vacation spot from childhood through adulthood. There is a cabin there called Oakie Cove. For six decades it's been a fixture in my life, the scene of countless happy memories, as you can imagine.

But in the past year, a growing sense of ambivalence began washing over me about it. The ambivalence transformed into confusion. For reasons that I will explain in the next chapter, I felt I would ultimately need to let it go, but that severance wouldn't come easily. I have deep generational ties to it. In 1960 my dad, mom, and us kids (my sister and brother and me) built it. You know, it took a thousand nails for just that one little cabin Oakie Cove, maybe more. My cousins on the island had constructed the nearby Dano farm, called Da-Brook, ten years earlier, representing both the Dano and Brooks sides of the family tree. They made their cottage with their own hands, same as us. I guess our part of the island was the territory of one collective clan who had the courage to stake it out years and years before my generation.

Today, besides those cousins, I have my kids, Jesse and Zak and Ashley of course; two younger siblings; nieces and nephews; and five grandchildren, ages four to eleven. We've all stayed at and enjoyed the cabin. I hoped it would be there for years to come. It's nice having a place you can always go to, even if only in your mind's eye and heart. I know my extended family feels the same.

An Eagle
Early this year, another of our clan passed. Uncle Bruce Brooks, my dad's brother, was a dentist, just like him. He was loved and respected by many.

My cousins took it hard, but the strong Brooks resolve pulled them through. Besides, Bruce had prepared and had made his wishes known when his time was at hand. He wanted to be cremated and have his ashes placed at both the family plot in Rochester as well as the Grindstone Island one.

My cousins asked for my help with the Brookses' plot service in the city. Bruce wanted a military type, being a veteran. I contacted the VFW here in town to help us, and they wanted me to officiate the service. No, I wasn't clergy, and the only experience I had for this was when my dad died many years ago. But hey, I knew "with the help of God" I could do it. So I followed a program my pastor recommended and lined up a couple of military personnel to play "Taps" and present the military burial flag to the girls, my cousins. I said a few words and a prayer and placed the half of Bruce's ashes next to my dad. It was a solemn, family-only affair.

A month or so later the girls scheduled a memorial service on Grindstone to honor Uncle Bruce for the many up north who knew him. Pastor Jeff McArn, from the Island Methodist Church there, officiated the service. It was a perfect sunny day at my cousins' cottage by the water's edge. Many kind words were said by the folks who knew Bruce well.

Pastor Jeff led the large gathering with a prayer, when up in the sky directly overhead came a gigantic, majestic bald eagle. He flew low to us to get our attention, continued away, then circled back towards us for another flyby. Uncle Bruce had been an air force paratrooper. We all were aghast, because eagles like that aren't often seen in the area. Of course, we all knew it was just like Uncle Bruce to arrange something like this.

"To Close or Not to Close"

Up until the time I was there to say goodbye to Uncle Bruce (his remains) on the island, I hadn't had the opportunity to even open the doors of Oakie Cove from the preceding year's winterizing, although my boat was in the water for me to get back and forth from the island. Tending to our cottage's needs was the last thing on my mind. I was faced with the reality that I could no longer take care of the place, but the thought of selling it was a huge burden. It was a reality that I skirted and prayed about for some time, ever since the stroke. When I say prayed about, I mean prayed *fervently* about.

I have never been an avid stargazer or astronomy scholar, but I do know and recognize a few constellations, like the Big Dipper I saw that night after I'd scaled Mount Kilimanjaro. When my family and I have gone out at night on the dock at Oakie Cove to look at the sky, I've located groupings everyone knows and which can point me in the directions of north, south, east, or west. I think this is the connection that stargazers have with the skies: a simple sense of direction plus a knowing of the universe's benevolence, resulting in a peace in one's soul. (That means even when things aren't so good otherwise—when situations are confusing.) A guiding light, like the North Star.

And the stars over Grindstone would guide me when I needed them. I was seventy-three this year, 2020, on September eighth. That day flipped a switch. I realized that as soon as I could, I needed to sell my beloved Oakie Cove. It had to happen soon. Why would I discard this personal haven, this place of Brookses' history and pride, so abruptly? While I was there, this is what I wrote in my journal one star-clad night to make a little sense of it:

I need to close the door on another chapter, but images will always remain in my mind. This is where my true heart is. Fall is in the air. Most people here are closing up for another year. A crazy year indeed, 2020. But we all will be facing a new reality that life will move on. Let the Brookses make the best of it with or without this old place.

I think you know where that was going…

WHERE I PASS THE TORCH ON TO YOU

Finish Line

"The Face in the Moon"

I looked and saw the moon last night
And said, "How could this be?
That face that's gazing down to earth—
It's looking right at me!"

I glimpsed you in the moon last night,
And now I really see
The moon's a mirror set in the sky.
You're looking back at me.

The moon, a distant orb, I think
Reflects our exiled love,
Though shines its frank assurance of
Our union there above.

Bespeak of forced estrangement, Moon,
That we must, sad, endure.
With promise of togetherness,
Reunion please ensure.

So when you see the moon on high,
And it is shining bright,
Know that our separation is
Grief only for tonight.

Us

The above poem was written by my father for a dear friend years ago. It speaks of the pain we feel when separated from a loved one or from our heavenly Father. It speaks of grief.

The year in which I wrote this book, 2020, was very, very hard. You know that. It brought with it all kinds of grief. I'm not certain that a person can compare it to ancient times, although I'm sure those generations lived through similar hardships. I surmise that modern people don't think like that. Now we tend to examine life as it affects us in the present tense only. Here in America we have currently been facing devastation from fire, fears about climate change, unemployment, intense racial unrest, and political turmoil, not to mention religious division. That's quite a script if you were to film a movie, but the drama we are experiencing is real.

However, the largest calamity we have had to go through this year has been the global pandemic. Millions have died. Millions more have been sick. The worldwide illness has tested our strength, patience, and sanity, both for individuals and communities. Today's trials have pulled us to our wit's end and shown us at our worst, our most vulnerable. Although in 2020 we are more technologically and medically advanced and evolved than we've ever been as the human race, we're going through a situation that is plenty scary. As Charles Dickens said in his famous novel about the French Revolution, "It was the best of times; it was the worst of times" (*A Tale of Two Cities*).

I hate to say it, but at the end of this year, my casket business really picked up. We are receiving many orders and increasing our business. Isn't that something to be happy about? No, not really. It's actually bad news. Why? Because caskets are used in "the worst of times." The casket orders are coming in for people who have lost their battle with Covid, succumbed to the virus. While a few types of businesses like ours have grown, most others have pathetically dwindled. It seems that so many things are upside-down. Billions of the rest of humanity find themselves dealing with uncertainty, anxiety, depression, even despair. No matter who we are, we have all felt at least some of those effects. We've become acquainted with loss, isolation, the need for coping, and forced adaptation that will certainly have far-reaching ramifications for years to come.

My father's poem, then, could be interpreted specifically in terms of the relationships we've lost through death and the social distancing and quarantining we've had to undertake in beginning our new decade. The Corona virus of 2020 has surely affected everyone's personal relationships. Around New Year's Day of this year, people were making cute little riddles and memes about 2020 having to do with perfect eyesight. Those were the days of innocence, when we could laugh. No one could ever have seen what was coming in this terrible year. Like the hymn writer of "Amazing Grace" wrote, we were "blind"—more like blindsided—and by the end of it, we couldn't wait to see 2020 fade away in the rearview mirror. Could it, though?

I had a bad dream one night this year. It wasn't like a regular dream, which is only make-believe. It made me relive a real, awful time from younger years. In the beginning of the dream, as it had occurred in reality, I was getting ready for a marathon, I think one of the ones I did in Toronto. Last time I ran it, I had temporarily fallen off the wagon and toed the line with a hangover—maybe still loaded. Not kidding. Miller Beer had sponsored the event, and I had taken advantage of the free and abundant alcohol.

My friend Mike broke 2:40, and that was my goal too. I think I ran it in 2:42. I had failed. It had turned excruciatingly hot during the race…many "soldiers" fell. My feet formed giant blisters, and I could barely see where I was going because of the toxins in my brain. Donna recalls that bloody sneakers were everywhere at the stadium finish, and people were passing out due to the heat. It was a battle scene you'd see only at the movies.

So why did I undergo this wicked flashback? Why did my mind dwell on that horrible race? The time, 2:42, wasn't bad, after all, if I hadn't had such insanely high expectations for struggling under intoxication. This episode showed up in my bad dream because it was the recollection of a major stress event, just like this year has been.

After I woke up and thought about it, it came to me that this was a metaphor for what we've all been going through. The setting of the dream itself was not the present or the future like regular dreams are. It was by definition *in the past*. Just like I went on after that race to be sober and be smart, achieving many goals and winning, victory will come once again to our world, and we will have set 2020 in the past.

We may be blind and stupid sometimes, like I was in the above anecdote of my race, but God isn't those ways, ever. He's all-seeing, the quintessence of intelligence. Really good questions would be: How does *God* see 2020? What does he think of it? Should it be left in the past, like my race and my bad dream, or is there anything to be learned from it?

Well, let's look at Biblical history. In my church's Bible study recently we discussed the Exodus story, and how it relates to us today. Are we as a people who believe in God surprised we are living in troubled times? And do we really believe that God is not in control?

The Israelites were living in troubled times under the regime of the Egyptians. They were miserable and forlorn and felt abandoned. But then victories were to come. With Moses as their leader, the Israelites fled from slavery and from the Egyptians. They escaped through the Red Sea with their slave masters chasing them. You know the story: the Israelites made it; the Egyptians didn't. That was victory number one. Then the Jews wandered in the desert wilderness for decades. They were thirsty and hungry and complaining the whole way. God miraculously provided them abundantly with water and food in the form of manna (like honey wafers).

That was victory number two. The Promised Land was eventually reached and they settled there, and that was victory number three. This story speaks of leadership, trust, faith, and adherence to laws—social, political, moral, and spiritual. There are too many parallels between this story and that of our present day to ignore. As a former health and safety engineer, I watched this year's virus hurt people and felt so very helpless. But I know that God will bring us out of this—together.

Me

Taking a cue from that story, now I'm going to tell you about how 2020 hit me personally, but then how things got better...

The train started to go off the tracks in early March, just about the time "Mr. Covid" (or *Ms.* Covid) came to visit our world. Donna lost her balance vacuuming and fell backwards, hitting herself on a piece of furniture. Not thinking too much about whether or not any back injury occurred, she continued her work. A couple of days later she was in severe pain, like can't-get-out-of-bed pain. Like a ten on the doctor's pain rating scale. It had become so increasingly painful that we eventually had to deal with it.

Now what? we asked. Because of the rising cases of Covid, our states were in crisis, in lockdown, and everything was moving at a snail's pace. The medical field was taking extreme caution, and getting any kind of attention other than for the virus was impossible. Seeing a doctor was absolutely out of the question, as they were terribly bogged down, but we tried. We called, and when we finally got some advice by phone weeks later, it was to get an x-ray. We did that, but the films didn't show much because of arthritis and her scar tissue from the previous scoliosis operations. The doctors, when we could reach them, said the best view would be from an MRI.

So then it was June, months later, when we finally were able to get her to a hospital for more sophisticated imaging. Talk about frustration! Donna could barely get into the car to go get her scan. I had to wait outside the hospital. Faith and patience were being tested.

After a half-hour or so, Donna came out and I was told they could not do that long-awaited MRI! Because of her previous cerebral aneurisms, she has metal clips in her brain which would not bode well for magnetic imaging. Another detour.

Meanwhile, I hadn't been up north to open the cottage, but the boat was out of storage, in the water and not being tended to. It was being smashed around by waves, just like we were. Also still on my plate was the work with my homeless crew making caskets, as well as my commitment to the leadership of our Caring Connection team at church. But these were the least of our problems. Donna was confined to upstairs, and because of her incapacitation, I was in charge of meals and daily care. She was in so much discomfort. Weeks turned into months as we tried to survive.

Eventually, we got some results from a neurosurgeon who is a spine specialist, and he was able to see the injury to her back. We discovered that Donna had cracked two vertebrae. She is now in a brace, my poor wife. The falling mishap has added insult to injury. The broken bones are around the area of her spinal fusion all those years ago, and as a result she cannot stand up straight anymore. She is having a very hard time these days. Her meds are many, and her pain is beyond what I can express. It seems like Donna and I do daily warfare with her doctor's office about pain pills, as they are a controlled substance, doled out minimally at a time. It has been a constant struggle making these opiate connections when the need for refills falls on a weekend and we can talk only to an on-call doctor who doesn't have the full story. She gets out-of-her-mind panicked with only one day's dose left. These tearful episodes leave us both even more drained.

Besides taking those strong medications for pain management, she is now faithfully doing physical therapy, and she's still by my side. She's still beautiful; she's still Donna. To me, she's still that young woman sitting by the pool on the summer's day, in the yellow bikini. Today, she continues to slowly improve, and that's an answer to prayer. Making sense out of this whole pandemic and what it has done in our lives has been an uphill battle for most people, me included. Good thing I was a marathoner, as this story is getting old. I'd say I'm a Romans 8:28 guy, patient in adversity. Patience is a good quality to continue developing, for anybody.

As far as my worry about the family's cottage I knew I couldn't handle anymore...a miracle happened. Against my own wishes, I listed with a realtor not here in Rochester but up north where the island is. It turned out to be the best decision so far this year. I took a couple of days to go up to Grindstone and meet with my new friend, Robin Lucas, and discuss the property and plan a path forward. I signed with her "as-is," listed on Zillow, and the next day, low and behold, we had multiple offers, one even over listing price. I accepted that offer, and it turned out that the new owner has roots on the island, likes the boat which went with the deal, knows the river, and has a brother who is a creditable building contractor who will love and respect our family-built cottage. What more could I have asked for? Amid all the chaos and tribulations of this year, I knew in my heart God had heard me, and he answers prayer. Well, the dilemma was in my prayers for a very long time. God had come through abundantly, like manna from heaven.

One of the most important stories I can remember of my running career involved the result of one of my few but gut-wrenching failures. In the middle of one of my long (and I mean long!) one-hundred-mile trail races, I missed a trail marker giving me direction to the next turn. I had already run over twelve hours. I was tired. I was alone, hungry, and all I wanted to do was get it over with. After running a mile or so after that, I realized I had lost the path. I began to tremble in fear. I couldn't see any way out of the maze. I became paralyzingly confused. So, I decided to calmly retrace my tracks to find out where I had missed the route. I really didn't want to run any extra miles (what a waste!), but how would I otherwise fix the situation?

Can you imagine how messed up your head gets after running twelve to fourteen hours, trying to go as fast as you can, and being solo? You get bombarded with negative thoughts. You get low. But you have to rise above situations like this. I finally did run the mile back to the overlooked juncture, saw that amazing little sign, resumed the correct leg of the trail, and recovered my mistake. I *did* finish my adventure. So, I really ran one hundred and *two* miles in those brutal twenty-one hours.

I recount this to say that we all miss the mark of our life adventure at points. But we have the opportunity, through free will, to turn it around, make a fresh start, pick up where we got lost. We don't have to live our life—or death—in crippling fear. I'm forever thankful that I was able to recover from a life without God. That was my biggest victory ever. From there, I got back on the path to a fulfilling life in which I've been given the chance to experience some more bumps in the road and wrong turns. These other, smaller failures (and here I'm speaking mostly about drug and alcohol addiction), were certainly there, but I always recovered them as well. My drinking was B.S.—that's right, "*b*efore *s*troke." After the stroke, I've not drunk a drop. I will move into my passing from an imperfect, perfect life and go be with my Lord with assurance. But I had to go through the hard things to make me the person I am today. I know now that all experience is sacred.

You

And how does this all apply to you, my friend? The significant and devastating emotional, financial, and social impacts of late have been felt not only in the individual human heart, not only in schools and businesses and churches, but in all the nations of the world. We are united in hard times, but also in rising understanding and empathy for our fellow human beings.

If you're like most of us, many of your pastimes and pleasures to help you get through life have had to be placed on hold while we wait for a vaccine. Many of them, like enjoying friends and family and your church family, have just about vanished. But I bet you now better appreciate what you had and look forward to the time you can do those things together again with your special people.

If you are a runner, social distancing hasn't halted your basic activity, just gathering for group work and events. Sadly, this was the first year, 2020, that ever precluded the Boston Marathon. More precisely, it was postponed, then cancelled, then relegated to virtual status. Can you believe it? After all these one hundred twenty-two years? What is "virtual racing," even? Virtual racing means running a race distance by yourself, unmanaged. You time yourself and pat yourself on the back when you finish. If you pay a virtual organizer, you can get a t-shirt and a finish metal. Sound like fun? Not. Well, I guess that was the best that we could do, considering.

But because running is such an individual type of sport, it doesn't absolutely have to be done together, with formality. Runners are lucky this way: you can still get out and temporarily forget the world's problems, focusing on the freedom of the run. And when our health and wellbeing in large groups are again better assured, we will restart our events and come together for competitions just like we always have.

So, fellow runners and readers, we retain hope for better days; God is in covenant with us and will move (or run) with us through this low spot in history. Take heart!: He is here, walking with us "through the valley of the shadow of death" as the Twenty-third Psalm says. And like it says in the "Footprints" poem that we all know and love so much, he is not only walking with us, but carrying us. He is almighty God, father, creator, and sustainer *of* it all, and he is our companion *through* it all. He is the Holy Spirit breathing through our lives every moment, and to prove his devotion he was incarnated as the Son, Jesus Christ.

Like the speaker in my dad's poem above, who sees his loved one's face reflected in the moon, if we try to imagine the divine incarnation standing near us, we see God's face shining through the human flesh of Jesus's. Still to this day, even without Jesus physically living among us, we can look up to the heavens and feel that connection with God. When we remember Jesus through prayer, psychologically we are reflecting his image from heaven to give us everlasting hope. Just because we don't see him with our limited physical vision doesn't mean he's not there. Regardless of his current invisibility, we just need to remember and believe. That is what's called faith!

Remember my ultramarathon-running hero, Yiannis Kouros? Here's a quotation from him about adversity and resilience: "Each horrid event should equip you with the necessary provisions so that you can confront the next one; it shouldn't make you yield. The continuous confirmation is that despair and hopelessness supply you with means—inconceivable at first, and they make you discover hidden, unexpected powers. Later, an unhoped-for tranquility and sobriety should follow so that you may pursue your goals with precision." Well, I've been *equipped*, so I can *confront*, and I won't *yield*, because I've got the *confirmation*. Confirmation is my launch pad from here. Kouros is right.

On my seventy-third birthday, I wrote the following on Facebook to recollect the day:

Today, I celebrate, like each day. It's another day. Life, liberty, and the pursuit of love. No cake or cards needed. Just happy that I can walk and talk. In my quiet space today, I'm reminded of the feeling of those morning runs… Just flowing along at one with nature. Before the rest of the world wakes up… In my mind, I've just finished up my run, still bathed with the glow of my runner's high. Just now I can feel this, even though sitting with my morning coffee and not running today, of course. I feel the love of God and am thankful for all that I've been able to enjoy and the family who will follow the trail I have walked. I'm happy that my book is being written. All this is enough.

Now that's the kind of memory of running I want to have more often! And that's the kind of gratitude I want to hold about today. Sure, I do miss the pre-Covid world like crazy, but I realize that I'm happy just where I stand (albeit three-legged) right now. I'm exactly where I need to be, where God can do his work. He is molding me and using me where he has equipped and trained me to be. With God by my side, I've survived to tell yet another story. The experience of the year 2020 isn't over yet. Can you see clearly what I do?

In my woodworking, I always see in a raw piece of wood a future chair, table, or shelf. I see the project before it's completed. I invite you: Look at that kid or adult, that person, yourself for that matter, as that finished, perfect work. The wood I'm speaking of might need some shaping, sanding, or rebuilding in order to get to that completed state. That equates to us being a work in progress. We are alive for a reason—to continue refining ourselves and to learn the lessons God sets before us. If you don't know what they are, get in tune with yourself. Journal, like I do. It will help you not only to express a healthy sense of gratitude, but to clarify all your thoughts and internal struggles. Then be a motivator, a change agent, a mentor to someone. Let God work in you; let God work *through* you.

My friend, have faith, be grateful for what you have, and be encouraged. Gratitude surely is an "unexpected power" like Kouros was talking about. You've got a 100 percent in life's track records for surviving bad days so far—right? And so has the world. That's quite an accomplishment, if you think about it. God has always brought us through. Thank him. Be happy. The verse I had written on my racing singlet back for all those years was as follows: "The joy of the Lord is my strength." Put some joy in your steps.

Know that the Lord will be with you when you're going through hell. You could come out smiling.

I am going to leave you now with two last cherished Bible verses. First, Isaiah 40:31, a verse that has always been near and dear to my runner's heart. "But those who trust in the LORD will find new strength. They will soar high on wings like eagles. They will run and not grow weary. They will walk and not faint." Remember that eagle who showed up at Oakie Cove? I believe he had a plan. He was there to inspire us. He was there to give us hope. Jeremiah 29:11 tells us that God has plans for me and you, "plans for good and not for disaster, to give you a future and a hope." Yes, we are overcomers. Take heart, because Jesus said, "I have overcome the world" (John 16:33). He *has* overcome the world, and through him, we will too. Remember, when you believe in him, you're going to be a winner! Keep moving forward. Whatever you're dealing with or striving for today, I pray that you can see that glorious finish line up ahead, or it won't be long until you do…

The End

ACKNOWLEDGMENTS

This book was really written by three people: myself, Irving Loder Brooks (my dad), and my fellow Rochesterian friend, collaborative writer Heather Beck.

My late father wrote all the poetry that is included before each chapter, and all the facts about my family history were distilled from his unpublished autobiography. Thanks, Dad, for all you inspired in me.

Heather helped me to "climb another mountain" and put pen to paper to achieve my vision and purposes. The African adventure I captured in a journal was the kickstart for writing my story. It sat on the shelf for fifteen years waiting for me to meet Heather to be my guide and companion in an even more fulfilling adventure—chronicling my life. We both agree it was a "God thing." Without her this book would never have been written. Thanks go also to Chris Boshnack of the runners' group Gold Rush, who put me in touch with Heather.

Thanks to Jim Castor for the look back into his journalism covering the Rochester races and to beta readers Alan Etkin, Laurel Fuller, Mary Jo Spallina, Nancy and Ward Abbett, Gerry Teal, and Chris Boshnack for their very fine suggestions. A huge thank you to my publisher, Kharis, for taking a chance on us and getting us to the "finish line" of publication.

In a broader scope, there are people too numerous to thank, but let me start with my family. First, my wife and "miracle mate," Donna Brooks; without her love, support, and solid memory, I'd be lost in the woods. Thanks to my children, Ashley and twins Jesse and Zachary; and to my grandchildren, Audrey, Morgan, Chloe, Zoe and Jacob, who all belong to the Brooks family tree that continues to grow. Thanks especially to my brother Jeff, who introduced me to a new life in the Lord.

To all of my mentors throughout my life, especially Pastor Mary Louise Edlin from Faith Temple church, and to all the runners I've ever coached, every one of my running pals and church friends at IUCC, and my coworkers at Kodak. Thanks so much. It's been a pleasure knowing you as the cast of characters in my life's drama.

And finally, I'm grateful to Father God and to his writers and apostles of history, who've spoken to regular humans like me in profound wisdom.

ABOUT
KHARIS PUBLISHING

KHARIS PUBLISHING is an independent, traditional publishing house with a core mission to publish impactful books, and channel proceeds into establishing mini-libraries or resource centers for orphanages in developing countries, so these kids will learn to read, dream, and grow. Every time you purchase a book from Kharis Publishing or partner as an author, you are helping give these kids an amazing opportunity to read, dream, and grow. Kharis Publishing is an imprint of Kharis Media LLC. Learn more at https://www.kharispublishing.com.

References:

Barton, Jeff. "The Incredible Feats of Yiannis Kouros." *Runner's Life*, March 21, 2020. https://medium.com/runners-life/the-incredible-feats-of-yiannis-kouros-a7fd8a01efb2.

Boston Central. "The Boston Marathon 2020." Accessed January 8, 2021.https://www.bostoncentral.com/events/boston-marathon/p900.php.

Brooks, Irving Loder. *Come Fly With Me: Poems by Loder.* 2011.

Brooks, Irving Loder. *The Story of a Lifetime: A Keepsake of Personal Memories.* 2011.

Centers for Disease Control and Prevention. "Stroke Signs and Symptom." Last reviewed August 28, 2020. https://www.cdc.gov/stroke/signs_symptoms.htm.

Crane, Marisa. "Genetics and Addiction: Is Alcoholism Hereditary or Genetic?" American Addiction Centers. Updated November 25, 2019. https://americanaddictioncenters.org/alcoholism-treatment/symptoms-and-signs/hereditary-or-genetic.

Dobbin, Ben. "A Kodak Moment: Olympic Flame Passes Through Rochester, N.Y." *APNews*, June 12, 1996. https://apnews.com/article/1c3f54230398778bbb9a01660e27735e.

Friel, Joe. *The Triathlete's Training Bible.* Boulder, Colorado: Velo Press, 1998.

Harvest.org. "Commandment #1." Accessed January 8, 2021. https://harvest.org/know-god-article/commandment-1-you-shall-have-no-other-gods-before-me-exodus-203/.

KalessinDB. "Looking for Recent Info on Kodak Cancer Clusters." Reddit, 2018. https://www.reddit.com/r/Rochester/comments/72qvwg/looking_for_recent_info_on_kodak_cancer_clusters/.

Livadas, Sheila. "Investigation of Cluster Requires Strong Link to Cause." *Rochester Business Journal,* June 19, 2015. https://rbj.net/2015/06/19/investigation-of-cluster-requires-strong-link-to-cause/.

Magellan Times. "When Scientists Drilled Into Mount Kilimanjaro, They Found A Biblical Secret Deep Within The Ice." Accessed January 8,

2021. https://magellantimes.com/science/earth-science/scientists-kilimanjaro-confirmed-bible-story/80/.

Matyszak, Philip. "Happy Plants and Laughing Weeds: How People of the Ancient World Used—And Abused—Drugs." History Extra. Updated August 1, 2019. https://www.historyextra.com/period/ancient-history/ancient-drug-use-history-how-what-for-opium-hemp/.

Necessary, Jeff. "What is the average mph of a typical long distance/marathon runner?" *Quora*, June 13, 2019. https://www.quora.com/What-is-the-average-mph-of-a-typical-long-distance-marathon-runner.

New York State Canal Corporation. "Canal History." Accessed January 8, 2021. http://www.canals.ny.gov/history/history.html.

"Rochester Parents Fret, and Sue, Over Cancer." *The New York Times*, March 2, 1998. https://www.nytimes.com/1998/03/02/nyregion/rochester-parents-fret-and-sue-over-cancer.html.

"Scree." *Wikipedia*, last updated January 4, 2021, https://en.wikipedia.org/wiki/Scree.

Thompson, et al. "Kilimanjaro Ice Core Records: Evidence of Holocene Climate Change in Tropical Africa." *Science* 298, no. 5593 (October 2002): 589-93. https://pubmed.ncbi.nlm.nih.gov/12386332/

CPSIA information can be obtained
at www.ICGtesting.com
Printed in the USA
JSHW050844300621
16392JS00004B/10